INVESTIGATIVE JOURNALISM:
DEAD OR ALIVE?

EDITED BY
JOHN MAIR
RICHARD LANCE KEEBLE

Published 2011 by Abramis academic publishing

www.abramis.co.uk

ISBN 978 1 84549 490 2

Printed and bound in the United Kingdom

Typeset in Garamond 12pt

Abramis is an imprint of arima publishing.

arima publishing
ASK House, Northgate Avenue
Bury St Edmunds, Suffolk IP32 6BB
t: (+44) 01284 700321

www.arimapublishing.com

Contents

Section 3. Alive and Well Locally?

vii

Acknowledgements

The editors would like to thank:

All the contributors to the conference and the book who worked *pro bono* (as did the editors).

The Vice Chancellor of Coventry University, Professor Madeleine Atkins, who has been unstinting in her support of the series and the Coventry Conversations over six years.

Pro Vice Chancellor David Pilsbury and Professor Martin Woolley, of Coventry University, who provided seed money for the March conference.

Our colleagues at the BBC College of Journalism who provided editorial and technical support for the conference.

Our publisher Richard Franklin at Arima for his sterling support.

Finally, our families who have had to live through commissioning, writing and editing at a non-academic speed in order to achieve our greatest aims – timeliness and impact. One day we will not wake up at the crack of dawn. One day.

The Editors

John Mair is Senior Lecturer in Broadcasting at Coventry University. He has won the Cecil Angel Cup for enhancing the prestige of Coventry University in 2009 and 2010. He invented and produces the weekly Coventry Conversations. He is a former BBC, ITV and Channel Four producer/director on a wide range of programmes from daily news to investigative documentaries on *World in Action* to more considered pieces on *Bookmark*. A Royal Television Society Journalism Award winner, he publishes widely in the media and journalism press including the *Guardian*, bbc.co.uk/journalism and journalism.co.uk. This is his sixth co-written or edited book. For the BBC, he co-wrote *Marx in London*, with Asa Briggs, in 1981. With Richard Lance Keeble, he edited *Beyond Trust* (2008) *Playing Footsie with the FTSE? The Great Crash of 2008 and the Crisis in Journalism* (2009), *Afghanistan, War and the Media: Deadlines and Frontlines* (2010), *Face the Future: Tools for the Modern Media Age* (2011), all published by Arima, of Bury St. Edmunds. He is on the editorial board of *Ethical Space* and chairs the Institute of Communication Ethics. He is also a judge for the RTS Journalism Awards and the Society of Editors Press Awards.

Richard Lance Keeble has been Professor of Journalism at the University of Lincoln since 2003. Before that he was the executive editor of *The Teacher*, the weekly newspaper of the National Union of Teachers and he lectured at City University, London, for 19 years. He has written and edited 20 publications including *Secret State, Silent Press: New Militarism, the Gulf and the Modern Image of Warfare* (John Libbey, Luton, 1997); *The Newspapers Handbook* (Routledge, 2005, fourth edition); *Ethics for Journalists* (Routledge, 2008, second edition); *The Journalistic Imagination: Literary Journalists from Defoe to Capote and Carter* (Routledge, 2007, with Sharon Wheeler) and *Communicating War: Memory, Media and Military* (Arima, Bury St Edmunds, 2007, with Sarah Maltby). He is also the joint editor of *Ethical Space: The International Journal of Communication Ethics*. He is the winner of a National Teacher Fellowship in 2011 – the highest prize for teachers in higher education.

Preface

Rumours of the Death of Investigative Journalism are Greatly Exaggerated

The *Guardian*'s campaign against the undue influence and the corrupt practices of some *News of the World* journalists has resulted in arguably the most dramatic shift in power in this country over the last three decades, according to Donal MacIntyre. Investigative journalism, he says in this Preface, is clearly in very robust shape

Reports of the death of investigative journalism have been greatly exaggerated. With apologies to Mark Twain, the obituaries have been written and its demise long foretold – and it was ever thus. This strand of journalism "far from dying a death" is, in fact, in very robust shape indeed.

As a matter of record, examine the triumphs in recent years – the journalistic scoops which testify to the health of the sector: the expenses scandal led by the Telegraph Group, Andrew Jennings' relentless FIFA investigations, even the *News of the World* hacking investigation driven by the *Guardian*, demonstrate that not only is British journalism engaged in effective and penetrating exposés but that its journalists are still hitting the big targets.

More than that, the creation of the Centre for Investigative Journalism at City University and its successful collaboration with a range of broadcasters and news organisations shows that this is an area that is advancing in ambition and dexterity. Indeed, the proliferation of online sites, blogs and magazines on the matters in hand indicate a healthy and expanding discourse on investigative journalism.

The RTS Journalism Awards judges said that this year's nominations were "among the strongest that anyone could remember". It is my view that the sector is strong and those pessimistic of investigative journalism's future have an overly restricted sense of what such journalism constitutes and secondly, overplay the role of money in such output.

In addition, those doomsayers perhaps are not in tune with all the work across the sector, those little investigative pockets from BBC Radio Current Affairs to programmes such as *Money Box* and even gems from the student journalism sector.

Indeed, the critics may not be entirely au fait with the continuing strength and depth of journalism in the regions across all media – online, newspapers and radio. As beacons of excellence BBC Belfast and BBC Scotland are continuing to making groundbreaking shows and developing a critical mass of experience and energy in investigative journalism.

The death of investigative journalism was predicted with the creation of commercial television in 1954. All through the 1990s I heard it while at BBC documentaries and *World in Action*. For the last decade as budgets got tighter and the information world changed at lightning pace the same arguments that gained currency in 1954, have now have become an accepted truth.

British investigative journalism – the envy of the world

Sounding the death knell of investigative journalism is a bit like being in opposition. It is easy to criticise and ease to undermine and that may serve as a purpose to cajole and encourage investment and standards, but it does not mean that the sector is at death's door. Rather, British investigative journalism is rightly the envy of the world. There has never been a greater number of investigative outlets, investigative documentaries and there are more output opportunities than ever before. From my own perspective, talking to commissioners and journalists alike across news, current affairs and even consumer programmes, the ambition to expose and hold to account is as strong as ever.

Indeed, the facilities to review, check and test the fruits of investigative journalism, again, are more abundant than ever. The tolerances are, therefore, tighter. Failures and weaknesses in our work are exposed faster and therefore our standards have to be tighter and more robust. That to my mind makes for improving standards and more steadfast results.

As an indication of the breadth and depth of the sector it must be recognised that there is more to investigative journalism than *Panorama* or *Dispatches*. There is no denying their bedrock of excellence over the years but that is to exclude other alternative and yet equally effective investigative analysis and exposés that comes from other quarters.

Magical mélange of comedy, agitation and investigation

Mark Thomas would never get a job on *Newsnight* but his magical mélange of comedy, agitation and sound investigative skills tore open the scandal of MEPs' interests and the secrecy surrounding that. His *The Mark Thomas Product* took a very different path to one John Ware would have taken but it was arguably more effective in terms of reach and impact.

From the same production stable, Bremner, Bird and Fortune's dissection of the grounds for the Iraq War was a brilliant, satirical and probing presentation of the key issues and its forensic approach matched with the comedic presentation resonates with the work of Michael Moore's *TV Nation* which preceded many of his Academy award-winning documentaries.

The winner of the 2010 Paul Foot Award for investigative journalism was freelance Clare Sambrook for her campaign against child detention – excellence in this quarter does not emanate exclusively from any particular broadcaster or newspaper. There was a time when that may have been the case but not now and that is to be applauded.

Clearly there is a wider scope to the sector than every before. Its investigations are encouraged and financed and produced by the busy local TV news team such as *London Tonight* (as I know from personal experience) including Ronke Philips' brilliant investigation into the culpability of Great Ormond St Hospital in the tragic death of Baby Peter. There is hunger and budgets for such work in these departments.

Internationally, Current TV, the new (relatively) online savy, broadcaster has built a youth audience based on original investigations and social conscious output. Based in the US, they work with many British producers and journalists, and have won Peabody and Emmy awards. The Discovery network has created Investigations Discovery, a television channel dedicated to revealing documentaries for the UK and Irish markets; mirroring their new venture in the US and online, journalists took their first Pulitzer Prize, the first of many, in 2010. The world is changing and the devices by which we consume and the ways which we present investigative journalism are changing too. But at its core, a driven curiosity to probe and examine still lies at its heart. Refusing to recognise these investigative outputs in all their diversity is at its best naive and at worst arrogance.

How Facebook and Twitter fuelled revolutions

New media has given oxygen to the sector. Facebook and Twitter created and fuelled revolutions and changed the world faster than any current affairs strand has ever done or ever will do. Crowdsourcing and even injunction breakers outside the jurisdiction have contributed to the investigative discourse. Investigative journalism can no longer be seen in isolation – its traditional linear narrative has been broken and never will be the same again. And it is the better for it.

And it's not all about money. David Cohen's brilliant work on *London's Dispossesed* in the *Evening Standard* was not driven by money and cash investment. It was driven by courage, ambition and a drive to connect with the community which he serves. I have no doubt that this award winning campaign was inspired and driven by Cohen's core journalistic instincts – commitment and curiosity in the public service sphere.

All too often among commentators, journalists and producers the complaint is of time pressure and lack of money. Resources do not drive the work of the *Guardian*'s David Leigh or the inimitable Andrew Jennings, both ex-colleagues of mine – they drive it themselves. Don't eliminate the x-factor from the investigative equation. While investment plays a role, I would argue that personality, that x-factor, plays a bigger role.

There are only a few Paul Foots and John Wares but there are a lot of people who can do a little of what they can and many of them have particular qualities which drive them to work long hours without extra remuneration, to live and breathe an investigation – qualities that elevate editorial requests and tasks into all-embracing crusades.

It is important that journalists are open to new ways of telling stories using new technology, embracing new movements (such as citizen journalism) rather than offer the all-too-familiar, knee-jerk rants, that "it was better in the old days". There are many ways towards the same truth be you a John Ware, or a Mark Thomas. We have long coveted diversity in news media and that extends not only to the people in the sector but also how we process and present the stories. It is clearly important as journalists to bring our stories to as wide an audience as possible, to connect and to elucidate and that means innovation in the way we present investigations. That "connectivity" enhances impact and that is what drives a lot of what we do.

Additionally, journalists are more efficient than ever before. Looking back over the years there was certainly a lot of fat in the departments and newspapers I have worked for. If budgets are tighter and that demands of us to be more efficient then that isn't all bad in a world of finite resources. Anybody who has worked in the bigger teams in BBC and ITV over the past 20 years will have to acknowledge that.

That is not to deny that cash and time are not key issues: they are; but they do not and should not exclusively rein back excellence in investigative journalism. It is an easy cop out – a get out of jail card. It reminds me of young filmmakers coming to me and saying: "I wish I could work in films." I always say: "Go and make your own." Making movies or investigations are not necessarily driven by money – that is a point I feel that is worth making.

Hacking scandal at the *News of the World*
One cannot address this subject without some discussion of the hacking scandal and the *News of the World*. Some have taken the view that such behaviour stains us all. I am not convinced. There is clear blue water

between tabloid title tattle and principled work that hold politicians, governments and big business to account.

Although I have a heritage in covert techniques I have never paid a policeman for information nor hacked into phone messages or emails and I caution those who, even with high-minded principles, feel it is their right to do so. There are some investigative journalists well away from the tabloids, who feel that they have to play dirty in a dirty world – who feel that sometimes the end justifies the means. I don't feel that any investigative journalist has the right to hack into anyone's mail, messages or communications. Standards are standards and playing the "Philosopher King" by allocating oneself the right to break the law is a dangerous game. It smacks of arrogance, the same kind of arrogance that has landed the *News of the World* in the mire and the funeral parlour.

If we are to accept, as some journalists in the quality newspapers do, that hacking is legitimate in some circumstances but not in others – where do we draw the line? If there is a line to be drawn, a distinction to be made then let it be made at full editorial level and not in the bunkers of investigative journalists, in the secrecy of their own heads, operating as lone wolfs without accountability or supervision. I do not believe that hacking is justified even in the public interest and I believe that such distinctions, rightly, leave journalists open to the charge of hypocrisy.

In summary, I believe that, despite the fashionable sentiments to the contrary, investigative journalism has never been stronger. There has never been more space for making noise, for digging, examining and exploring those issues that are critical to a working democracy. Notwithstanding the advance of new technology and social communications which offers us the magic of Twitter and Facebook as vehicles for information sharing and collecting, investigative journalism in this country has been on a rising trajectory for the last decade and continues apace.

Let's celebrate that. The demise of the *News Of the World* has even shown the capacity of the media here to devour and investigate its own. The *Guardian*'s campaign against the undue influence and the corrupt practices of some *News of the World* journalists has resulted in arguably the most dramatic shift in power in this country over the last three decades. Against that backdrop how can it be said that investigative journalism is at death's door? Judging by the fruits of its labour, the future of investigative journalism appears to be very bright indeed

Note on the author

Donal MacIntyre is an award-winning investigative journalist and documentary director specialising in hard-hitting investigations, undercover operations and television exposes. He has won praise for his courage, and campaigning zeal particularly his consistent work in the area of care homes for the elderly and the learning disabled.

Section 1. Alive and Well –
With Scoops Galore

More than just WikiLeaks

John Mair

It appeared to be dead or dying then along came WikiLeaks in 2010 with the Afghan War Files and and then in April 2011 came the "Cablegate". In no time revelations about the US-led "war on terror" were all over the *Guardian*, *The New York Times* and others newspapers worldwide. Investigative journalism seems to be having a new dawn, a renaissance. Julian Assange was its saviour!

Investigation and revelation has a proud tradition in British and American journalism. It is time consuming and expensive. Too expensive in a media recession especially when the legal risks are taken into account. It reached the zenith of its influence in Britain with *The Sunday Times'* "Insight" Thalidomide revelations in the 1960s (when Harry Evans was editor) and Bob Woodward and Carl Bernstein targeting and getting rid of President Nixon over Watergate in the USA in 1974. All this gave birth to a generation of journalism students many of whom wanted to be

Woodwards/Bernsteins. Today, how many would know who they are? Investigations seemed to beat a nadir.

This volume – the fifth in a series of contemporary and very relevant volumes edited by Richard Lance Keeble and John Mair – has its roots in a joint Coventry Conversations, BBC College of Journalism, Lincoln School of Journalism conference at Coventry University in March 2011. There, practitioners such as Donal MacIntyre, David Leigh and Mark Daly were brought together with "hackademics" such as Richard Keeble, of the University of Lincoln, and Paul Lashmar, of Brunel University, to examine the big question: investigative journalism: dead or alive?

It was a very productive encounter as have been the three previous such hack/academic conferences and the one since (the book of that – *Mirage in the Desert? Reporting of the Arab Spring* – is out in October). This is the result of the papers given and chapters written and submitted since. In this first section we look firmly for signs of life.

Technology has helped the art of investigation. Tools such as secret video cameras have simply become much smaller and easier to use. Easier to overuse as well. Undercover journalism became a bit of a vogue in the UK in the late 1990s and after. Much of that was down to one brave young journalist – Donal MacIntyre, of *World in Action*. McIntyre went undercover as a nightclub bouncer for *WiA* in 1996 to investigate the sources of the City's drug trade. All routes he found led to the door(men). They were the spiders at the centre of the web. That won two Royal Television Society Awards.

MacIntyre followed this up with a long range and well-financed series for the BBC, *MacIntyre Undercover* (1999) in which he or a member of his small team immersed themselves in groups ranging from football hooligans to fashion models. Under the covers they found much that was wrong and results soon followed. Here, MacIntyre, in the Preface, examines the lessons to be learned from the *News of the World* hacking scandal. And he argues that investigative journalism has never been stronger: there has never been more space for making noise, for digging, examining and exploring those issues that are critical to a working democracy.

Sir Harold Evans has been voted by British journalists the all-time greatest British newspaper editor. As editor of *The Sunday Times* for 14 years, he led its crusading style of investigative journalism – exposing the Thalidomide children scandal and Kim Philby as a Soviet spy. In an interview conducted specially for the Coventry conference, he considers the state of long-form journalism in the age of Twitter and Facebook. But he warns that as journalists increasingly use online searching techniques "the need for scrupulous, intelligent journalism, not just in discovery, but also in checking, is paramount".

Phillip Knightley is truly the doyen of the investigative trade. He was the backbone of *The Sunday Times*'s "Insight" team in its heyday. Here, he recalls his best story – Lord Vestey the tax avoider – which simply resulted from a "walk in" to the newspaper's offices and a year of hard work to get to the printer's stone. Knightley is short, simple and to the point in classic journalistic fashion.

Bob Woodward is another journalism legend – this time from the other side of the Atlantic. He and Carl Bernstein brought down a President who was lying and covering up over the "dirty tricks" he had used against his opponent. They then wrote the story of their story in *All the Presidents Men* which was made into a Hollywood film in 1976 starring Robert Redford as Woodward. Here, in a *Washington Post* interview shown at the Coventry conference, Woodward outlines what makes good investigative journalism or even just good journalism with an early lesson he learned about fact checking.

John Ware is a British investigative legend. First for Granada's *World in Action* and more recently for the BBC's *Panorama*, he has conducted detailed and forensic investigations in the most difficult of terrains such as Northern Ireland and Afghanistan. His *Panorama* on the Omagh bombing in 2008 is seen as a classic. Here he looks at the state of his art in an interview specially conducted for the Coventry conference.

Signs of life in the investigative journalism body can now be seen in the papers and on screens every day. Paul Lewis, of the *Guardian*, painstakingly pieced together the events leading up to the death of newsvendor Ian Tomlinson on the fringes of the G20 protest demonstration in the City of London in April 2009. Destroying the police version of the events, his work has resulted in PC Simon Harwood facing trial at the Old Bailey for manslaughter as this book goes to press.

The *Guardian* is an oasis of good investigation in a desert of celebrity and similar reporting in the UK press. Not just WikiLeaks and Tomlinson but also the relentless digging of Nick Davies on the phone hacking story over several years. Relentless and fruitful ultimately. Davies has proved that far from the "one rogue reporter" Clive Goodman as News International claimed, supported by a supine Scotland Yard, for years the culture of phone tapping was endemic in the *News of the World* and went right to the top. Sean Carson tells the story of this rapidly changing and ever-escalating investigation.

Andrew Jennings is a one man investigative team. He gets results through his persistent, some say irritating, work especially on the BBC's *Panorama* on international sporting bodies. Sometimes it takes a decade for the results; the International Olympic Committee is finally transparent twenty years after Jennings's first programmes. Results are faster coming through on FIFA – the world football governing body – after another decade of digging.

On 20 June 2011, FIFA vice president Jack Warner resigned rather that face an ethics tribunal on alleged bribery. A leaked report seemed to show him and wannabe President Bin Hamann were guilty of little short of bribery. Incumbent FIFA President Sepp Blatter is firmly in the Jennings cross hairs. His demise cannot be far behind. John Mair tells the story of Jennings v the World. Usually, Jennings wins.

Barnie Choudhury is a poacher turned gamekeeper. A former BBC News Community Affairs Correspondent (itself a misnomer) turned "hackademic", here he explores the problems of investigating your own community even if your skin is the same colour as theirs. No investigations are easy and they take a special sort of journalist such as Choudhury to see them through.

Peter Hill is a TV veteran and investigative legend. He invented the BBC series *Rough Justice* which re-examined miscarriages of justice and managed to free eighteen wrongly convicted people. The series also firmly got up the noses of some of the judiciary which showed its effectiveness. Hill argues that the BBC lost its nerve with *Rough Justice* when he was forced to step down and has lost its nerve more since. He sees the internet as a possible saviour.

Mark Daly had an incredibly difficult task as an undercover reporter. He had to join the Greater Manchester Police in 2003 as a trainee policeman in their training school at Warrington. Secretly filming over nine months he found a culture of racism, sexism and other isms. The revelation of his work led to the balloon going up at GMP and a threat to stop the programmes. Once that panic balloon came down, practice in training policeman has changed for the better. In this piece written specially for this volume, Mark Daly talks frankly about the many tricky ethical dilemmas he faced while filming his Bafta-winning investigative programme, *The Secret Policeman*.

How the Media Failed to Warn America Before 9/11: Wake up!

An interview with Sir Harold Evans

You've headed the London *Sunday Times*: you helped make it distinctive by giving it a strong investigative arm. Do you see that kind of strength in reporting and in news outlets these days? And what sort of thoughts might you have about whether this shift towards online journalism creates a pressure against that or limits that in any way?

There has been a reduction in the amount of long-form investigative journalism and that's a great pity because some stories actually need space to investigate and put the qualifications in and so I regret that to some extent – to a large extent, in fact. It can be done online, I mean the Daily Beast [www.thedailybeast.com, edited by Sir Harold's wife, Tina Brown] does some, but generally speaking the longer forms of journalism are more suitable to print than to the web. Generally when we are on the web we are in a hurry. I think they are both complimentary, you need both.

It's a real challenge to do what we should do. For instance, before the financial meltdown, there was very little reporting of what was going on. Gretchen Morgenson, in *The New York Times*, was absolutely brilliant about the rating agencies and the way they were behaving or about Freddy and Fanny and the housing crisis, but there wasn't the continuous, concerted attention to say: wake up. The same thing with 9/11.

Senator Hart and Senator Warren Rodman went round the world at the behest of President Clinton and came back and reported that America was in great disfavour, particularly in the Muslim countries and they warned. Hart actually had a sentence in his report asking: do we have any means of rescuing people from a high building in case of fire.

That report was launched at a Senate office conference in 2000. The attention it got in the Senate and in the press was absolutely minimal. And Hart went along to see Condoleezza Rice [President Bush's National Security Adviser and later US Secretary of State 2005-2009] because of the newspapers – *The New York Times* didn't do it at all. This was a major investigation and it was saying: wake up America. Well, you might have said wake up America (whispered) because the press take up on that was terrible.

This is what I mean, what I worry about in journalism. I like to think that if I had been editing and I had been told about it that I would have made a big fuss about it. Who knows – I might have missed it too. That kind of omission really bothers me because it is clearly the job of a newspaper to obtain the earliest and most correct intelligence and convey it to the public. And we didn't do that. Either with the financial meltdown or with 9/11.

Before 9/11, Gary Hart went to see Condi Rice and she was concerned. She was very aware of the importance of the report, she said you've got to do something about it, but don't worry, Dick Cheney is studying it and he's going to report in October. Of course, the 9/11 attacks came before October – who was to know that. But those are the kind of things that a really good newspaper, or really good website or agency should be on continual alert for. What are we missing, what's going on now, that we should be alerting people to?

That's interesting because we have talked about there being less room in the newspapers and media for that sort of longer, investigative journalism. On the other hand, as you note with the Daily Beast, we have this proliferation of websites and blogs and there is commenting, digging, investigating and the web has essentially created an open forum for that. I wonder, even as we see less long-form journalism, do we have essentially another golden age of journalism ahead of us because of the opportunities created by the web?

I think we do have a golden opportunity because it is much easier to do research with all the browsing sites, particularly Google. So you can get a lot done which would have taken a long time before, but you have to be particularly careful about some of those researches because it is not particularly accurate so you still have the checking to do. But it is marvellous in the sense that today, even though I don't want to go on too much about Twitter and Facebook, but because of websites like The Beast and the Huffington Post and so on, you've got a much more immediate sense of what is concerning people.

The first instance which struck me was when the ethnic cleansing was going on in Pristina in the Balkans and there were no reporters there. But somebody was in a house in Pristina and saw the military going around killing people and put it on to an electronic message and that was the first sign from Pristina of the citizen reporter.

Since then we know of citizen reporting through Twitter, Tahrir Square in Cairo, Egypt, and so on but we still need to be careful about this. In Iran, first of all they know where you live, because you have done your email or whatever it may be and secondly (in Iran this is particularly true) the authorities can flood the sites with bogus messages. So the need for scrupulous, intelligent journalism, not just in discovery, but also in checking, is paramount.

Note on Sir Harold Evans
Sir Harold was the editor of *The Sunday Times* and *The Times* (and earlier of the *Northern Echo* and assistant editor of the *Manchester Evening News*). A graduate of Durham University, he has written a number of best-selling histories. He followed the late Alistair Cooke in commentaries on America for the BBC. He holds the British Press Awards' Gold Award

for Lifetime Achievement of Journalists. In 2001, British journalists voted him the all-time greatest British newspaper editor. He was knighted in 2004.

Mundane Reality Behind the Myth of the Dashing, Devil-May-Care Super Sleuths

Phillip Knightley, one of the country's most distinguished investigative journalists, has never gone undercover. For him, investigative reporting involves long, boring hours in libraries, looking things up, tracing people, studying court reports, attending legal conferences, typing up memos and listening to outlandish conspiracy theories: that sort of thing. Here he offers six top tips to an aspiring sleuth

There are lots of myths about investigative journalism. It is thought to be exciting and glamorous. Its practitioners are seen as dashing, devil-may-care reporters who made the leap from suburban courts to "under-cover" work exposing the wrong-doers in our society and obtaining justice for those who had suffered at their hands.

Investigative journalists, so the myth goes, persist when ordinary reporters give up, have flashes of inspiration and insight, persuade reluctant insiders to confide in them and then, at the right moment, confront the guilty men (seldom women) and reveal all.

It must have sometimes happened that way, Watergate for example. But not in my experience. I got into investigate journalism by accident. I never went "undercover" in my whole career. I never pretended to be other than what I was – a reporter on *The Sunday Times*. Most of the exposures that I worked on involved long, boring hours in libraries, looking things up, tracing people, studying court reports, attending legal conferences, typing up memos and listening to outlandish conspiracy theories. Yes, there were occasional long lunches with new sources but I was usually too busy to take lunch at all. In fact, the investigation of which I am most proud, *The Rise and Fall of the House of Vestey*, came to me because I was not out to lunch.

On a quiet Wednesday in 1979 at *The Sunday Times* building in Gray's Inn Road my telephone rang. It was the commissionaire at the front door. "There's a Canadian gentleman here who wants to see Stephen Fay," he said. "But he doesn't appear to be in." I shared an office with Stephen and we fielded each other's callers. "Send him up," I said.

In those days a lot of stories walked in off the street because newspaper offices were in the centre of London and easy to contact.

Lesson One: make it easy for potential whistleblowers
Make it easy for potential whistleblowers to heed their impulse to talk to a reporter. The Canadian turned out to be an economist who was living in Australia at the time and working for a group of cattlemen in Queensland who sold their beasts to the Vesteys, best known for Dewhurst, a chain of British butcher shops. His assignment was to try to improve the price the Vesteys were paying for beef cattle.

He had started his task by drawing up an organisational chart showing all of the Vestey's worldwide companies and their interlocking structure. At first the chart occupied the top of his desk, then the floor of his study and finally his whole garage. "Don't you think that's interesting," he said.

I could not see a story but to humour him I called the library and ordered up the clippings on the Vestey family and their companies. In view of what he had told me, I expected several bulging packets. There was one packet which contained only one clipping – a story about Lord Vestey playing polo with Prince Charles. "You see," the economist said.

"There's something odd going on here."

Lesson Two: be prepared to believe improbable stories

Be prepared to believe the most improbable stories that whistleblowers tell you. Enough stories will turn out be true to make it worth your while.

We mapped out a plan. He would return to Australia after his holiday in Britain and continue his research. Meanwhile I would try to find out more about the Vestey family. We would share our results and if there were, indeed, a worthwhile story, *The Sunday Times* would pay him a handsome freelance fee. I dropped everything and started work on the Vesteys that afternoon.

Lesson Three: work for an overstaffed newspaper

Try to work for a newspaper that is so overstaffed that it can afford to allow you limitless time to pursue your hunch that your story will eventually stand up.

My Vestey investigation took a year and involved enquiries around the world. It revealed that the Vesteys, one of Britain's richest and most respected families, had been tax avoiders to the tune of millions of pounds for more than 60 years.

It soon became evident from the Canadian's research that the whole structure of the Vestey empire was created to avoid taxation. They ran the biggest privately-owned multi-national in the world. They were the world's biggest retailers of meat. They owned woollen mills in Yorkshire, textile factories in Hong Kong, and cattle ranches in South America, Australia and New Zealand. The family had interests in 27 countries, including grocery wholesalers, supermarkets, guard dogs, insurance, shipping lines and travel. But it was with meat that the Vesteys made their millions. At their peak, it was difficult to eat a chop or slice of beef in Britain that had not come from a Vestey animal.

They owned the ranches and farms where the animals were raised, the slaughterhouses and packing plants that processed the carcasses; the shipping lines that brought the meat to Britain, the insurance companies that insured the ships and their cargoes, the wholesale companies that took delivery and the butcher shops that sold the meat to the housewives.

This meant that they were able to take their profit at any stage down this chain and naturally they took it where they paid the least tax. So the

Vesteys set off profits in one part of their empire against losses in other parts, a practice which is entirely within the law. But it meant that, in one year for example, the Dewhurst butcher shop chain turned over £152.5 million and their pre-tax profits were £2.3 million.

Their tax bill was £10.

The real problem for the Vestey's was to avoid tax on their personal income and yet still be able to live in Britain. In 1919, the family had found a brilliant accountant, Edward Brown. Brown was a tax genius and he created for the family the famous Paris Trust, to this day a source of the Vestey's wealth.

The scheme, with all its intricate subtleties, requires hundreds of pages of legal jargon to set out, has been pored over, dissected and examined by some of the greatest legal minds of the century. Generations of Revenue officers and their legal advisers have tried to crack the Vestey Trust, all without success.

The Vesteys have always fought any attempt to break the trust, or tax its pay-outs, and have always been prepared to go to the House of Lords. And, in the end, they have always won. Revenue officers have summed up what fighting the Vesteys generation after generation, has been like. One described the genius of Edward Brown: "It was as if he had peered into the minds of the Revenue, and anticipated their every move, not only for now, but for years to come." Another said: "Coming to grips with the Vesteys is like trying to squeeze a rice pudding."

They had social clout as well. The Vesteys were pillars of the British establishment – friends of the Royal family, peers of the realm, Old Etonians, High Sheriffs, Deputy Lieutenants of the country, Masters of Hounds. Lord Vestey liked to joke that he was the only butcher in the House of Lords, but at weekends he would often entertain the Waleses, the Westminsters, the Beauforts, the Astors, the Hoares and the Cobbolds.

Lesson Four: you must not be afraid to take on the powerful
You must not be frightened of taking on powerful people but it is wise not tell your editor in advance how powerful they are.

So I plugged away at the story because it seemed to me to confirm my definition of what investigative journalism is all about. The story should reveal a major injustice or scandal which has been there untouched for some time. The guilty parties should be people of substance. ("Don't expose people who earn less than you do," Paul Foot used to say.) The investigation should lead to setting matters right and then legal reform so it won't happen again. Although it should arouse indignation, it must be a good read.

Gradually the Vesteys emerged as a Victorian family whose obsession with making money was almost pathological. The brothers who founded the fortune, William and Edmund, considered business not simply a way of making a living but life itself. They worked six days a week, kept modest houses and had no outside interests whatsoever.

They refused to live on income or even the interest on capital. They lived on the interest on the interest. William believed business to be so important that when he was on his honeymoon in 1924 in Ceylon (now Sri Lanka) with his new wife and there was a fire in the Vestey meat plant in Brazil, he packed her off on the next steamship to Rio to sort out the trouble, while he went back to London.

The brothers maintained their own debt collection department to handle small traders who could not pay for their meat, or tenants who had fallen behind in their rent. It was their policy to sue in the county court for any debt of £1 or over and evict any tenant who was more than £4 behind with the rent. Employees were treated fairly but without sentiment. It was Vestey policy, for example, to promote three times a good workman in their Argentine meat plants. But when the man became due for a fourth promotion, he was instead sacked – on the grounds that he had already given his best for the company and could now only decline.

None of this was generally known about them because of the family's obsession with secrecy. How was I to penetrate this? What I had learned about the current head of the family, Lord Vestey, did not suggest that he would be forthcoming at an interview, although it was obvious that sooner or later I would have to put my allegations to him and give him an opportunity to comment.

The experience of Anthony Gardener, a magazine writer, was not encouraging. Lord Vestey met him and remained aloof but courteous until there was a mix-up over an appointment. Then Lord Vestey told him: "You are the most disgusting little shit I have ever come across…How dare you come bursting into my office without an invitation. Do I have the right of veto on this article? No? Out! Out! You'd better bloody get it right, sonny, or I'll sue you until your feet don't touch the ground."

When I was nearly ready, I wrote to Lord Vestey suggesting a meeting. He replied saying that he had been well-aware that I had been making enquiries about his family for a long while but he had no interest in speaking with me. Far from a reassurance, this alarmed me.

Lesson Five: use the crucial confrontational interview to test conclusions

The confrontation interview can be crucial. It is your chance to test your conclusions and confirm their accuracy. Without such an interview it becomes doubly important that you've got it right.

Had I got it right? Hundreds of highly-skilled accountants and expensive lawyers had pored over the Vesteys' tax affairs for years. Was I not presuming too much to imagine that I could tell their story without making serious errors for which I would be severely punished?

One of the advantages of living in a bureaucratic society is that everything is written down somewhere. It is just a matter of finding it. I had heard rumours that a senior Revenue officer with a literary bent had written for posterity a small book that set out the story of the battle between the Vesteys and the Revenue. I was told that the book might be available in the House of Lords library. I contacted the librarian who said: Yes there was such a book and it was in the library. Could I borrow it? He said no journalist had ever asked to borrow a book from the House of Lords library but as far as he could see there was no rule against it.

The book became my bible that enabled me to check everything I had written about the Vesteys and after a long bout with the defamation lawyers, *The Sunday Times* proceeded to publication in October 1980 under the headline "The Gilded Tax Dodgers". On the Monday, readers' letters poured in full of praise – for the Vesteys. Three out of four letters attacked me and the newspaper and supported the Vesteys. The newspaper was accused of "gutter journalism", "pandering to envy", and "humbug".

Lesson Six: readers may not necessarily support your investigations

Do not expect all your readers to agree with your investigation. There will always be some who consider any media enquiry to be an invasion of privacy, sensationalism and designed solely to sell papers. There is nothing you can do about this.

I had some success. The tax laws were changed but too late to make any difference to the Vesteys. In 1993 when Lord Vestey heard that the Queen had agreed to pay income tax, he smiled and said: "Well, that makes me the last one."

Conclusion

I am sure there are stories like the Vesteys out there now waiting for someone to find them and investigate them. The trouble is finding the finance. If no one is willing to do so, we may have to put up the money ourselves.

Note on the author

An Australian by birth, Phillip Knightley became part of the celebrated *Sunday Times* "Insight" team from the 1950s to the 1970s, breaking such famous stories as the Kim Philby spy scandal, the Profumo sex scandal and exposing the effects of Thalidomide on new-born babies. Now an acknowledged expert in the dark arts of warfare, having written the seminal text on wartime propaganda *First Casualty*, he lives in London and works as a freelance journalist for publications all over the world. He is the author of some 10 books, covering in depth some of the biggest stories of recent times. Most recently he has written his autobiography *A Hack's Progress* and the critically acclaimed history *Australia: A Biography of a Nation*.

How to Get to a Story

Bob Woodward cracked Watergate nearly four decades ago. He still works as a journalist for the *Washington Post*. In this interview, he talks about basic journalism skills

One of the questions which persists in journalism is: Where do we get our information? And there are actually three tracks which, I think, apply to any story. The first, obviously, is people and that doesn't mean just going to one person or one source, it means checking everything, talking to half a dozen or even a dozen people for a day. If it's something longer you want to totally surround and saturate the subject.

Second track is documents. I have not really ever seen a story in a newspaper or on TV or even on radio that couldn't be enhanced with some kind of documentation which would support or add more detail to what the story is about. And the third track – often if you ask people what's the third they don't get it and I would tell an anecdote from my early reporting career to illustrate the importance of the third track.

In the first months I started working at the *Washington Post* in 1971 I had developed a source in the local District of Columbia Health Department and they were doing inspections of restaurants, many of the famous restaurants in Washington, and closing them down for sanitation violations, so we were doing front page stories on this. And one day the source called me up and said we have the worst score that any restaurant in the District of Columbia has ever received and I won't go through the gross details of what was floating in the food.

So I went and got the document – at a newspaper even then they liked to get early copy so I wrote out the story about lunch time, maybe even before lunch. The story said that the document made it clear that the Mayflower coffee shop, as it was called, was the restaurant which had been closed down with the score of less than 50 points. I wrote up the story based on the document about the coffee shop at the Mayflower hotel, one of the famous restaurants in Washington, and handed it to the city editor.

I said: Here's early copy and he was delighted and he said: Wow, this is a front page story, that's an awful series of violations and then he said have you been there? And I said no, I've got the document, I know it is authentic. And he said well, it's two blocks away, get your ass out of the chair and get over there. So I went to the Mayflower hotel and I asked to visit the coffee shop. Everyone there said we don't have a coffee shop. We have a famous Jean Louis or something restaurant, we have the buffet, but no coffee shops. So I looked at the address of the Mayflower coffee shop and it turned out not to be in the Mayflower hotel but in the Statler Hilton hotel which was a half a block away from the *Washington Post*.

So I went over there and found the Mayflower coffee shop and they had a big sign saying closed for repairs. The man who ran the restaurant happily but reluctantly acknowledged that they had been closed down for all of these violations. I went back to the *Post* and asked the editor for the copy back. I said I had a few minor changes to make. And if we had run this story without me getting my ass out of the chair and going to the scene we probably would have had to run a front page correction

Is investigative journalism alive in the USA?

I think that there will always be investigative or in-depth reporting. Clearly the newspapers are going through a convulsion now. It may last a long time, but young people are going to develop new business models. Everyone, all age groups, realise that it is important to have good data, good information about what government does. I asked Ben Bradlee, who was the editor of the *Post*, what he thought and he said look it's going to change. But then with great passion he said that there will always be a group of people, a band of brothers and sisters working to get to the under-layer of what's going on and they will find a way to publish or broadcast what they believe the truth to be.

Note on Bob Woodward

He has worked for the *Washington Post* since 1971 as a reporter, and is currently an associate editor. While a young reporter in 1972, Woodward was teamed up with Carl Bernstein; the two did much of the original news reporting on the Watergate scandal which led to numerous government investigations and the eventual resignation of President Richard Nixon on 9 August 1974.

Investigative Journalism: The state we're in

An interview with John Ware

I think some newspapers are still doing some really valiant and important stuff. Clearly overall the economic model for newspapers is not conducive to serious money being put into serious long-term investigations. But still, newspapers, particularly like the *Guardian*, the *Sunday Telegraph*, to an extent, the *Telegraph* and *The Sunday Times* are still cracking pretty big blocks of ice.

Investigation on television

Now broadcasting –there isn't any investigative journalism on ITV. We hear that ITV wants to become more serious so that will be a good thing. *Dispatches* – doing pretty well, the BBC – there's some good stuff on the BBC but certainly I think that the financial risk-taking which used to underpin a lot of the stuff that I was really privileged to do when I joined the BBC 20 something years ago, I think that has fallen away. The BBC is still doing some very good stuff, but I think its ambition has narrowed and I think that's a function of tighter money, and also the dominant position of commissioners, I should say controllers, who have become in my view pretty autocratic. They have induced an unhelpful ethic which is that everybody is now looking over their shoulder, trying to second guess what would appeal to them.

Editors want an assurance that you are going to get home on this target. Investigative journalism is a very expensive business. It's hugely time-consuming and it often fails. You have to be prepared to fail. I'm not saying that editors, Tom Giles, for example, of *Panorama*, is very keen on investigative journalism, but he has to live in the real world and there is a limit to the kind of risks that he can take financially and I know he pushed the boat out as far as he can, but it is not as far as editors in previous regimes were able to push it. That's the reality.

Note on John Ware

John Ware joined the *Panorama* team as a reporter in 1986. He began his journalistic career as a reporter on the *Droitwich Guardian*, before moving to the *Worcester Evening News*. He worked for the *Sun* in Belfast from 1974 to 1977 before becoming a researcher on *World in Action*. He was promoted to producer on the programme in 1981, leaving five years later to join the BBC. Between 1992 and 1997, in addition to his work on *Panorama*, John Ware also presented *Rough Justice*, *Taking Liberties* and *Inside Story*. Several of the cases he covered were referred back to the Court of Appeal and some of the convictions were quashed. One of John Ware's specialities has been the conflict in Northern Ireland which he has covered regularly since 1974. He was named Broadcast Journalist of the Year at the RTS Journalism Awards in February 2001 for *Who Bombed Omagh?* and *Spin Doctors* which was an investigation into the truthfulness of government claims about NHS spending and new initiatives. *Who Bombed Omagh* also received the Current Affairs Home Award.

How "Citizen Journalism" Aided Two Major *Guardian* Scoops

Paul Lewis shows how Twitter helped the *Guardian* in its investigations into the deaths of news vendor Ian Tomlinson at the London G20 protests and Jimmy Mubenga, the Angolan detainee, while he was being deported from Heathrow

Investigative journalists traditionally work in the shadows, quietly squirrelling away information until they have gathered enough to stand-up their story. That silence reassures sources, guarantees targets do not discover they are being scrutinised and, perhaps most importantly, prevents competitors from pinching the scoop.

But an alternative modus operandi is insurgent. It is counter-intuitive to traditionalist mind-set, but far more consistent with the prevailing way readers are beginning to engage with news.

Investigating in the open means telling the people what you are looking for and asking them to help search. It means telling them what you have found, too, as you find it. It works because the ease with which information can be shared via the internet, where social-media is enabling collaborative enterprise between paid journalists and citizens who are experts in their realm.

Journalism has historically been about the hunt for sources, but this open method reverses that process, creating exchanges of information through which sources can seek out journalists. There are drawbacks, of course. This approach can mean forfeiting the short-term scoop. At times, the journalist must lose control of what is being investigated, how and by whom, and watch from a distance as others make advances on their story. They have to drop the fallacy that their job title bestows upon them a superior insight to others. But all these are all worthwhile sacrifices in the context of what can be gained.

This is illustrated by *Guardian* investigations into the deaths of Ian Tomlinson, the newspaper seller who died at the London G20 protests in 2009, and Jimmy Mubenga, the Angolan detainee who died while being deported from Heathrow on 12 October 2010. In both cases, eliciting cooperation through the internet – particularly Twitter – allowed us to successfully challenge the official accounts the deaths.

Disproving the police account of Tomlinson's death
The investigation into Tomlinson's death began in the hours after his death on 1 April 2009, and culminated, six days later, in the release of video footage showing how he had been struck with a baton and pushed to the ground by a Metropolitan police officer, Simon Harwood. The footage, shot by an American businessman, was accompanied by around twenty detailed witness accounts and photographs of the newspaper seller's last moments alive and successfully disproved the police's explanation of the death.

The result was a criminal investigation, a national review of policing, multiple parliamentary inquiries and, by May 2011, an inquest at which a jury concluded Tomlinson had been "unlawfully killed". At the time of writing, Harwood, who was on the Met's elite Territorial Support Group, was awaiting trial for manslaughter.

In media studies, the case was viewed as a landmark moment for so-called "citizen journalism". Sociologists Greer and Laughlin argue the Tomlinson story revealed a changing narrative, in which the powerful – in this case, the police - lost their status of "primary definers" of a controversial event.

> Significantly, it was the citizen journalist and news media perspective, rather than the police perspective, that was assimilated into and validated by the official investigations and reports. Ultimately, it was this perspective that determined "what the story was", structured the reporting of "what had happened and why" and drove further journalistic investigation and criticism of the Metropolitan Police Services[1].

The initial account of Tomlinson's death put out by police was that he died of a heart attack while walking home from work in the vicinity of the protests, and that protesters were partly to blame for impeding medics from delivering life-saving treatment. Neither of these claims were true, but they fed into coverage that was favourable to police. A public relations drive by the Met and City of London police was bolstered by "off the record" briefings to reporters that suggested – also wrongly – that Tomlinson's family were not surprised by his death and upset by internet speculation it could be suspicious. These briefings contributed to a broader media narrative that endorsed police and criticised protesters.

How the police account left so many questions unanswered

The morning after father of nine died, the newspaper he had been selling outside Monument tube station, the *Evening Standard*, carried the headline: "Police pelted with bricks as they help dying man." But it was plain to us, even at an early stage, that there could be more to the story. The overly-defensive police public relations campaign gave the impression there was something to hide. Embedded in the small-print of press releases, there were clues – such as the Independent Police Complaints Commission's notification of the death – that left unanswered questions.

Most obviously, anyone who had ventured near to the protests near the Bank of England on the evening Tomlinson died would have known he collapsed in the midst of violent clashes with police. It seemed implausible, even unlikely, that the death of a bystander would not have been connected in some way to the violence. But pursuing this hunch was not easy, given the paucity of reliable information being released by police, who at times actively discouraged us from investigating the case.

All that was known about Tomlinson in the 48 hours after his death was that he had been wearing a Millwall football t-shirt. That, though, was enough to begin pursuing two separate lines of inquiry. One involved old-school "shoe leather"; trawling through notepads to identify anyone who may have been in the area, or know someone who was, who could identify Tomlinson from press photographs of him lying unconscious on the ground.

That yielded one useful eye-witness, with photographic evidence of Tomlinson alive, with images of him walking in apparent distress, and lying at the feet of riot police 100 yards from where he would eventually collapse. Why was Tomlinson on the ground twice, in the space of just a few minutes? And if those photographs of the father of nine stumbling near police officers, moments before his death, were put online, would anyone make the connection?

Becoming part of a virtual G20 crowd

The answer was yes, as a direct result of the second line of inquiry: by open sharing information online, both through internet stories and Twitter, we became part of a virtual G20 crowd that had coalesced online to question the circumstances of his death. In this environment, valuable contributions to the debate, which were more sceptical in tone than those adopted by other media organisations, worked like online magnets for those who doubted the official version of events. Twitter proved crucial to sharing information with the network of individuals who had begun investigating the death of their own accord.

I had signed-up to the social media website two days before the protest, and became fascinated with the pattern of movement of "newsworthy" tweets. For example, a YouTube video uploaded by two protesters who did not see the assault on Tomlinson, but did witness his collapse minutes later and strongly disputed police claims that officers treating him were attacked with bottles, was recommended to me within seconds of being uploaded. Minutes later, Twitter investigators had identified the protesters in the film and, shortly after that, found their contact details.

Similarly, those concerned to document Tomlinson's last moments alive, including associates of the anarchist police-monitoring group Fitwatch, were using the internet to organise.

Through Twitter I discovered there were Flickr albums with hundreds of photographs of the vicinity of this death, and dissemination of blog-posts that speculated on how he may have died. None of these images of course could be taken at face value, but they often contained clues, and where necessary the crowd helped locate, and contact, the photographer.

Journalists often mistakenly assume they can harness the wisdom of an online crowd by commanding its direction of travel. On the contrary, in digital journalism, memes (namely, concepts that spread via the internet) take their own shape organically, and often react with hostility to anyone who overtly seeks to control their direction. This is particularly the case with the protest community, which often mistrusts the so-called mainstream media. Hence it was incumbent on me, the journalist, to join the wider crowd on an equal playing-field, and share as much information as I was using as the investigation progressed.

Establishing authenticity and context

There were times, of course, when we had to hold back important material; we resisted publishing images of Tomlinson at the feet of riot police for four days, in order to establish properly their authenticity and context.

Internet contact usually does not suffice for verification, and so I regularly met with sources. I asked the most important witnesses to meet me at the scene of Tomlinson's death, near the Bank of England, to walk and talk me through what they had seen. We only published images and video that we had retrieved directly from the source and later verified.

A different standard applies to sharing images already released on Twitter, where journalists such as National Public Radio's Andy Carvin in the US have proven the benefits from sharing information already in the public domain to establish its significance and provenance. The break, though, as with most scoops, was partly the result of good luck, but not unrelated to the fact that our journalism had acquired credibility in the online crowd.

Chris La Jaunie, an investment fund manager, who had recorded the crucial footage of Harwood pushing Tomlinson on a digital camera, had become part of that crowd too, having spent days monitoring coverage on the internet from his office in New York. He knew the footage he had was potentially explosive. The options available to Mr La Jaunie were limited. Fearing a police cover-up, he did not trust handing over the footage. An alternative would have been to release the video onto YouTube, where would it lack context, might go unnoticed for days and even then could not have been reliably verified.

He said he chose to contact me after coming to the conclusion that ours was the news organisation which had most effectively interrogated the police version of events. It was more than a year later that my colleague Matthew Taylor and I began inquiring into the death of Mubenga. By then we had recognised the potential reach of Twitter for investigative journalism and our decision to openly investigate the death of the Angolan failed asylum seeker was a deliberate one.

Not all investigations are suited to transparent digging, and, indeed, many stories still demand top secrecy. This has been true for the three outstanding UK investigations of our times: the *Telegraph*'s MPs' expenses scandal and, at the *Guardian*, the investigations into files obtained by WikiLeaks and phone-hacking by the *News of the World*. However, Tomlinson had shown that open investigations can succeed, and there were parallels with the death of Mubenga.

Investigating Mubenga's death

His death had been similarly "public", occurring on a British Airways commercial flight to Angola surrounded by passengers. As with Tomlinson, there was a misleading account of the death put out by the authorities, which we felt passengers may wish to contest. Within days, open journalism established that Mubenga had been handcuffed and heavily restrained by guards from the private security firm G4S. He had been complaining of breathing prior to his collapse. After the investigation was published, three G4S guards were arrested and, at the time of writing, remained on bail and under investigation by the Met's homicide unit.

Our strategy for finding out more about Mubenga's death centred on two approaches, both aided by Twitter. The BA flight, which had been due to depart on 12 October, was postponed for 24 hours, and by the time we began investigating the following day the passengers had left Heathrow and were on route to Angola's capital, Luanda. Raising our interest in the story via Twitter, we asked for help in locating someone who could visit the airport to interview disembarking passengers.

A freelance did just that, and managed to speak to one who said he had seen three security guards forcibly restrain Mubenga in his seat. We instantly shared that breakthrough, in the hope that it would encourage more passengers to come forward. At the same time we were publishing what we knew about the case, while being candidly open about what we did not know.

Hence the very article, published before any passengers had been tracked down, stated: "There was no reliable information about what led to the man's death of how he became unwell." It added, perhaps controversially: "In the past, the Home Office's deportation policy has proved highly controversial." The tone was necessarily speculative, and designed to encourage witnesses to come forward. So too were the tweets. "Man dies on Angolan flight as UK tries to deport him. This story could be v big," said one.

This articles and tweets, contained relevant search-able terms – such as the flight number – so that they could serve as online magnets, easily discoverable for any passengers with important information and access to the internet. Another tweet said: "Please contact me if you were on BA flight 77 to Angola – or know the man in this story."

One reply came from Twitter user @mlgerstmann, a passenger on the flight who felt inappropriate force was used against Mubenga. He had come across the tweet – and then read the article – after basic Google searches. "I was also there on BA77 and the man was begging for help and I now feel so guilty I did nothing," he tweeted. Within hours, his shocking account of Mubenga's death was published alongside several other passengers who had found us via the internet. An interactive graphic of the seating arrangements on the aircraft was created, enabling users to listen to audio clips of the passengers give personal accounts of what they had seen.

How verification was crucial
As with the Tomlinson investigation, verification, something paid journalists do better than their volunteer counterparts, was crucial. The fact the passengers had disseminated to remote parts of Africa –

@mlgerstmann was on an oil-rig – explains why the only way to contact them was through an open, Twitter-driven investigation.

But this methodology also poses problems for authenticating the validity of sources. Journalists are increasingly finding that a danger inherent in opening up the reporting process is that they become more susceptible to attempts to mislead or hoax. This is particularly the case with live-blogs which need regular updates, require authors to make split-second decisions about the reliability of information and take care to caveat material when there are questions.

For journalists with more time, it is incumbent, therefore, to apply an equal if not more rigorous standard of proof when investigating in the open. In the Tomlinson case, when sources were encountered through the internet it was mostly possible to arrange meetings in person. That was not possible when investigating Mubenga, where there was an attempt by a bogus passenger to supply us false information.

In lieu of face to face meetings, we were able to use other means, such as asking prospective sources to send us copies of their airline tickets, to verify their accounts. What the investigations into the deaths of both Tomlinson and Mubenga show is that journalists don't always need to investigate into the dark. Through sharing what they do know, they are most likely to discover what they don't.

Note
[1] Greer, C. and McLaughlin, E. (2010) "We Predict a Riot!" Public order policing, new media environments, and the rise of the citizen journalist, *British Journal of Criminology*, Vol. 50, No. 6: pp 1041-1059

Note on the author
Paul Lewis is Special Projects Editor for the *Guardian*. He was named Reporter of the Year at the British Press Awards 2010 and won the 2009 Bevins Prize for outstanding investigative journalism. He previously worked at the *Washington Post* as the Stern Fellow. He studied at Cambridge University and Harvard University.

Revealed: Dogged Digging Behind the "Hackgate" Scandal

Sean Carson examines the extraordinary twists and turns as the *News of the World*'s ever-escalating hacking scandal unravelled. And he concludes that while Twitter may help make us all "citizen hacks" in trivial "human interest" stories, the trained nose of an experienced investigative journo is needed to sniff out the hidden facts in big, legally complex stories such as "Hackgate"

Is investigative journalism dead or alive? The answer, in a word: alive. And what better example to prove it than the *News of the World* phone hacking scandal. Dogged digging for facts, perseverance and a determination to search out the truth were at the forefront of the journalistic investigation powered by the *Guardian* that revealed the dodgy goings-on at the jewel in the crown of Rupert Murdoch's newspaper empire.

The kick-off – royal phone hacking scandal
On 8 August 2006, Clive Goodman, the *News of the World*'s Royal Editor, and his associate Glenn Mulcaire, a private detective employed by the

NoW, were arrested in connection with allegations that the duo illegally hacked into the answer phone voicemail message of certain members of the royal family.

A relatively unimportant article by Goodman in November 2005 claimed that Prince William had borrowed some editing gear from ITV's royal correspondent, Tom Bradby. Both were fairly miffed at how the story had got out, and following the publication of another article detailing William's appointment with a knee surgeon – again an unusual and fairly trivial story – the pair met to tie down the leak. As only two other people were aware of the arrangement they eventually tracked it down to the infiltrated mobile phone voice mail boxes of William's staff[1].

With more and more evidence coming to light regarding the extent to which the duo had gone to secure exclusive stories for the paper, Goodman was jailed for four months on 26 January 2007, pleading guilty to charges of illegally obtaining phone messages. Mulcaire, who was rumoured to have been paid £100,000 for services rendered, was jailed for six months but tellingly, on the same day, Andy Coulson, then Editor of the *News of the World*, resigned immediately to be replaced by Colin Myler. Although the soon-to-be Chief of Communications for the Conservative Party consistently denied any knowing or involvement of the alleged dealings, it did not exactly cover the new master of spin in glory.

The jailing of Goodman and Mulcaire kicked off a criminal investigation that burgeoned from the Prince as the sole victim to MPs, cabinet ministers, military top brass, premiership footballers and the ubiquitous celebrities.

Further evidence comes to light – the *Guardian* wades in

Beginning with Nick Davies's article on the 8 July 2009 – "Trail of hacking and deceit under nose of Tory PR chief"[2] – the *Guardian* made a series of allegations that the *News of the World*/Royal family telephone tapping scandal was but the tip of the iceberg of the paper's involvement in the illegal acquisition of voicemail messages.

Among the individuals thought to have been snooped on by *News of the World* employees were figures such as John Prescott, Sir Alex Ferguson, Tessa Jowell, Boris Johnson, Max Clifford and even Rebekah Brooks, while Editor of the *News of the World's* sister newspaper, the *Sun*. Owners of the paper, News International, countered the *Guardian's* claims with an official press release stating:

> All of these irresponsible and unsubstantiated allegations against *News of the World* and other News International titles and its journalists are false. The *Guardian* has been selective and misleading in its coverage of the report and investigation by the Information Commissioner. There has been and is no connection between the Information Commissioner's investigation and the allegation of hacking into telephones or accessing telephone voicemails. Furthermore, we are inviting the *Guardian* to supply the Metropolitan Police with any new evidence they claim to have[3].

After inviting the *Guardian* to share any evidence it may have compiled with the Metropolitan Police, the Met declined to re-open the investigation citing "no additional evidence has come to light since this case has concluded; we therefore consider that no further investigation is required"[4].

The *Guardian* did not give up, though. Davies later reported that three mobile telephone networks believed that more than 100 numbers registered to their networks had had the answer phone messages hacked[5] and that a Freedom of Information request had turned up 91 pin codes from the amassed evidence used to access voicemails illegally by Mulclaire and Goodman. In April 2010, mobile phone operators went on to identify the individuals in question to the Crown Prosecution Service after the police disclosed information including more than 4,000 names and nearly 3,000 full or partial mobile phone numbers recovered from evidence seized from the possession of the duo.

Rusbridger resigns from PCC committee

And so the *Guardian* continued to plug away, revealing that more than £1 million was paid to three people, including a £700,000 out of court payment to Gordon Taylor, Chief Executive of the Professional Footballers Association[6]. Next *Private Eye* highlighted that the out-of-court agreements reached between the *News of the World* and the three individuals, including Taylor, were signed off by the directors of News International[7]. This new evidence prompted the Press Complaints Commission to continue the investigation into whether the *News of the*

World had been in breach of its code of conduct. When it finally ruled that it had not been "materially misled", Alan Rusbridger, Editor of the *Guardian* and member of the PCC's code committee, resigned, branding the report as "worse than pointless"[8].

Further payouts were to come with PR consultant Max Clifford receiving a rumoured £1 million plus – although not described as damages – as well as legal expenses on top[9]. The case was a breakthrough since, as part of ruling, the newspaper and Mulclaire had to disclose the names of journalists involved in hacking, and party to the transcripts, of the answer-phone messages.

Tugging at the *News of the World*'s dangling thread

The fabric of the *News of the World*'s case was to unravel further when in April 2010 the original police investigation attracted renewed interest after it emerged that the assistant commissioner of the Metropolitan Police, Andy Hayman – the man responsible for overseeing the *News of the World* inquiry – left the Met to work for News International as a columnist[10].

A further rigorous journalistic investigation was still to come courtesy of *The New York Times*. In September 2010, the newspaper published an investigation suggesting it was unlikely that Coulson was unaware that phone hacking was being practised by his staff thanks to the "do whatever it takes mentality" employed by the then-editor, even citing the method the hackers used to crack the mail boxes.

> Around the newsroom, some reporters were getting stories by surreptitiously accessing phone messages, according to former editors and reporters. Often, all it took was a standard four-digit security code, like 1111 or 4444, which many users did not bother to change after buying their mobile phones. If they did, the paper's private investigators found ways to trick phone companies into revealing personal codes. Reporters called one method of hacking "double screwing" because it required two simultaneous calls to the same number. The first would engage the phone line, forcing the second call into voice mail. A reporter then punched in the code to hear messages, often deleting them to prevent access by rival papers. A dozen former reporters said in interviews that hacking was pervasive at *News of the World*. "Everyone knew."

One former editor said Coulson talked freely with colleagues about the dark arts, including hacking. "I've been to dozens if not hundreds of meetings with Andy" when the subject came up, said the former editor, who spoke on condition of anonymity. The editor added that when Coulson would ask where a story came from, editors would reply: "We've pulled the phone records" or "I've listened to the phone messages."

Sean Hoare, a former reporter and onetime close friend of Coulson's, also recalled discussing hacking. The two men first worked together at the *Sun*, where, Hoare said, he played tape recordings of hacked messages for Coulson. At the *News of the World*, Hoare said he continued to inform Coulson of his pursuits. Coulson "actively encouraged me to do it", Hoare said[11].

In his new job as David Cameron's Communications Director, the outlook was not looking too bright for Coulson after the account from *The New York Times*'s investigation was independently corroborated one month later by another former unnamed senior journalist at the *News of the World* alleging that Coulson had listened to the hacked answer phone messages personally[12].

Coulson denied all knowledge of the uncovered chain of events as well as knowing Mulcaire. But former News International employee and Editor of the *Sun*, David Yelland – a man well-placed to comment on events – was sceptical: "As an editor, I can't believe a fellow editor would not know phone tapping was in action, especially with the rumoured remuneration of £100,000 to a private detective in the *News of the World*'s case. Anything more than £1,000 would have to be signed off by someone in deep carpet land. It would be impossible for anyone at News International to not know what was going on."[13]

In December 2010 it came to light that witnesses interviewed by the Met, including those who had previously hurled allegations through "media outlets", had not been willing to provide evidence[14].

On 21 January 2011, though, Coulson resigned, citing "growing questions about his role in illegal phone-hacking during his time as editor of the *News of the World*". Just five days later, the Metropolitan Police declared that it would commence a fresh investigation into the phone hacking scandal as a result of new evidence relating to the conduct of *News of the World* employees. On the same day, the newspaper's owner, News International, announced the dismissal of Ian Edmondson, a senior executive at the *News of the World*, on the grounds of evidence it had disclosed to the police suggesting that, contrary to Edmondson's previous refutation of knowledge of the phone hacking scandal, the executive was actually aware of the illicit actions of *News of the World* journalists at the time[15].

Along with Edmondson, *News of the World* chief reporter Neville Thurlbeck and a third employee, James Weatherup, were arrested on suspicion of illegally intercepting voice messages. It was then left for News International to concede responsibility in some, but not all of the cases being brought against the newspaper with respect to voice mail hacking. The company extended full apologies to the eight claimants, including Sienna Miller, Sky Andrew (sports agent), Nicola Phillips (PA to Max Clifford), Tessa Jowell and her estranged husband David Mills.

An acknowledgement of guilt – Sienna settles as News Corporation apologises

After a short hearing at the High Court, London, the corporation that owns and operates the *News of the World*, Rupert Murdoch's News Corporation, issued a formal "sincere apology" to actress Sienna Miller for hacking in to numerous mobile phone voicemail accounts registered to Miller, admitting the information was obtained by hacking and should never have been brought to the *News of the World's* attention in that manner or published.

The actress settled for £100,000 damages and was pleased to confirm it was not family or friends who were leaking to the media details of her private life that appeared in the News Group publication throughout 2005 and 2006[16].

Truth rewards tenacity

Just when we thought News International had finally shipped off its last skeletons from its very deep closets to an autopsy by the PCC and the Met – going some way to righting the wrongs of hacking celebrity voicemail boxes, with an apology to those affected in the meantime – the saga took an unforeseen and, for the *News of the World*, exponentially damaging turn.

With the revelations reported in the *Guardian* on 4 July 2011 that Scotland Yard had found evidence suggesting the already disgraced Glenn Mulcaire had collected information surrounding the family of the murdered school girl Milly Dowler (who disappeared in 2002) by hacking into her voicemail box, the scandal exploded.

Hacking the mail box of a murder victim days before the body was found and allegedly deleting voicemail messages, potentially corrupting significant evidence in the case not only changed the character, but the nature of the phone-hacking scandal. It moved many in Westminster who previously regarded the story as a question of interest only to those excited by media ethics or the privacy of celebrities, and meant that for the first time Rupert Murdoch, proprietor of News International and the *NoW*, Rebekah Brooks, NI Chief Executive, and David Cameron, the Prime Minister, became aware that the hacking story was provoking widespread public anger[17].

The methods the newspaper allegedly employed to access information were shocking, highly unethical and more importantly, illegal. It was also alleged that messages from the mailboxes of victims of the 7/7 London bombings and dead British Army soldiers may have been accessed by journalists at the *News of the World* after personal details and phone numbers of deceased servicemen were said to have been found in files kept by Mulcaire.

The final straw for the *News of the World*, however, was the revelation that the Metropolitan Police – the authority that carried out Operation Weeting, the investigation into the initial stage of the phone hacking scandal – were fully embroiled in the scandal having received payment in return for information that would be used to generate stories for the paper: "News international has uncovered emails that indicate payments were made to the police by the *News of the World*, during the editorship from 2003 to 2007 of Andy Coulson."[18]

Not only had the integrity of the police been drawn into question, but so too the security of the royal family after email evidence between Goodman and Coulson (who had previously denied any knowledge of royal phone hacking or that he knew private investigator Glenn Mulcaire) showing requests for cash sums in the region of £1,000 to buy a confidential directory from a police officer in royal protection was further uncovered. The directory, or the "Green Book", contained the royal family's landline telephone numbers and all the phone numbers, including mobiles, of the household staff[19].

Consequently Coulson was arrested for conspiring to intercept communications and later bailed. News Corporation, the parent company to News International then announced, that the *News of the World* was to be discontinued after 168 years in print, the proceeds from the last issue being donated to charity. Days later, as concerns grew across all parties in Parliament about Murdoch's intention to take over satellite broadcaster BSkyB, News International dramatically withdrew its bid. The Culture Secretary, Jeremy Hunt, had referred Murdoch's bid to acquire the 61 per cent of shares it did not already own in BSkyB to the Competition Commission. The Prime Minister went on to announce the formation of a judge-led inquiry to examine "the culture and unlawful practices of some parts of the newspaper industry, the relationship between the police and media, and the nature of regulation". And so the controversy rumbled on. To what conclusion: who knows?

Size matters – and so does Twitter

In the case of the *News of the World* scandal, investigative journalism, led by the *Guardian*, has achieved amazing results. But what if the subject of the investigation is an unnamed premiership footballer who has allegedly had an extra-marital affair? Is this really worthy of being called "investigative reporting"?

What *is* certain is that we don't need reporters any more to do the probing into this kind of "human interest" story – not when we've got Twitter. During the Ryan Giggs and Imogen Thomas affair in June 2011, if you had a Twitter account it was easy to access information to help you conduct your own bit of investigative journalism.

But as *News of the World* scandal proves, some controversies are just too big and significant and require the trained nose of an experienced investigative journo to sniff out the excrement that has been banished, supposedly, out of sight.

Notes

[1] See Mail Online, (2006) Moment Prince William discovered "voicemail scam", 9 August 2006. Available online at http://www.dailymail.co.uk/news/article-399814/Moment-Prince-William-discovered-voicemail-scam.html, accessed on 15 May 2011

[2] See Davies, N. (2009) Trail of hacking and deceit under nose of Tory PR chief, *Guardian*, 08.07.2009. Available online at: http://www.guardian.co.uk/media/2009/jul/08/murdoch-newspapers-phone-hacking, accessed on 15 May 2011

[3] See News Corp (2009) News International Statement on *Guardian* article. Available online at: http://www.newscorp.com/news/bunews_40.html, accessed on 15 May 2011

[4] See Yates, J. (2009) Statement from AC John Yates. Available online at: http://cms.met.police.uk/met/news/major_operational_announcements/statement_from_ac_john_yates, accessed on 15 May 2011

[5] See Davies, N. (2010) News of the World pair hacked into 100 mobile accounts, *Guardian*, 1 February. Available online at http://www.guardian.co.uk/media/2010/feb/01/now-phone-hacking-scandal, accessed on 15 May 2011

[6] See Robinson, J. (2009) MPs' phone-hacking report delayed as Rebekah Brooks called to give evidence, *Guardian*, 9 December. Available online at http://www.guardian.co.uk/media/2009/dec/09/phone-hacking-report-rebekah-wade, accessed on 15 May 2011

[7] See *Private Eye*, 27 July 2009. Issue 1241

[8] See Tryhorn, C. (2009) Alan Rusbridger: PCC phone-hacking report is "worse than pointless", *Guardian*, 9 November. Available online at: http://www.guardian.co.uk/media/2009/nov/09/alan-rusbridger-pcc-phone-hacking, accessed on 15 May 2011

[9] See Evans, R. (2010) Max Clifford drops *News of the World* phone hacking action in £1m deal, *Gaurdian*, 9 March 2010. Available online at: http://www.guardian.co.uk/media/2010/mar/09/clifford-news-of-the-world-phone-hacking

[10] See Davies, N. (2010) *News of the World* pair hacked into 100 mobile accounts, *Guardian*, 1 February 2010. Available online at: http://www.guardian.co.uk/media/2010/feb/01/now-phone-hacking-scandal, accessed on 15 May 2011

[11] See Van Natta Jr et al. (2010) Tabloid Hack Attack on Royals, and Beyond, *The New York Times*, 1 September. Available online at http://www.nytimes.com/2010/09/05/magazine/05hacking-t.html, accessed on 15 May 2011

[12] See Van Natta Jr et al. (2010) Tabloid Hack Attack on Royals, and Beyond, *The New York Times*, 1 September. Available online at: http://www.nytimes.com/2010/09/05/magazine/05hacking-t.html, accessed on 15 May 2011

[13] See Carson, S. (2010) "Cov Con" Live Blog – David Yelland: My life in and out of the *Sun*, 25 November 2010. Available online at: http://cutoday.net/2010/11/25/cov-con-live-blog-david-yelland-my-life-in-and-out-of-the-sun/, accessed on 15 May 2011

[14] See Washbrook, C. (2011) UK: Coulson resigns due to phone-hacking scandal, Mediaspy.org, 21 January 2011. Available online at http://www.mediaspy.org/report/2011/01/21/uk-coulson-resigns-due-to-phone-hacking-scandal/, accessed on 15 May 2011

[15] See Peston, R. (2011) News International's new hacking evidence, BBC online, 26 January 2011. Available online at: http://www.bbc.co.uk/blogs/thereporters/robertpeston/2011/01/news_internationals_new_hackin.html, accessed on 15 May 2011

[16] See BBC (2011) Timeline: News of the World phone-hacking row, BBC online, 8 June 2011. Available online at: http://www.bbc.co.uk/news/uk-politics-12253968, accessed on 5 July 2011

[17] See Robinson, N. (2011) Phone-hacking saga 'changes character', BBC online, 5 July 2011. Available online at: http://www.bbc.co.uk/news/uk-politics-14025134, accessed on 5 July 2011

[18] See Peston, R. (2011) *News of the World* "paid police for stories", BBC online, 5 July 2011. Available online at: http://www.bbc.co.uk/news/business-14039915, accessed on 5 July 2011

[19] See Peston, R. (2011) *News of the World* "paid royal police officer", BBC online, 11 July 2011. Available online at: http://www.bbc.co.uk/news/uk-14107410, accessed on 12 July 2011

Note on the author

Sean Carson is studying for an MA in Automotive Journalism at Coventry University. He graduated from the University of Liverpool in 2009 with a BSc in Geography.

Bent Cops, Honour Killings and No-go Zones

Barnie Choudhury focuses on his work investigating minority communities and concludes that investigative journalism will survive so long as reporters maintain their insatiable curiosity

The Big Question

The big question in this book is whether investigative journalism is dead? My response to that is an emphatic *no*. Basically, we will have investigative journalists so long as reporters maintain their insatiable curiosity. Ultimately, no subject is too boring or too taboo to investigate.

In my case, I decided to pursue a particular genre of investigative journalism – reporting minority communities. When I began to study this area, nearing the end of the 1980s, it appeared completely unfashionable. This was even though there had been the headline-hitting riots in Toxteth[1], Brixton[2] and Broadwater Farm[3] while the *Scarman Report*[4], the forerunner to the influential *MacPherson Report*[5], had received substantial coverage.

The problem I felt was that for too long ethnic minority communities had been misreported by the main stream media. My contention is that all too often, journalists get it wrong. It is not always their fault: it is because they don't understand Black Minority Ethnic communities. How can they? Theirs is often the journalism of short hand, the journalism of stereotype and the journalism of the negative. Not only that, most of them have not lived in these communities and cannot hope to understand the subtle nuances. This is just the same for any of us who have never been to Eton or Oxbridge. We can never hope to understand the rarefied air these graduates breathe. Keeble[6] quite rightly explains that many journalists fight against discrimination but sometimes get it wrong. He reports (p. 177):

> Analysis of television coverage by Cardiff University School of Journalism found similar stereotyping and lack of appropriate sourcing on statistics. Archive footage, often showing men climbing fences in Sangatte [a refugee camp in Calais], was regularly shown whenever the topic of asylum seekers was dealt, thus reinforcing a negative image of them.

Consider then the incendiary comments from the former Metropolitan Police Commissioner, Paul – now Lord – Condon. He got into huge trouble when he suggested that most muggers were black.[7] Of course, he conveniently forgot to mention that black people were, at that time, at least four times more likely to be stopped and searched than white people[8]. Today it is even higher – you are seven[9] times more likely to be stopped and searched if you are black. Some newspapers do, of course, see positive stories or lobbying by pressure groups as "political correctness". Other newspapers even fall into the trap of being open to the accusation that they are institutionally racist[10]. Ironically, Condon never accepted his force was institutionally racist[11] even though he said about the inquiry following the murder of Stephen Lawrence in 1993:

> I recognise that individual officers can be, and are, overtly racist. I acknowledge that officers stereotype, and differential outcomes occur for Londoners. Racism in the police is much more than "bad apples". Racism…can occur through a lack of care and lack of understanding. The debate about defining this evil, promoted by the Inquiry, is cathartic in leading us to recognise that it can occur almost unknowingly, as a matter of neglect, in an institution. I

acknowledge the danger of institutionalisation of racism. However, labels can cause more problems than they solve.

Reporting black and Asian communities has usually been the domain of the minority journalist. Some may consider this, in itself, institutionally racist. But consider for a moment: if they have some understanding of the communities they are reporting on, is it not better than someone who comes blundering in with an agenda or a set of stereotypes? Similarly, is it not better that a reporter is well versed in the customs and nuances so the wool isn't pulled over their eyes, they don't offend and they don't appear naïve?

So this chapter aims to help highlight the basic tools needed to report responsibly, fairly and ethically these communities while producing potentially award winning stories. I will focus on three stories which I investigated to draw out some useful learning points and hopefully to stop any journalist from being labelled racist – and so becoming part of the story.

Bent cops

The "bent cop" refers to "the disgraced top cop Ali Dizaei". If you read his book *Not One of Us*[12], you are left with an overwhelming sense that had he not been so righteous, confrontational or litigious, his life may well have turned out so differently. But all these character flaws do not necessarily mean that someone is corrupt. The Metropolitan Police investigated Dizaei after they received a complaint that he was corrupt from the mother of one of his former girlfriends. They code-named this case "Operation Helios". Dozens of officers spent more than a year investigating the officer. They put him under almost constant surveillance. They secretly recorded 3,500 telephone conversations he had with friends and colleagues. Some taps were illegal. They even tried to set up a sting operation, involving the FBI. It did not work. Estimates put the cost of this operation at between £2 million and £7 million.

The basis of many a journalistic investigation begins with the sentence: "Something just doesn't smell right." Journalists rely so much on instincts. And so it proved with this case. Other elements of investigative journalism are luck and the continual appetite for creative risk taking. I was lucky because BBC2's *Newsnight* decided to take a risk. My investigation started in the middle of 2001, months after Dizaei's story had been in the newspapers, and finished in September 2003. Elliot Choueka was the researcher, Claudia K Milne the producer and I was the reporter. The timing of the legal case meant that the story was spread over two years. We had to dip in and out, keep notes and communicate with one another ad-hoc.

We needed to be forensic in our examination of the conclusions reached by the investigators. We needed to challenge Dizaei's arguments, put ourselves in the place of his accusers and really test his responses. Why is this particular case racist and a witch hunt? Just because the Metropolitan Police was found to be institutionally racist, does not necessarily mean this is one of those cases. So why did he order needles, if not to inject himself? Did he use prostitutes? And was he merely playing the race card?

We asked all these questions and more. We needed to convince ourselves, beyond all reasonable doubt, that what Dizaei was saying was credible. And then we looked at the Met's own investigation. Why would they ask police canteens whether Dizaei ate there and more specifically whether they served Halal meat? Furthermore, what use was it to spend hours traipsing the restaurants of London to check whether they were Halal? Our job was to put these facts in front of the British public and leave them to make up their own mind. It was never a crusade.

Investigative journalists also have to absorb a lot of pressure. You have a right to ask uncomfortable questions. You have a right to think independently. And you have a right not to follow the pack. For these things we came under pressure from the police who were annoyed we did not tow the line. The late Mike Todd was the man who suspended Dizaei. When I met him with colleagues he was the Chief Constable of Greater Manchester. One conversation sticks in my mind. He told us: "If you've seen the evidence I've seen, you wouldn't touch this story or Ali with a barge pole." Todd was persistent. He rang me a few weeks later when I was cutting this film to say he had seen even more evidence which showed Dizaei was guilty. He was trying to convince us to lay off the story. He was not alone. We know it was the police's job to spin. But we went away thinking: "You know what, you're just protesting *too* much." In the end, Dizaei was cleared and returned to work.

Yet my film exposed fundamental flaws in the police investigation because no-one challenged assumptions or defective leaps of logic. If *we* did that, why didn't the police? Clearly this investigation showed that some in the mainstream media are often complicit, unwittingly or deliberately, in accepting what the police say. During this episode, I felt exposed. Only the *Guardian*, *Newsnight* and the *Today* programme, on which I was working, challenged the Met to any meaningful degree. Exposing this case on prime-time television helped Dizaei demand an inquiry. It was called the Morris Inquiry [13] and was an independent public examination of professional standards in the Metropolitan Police.

It exposed flaws in police methods. The Dizaei investigation was a perfect example that even the best can fall foul of what was coined by one witness, Deputy Assistant Commissioner Stephen Roberts, the "Al Capone model " (see the *Morris Report* Section 7.39:144):

> Discipline inquiries can be quite different. You can start off at one extreme – and I have christened it the "Al Capone model" – where it is very clear that you have somebody who is definitely engaged in criminal corrupt behaviour; that might well be based on intelligence that you could never use in court, but you have a very clear view: here they are; they are guilty; now the problem is finding sufficient evidence to essentially get them out of the organisation and preferably into prison: the "Al Capone model". It does not matter what you get him for, you can get him for tax evasion, as long as you get him for something.

The result of this investigation is that it reinforced my core belief as a journalist: don't take anything at face value. It does not matter if your source is God, be healthily sceptical and check and re-check what you are being fed. The result was an affirmation for me that the media need to be careful about being exploited by those whose bosses admit to being on crusades. The then-Met Commissioner Sir Paul Condon said of weeding out bent cops: "This has been a crusade for me over the years."[14]

But this story has not yet ended. Dizaei was jailed in February 2010 and was no longer a top cop but a disgraced cop[15]. He was serving a four-year sentence for assaulting and falsely arresting a man over a £600 dispute. But at the time of writing, Dizaei's conviction was quashed by the Court of Appeal in May 2011[16]. During his appeal, the court heard how Dizaei's accuser lied about who he was and fraudulently claimed benefit using his dead father as cover[17]. Astonishingly the evidence was uncovered by Ali's

Iranian wife who took on the misogynistic Iranian system and testified in court to get her husband freed. Talk about investigating and campaigning for a truth. After serving fifteen months for a crime he says he did not commit, Dizaei is waiting for a re-trial. I met him at his home a few days after his release and he remained defiant, stating that his "integrity remained intact".

Sometimes, as an investigative journalist, you *just* have to trust your instincts about whether you can take a person at their word. The *Daily Mail* accused me of being a cheer leader[18] for this former officer. Unfortunately, neither Stephen Wright nor Richard Pendlebury, who I think is a brilliant journalist, bothered to speak to me. The article is inaccurate and as an investigative journalist you simply need to develop a thick skin. I remain simply a deep sceptic, refusing to accept things which simply do not add up.

Honour killings

One of the things you have to do if you want to be a successful muckraker is to have the temerity to offend, when necessary, in the public interest. No matter how insensitive it may appear, no subject is taboo, no question is off limits and no cow is too sacred. "Honour killings" is one of those subjects where you get hidden truths and have to confront communities and colleagues to uncover inconvenient truths.

In 1998, police in Derby were investigating a murder. The body of a pregnant teenager of Pakistani origin had been found dumped in bags, tied up, a hundred miles north of the city. It turned out that her brother had murdered her and her mother helped him. It brought into sharp focus to the British public the concept of "honour killings". This was one of the first reported cases in the UK.[19] To investigate this story, I remember having to walk on egg shells. I spent weeks winning the trust of people in this community where everyone knew what had happened, knew who was responsible, knew a wrong had been committed but did not talk about it. Eventually, I managed to persuade some to go on the record and speak on television.

How do you do that? According to Steven Covey in his *The Seven Habits of Highly Effective People*[20] we need to build up "an emotional bank account". What does this mean? Think of a bank deposit account before the world-wide recession. The more money you put in, the more interest you earn and the more money you get back. If you keep on putting in money, the bank gets to know you and starts to treat you as one of their valued customers. Very soon you are on first name terms with the manager. Very soon you will end up playing golf with them or being invited to social gatherings. So it is with minority communities. Journalists need to show that they are there for the long run. They need to show they can be trusted. And above all they need to earn that trust. If journalists take the trouble to research political parties, why don't they do that with minority communities? It is common sense and it makes business sense.

During this investigation I made sure I checked and re-checked every fact I found. I ran the finished script past Muslim colleagues and friends. And yet I got into trouble for a piece which went on to win me my first award. It is strange isn't it, how words can land you into trouble? It was two words: "practising Muslims". You see, a BBC colleague was so offended by my reporting he got someone in his community to complain to the BBC. For that I was hauled before a BBC Regional Advisory Council. I was cleared. My argument was that you can be born a Christian, Muslim, Hindu, Sikh and not be practising. I know some Muslims who drink alcohol and eat pork. I know some Hindus who eat beef. I know some Sikhs who cut their hair. Strictly speaking are they practising their religion? It was, unfortunately, a reflex reaction to try to deny and censor the freedom to investigate.

What was the outcome of my investigation? I revealed that some in the South Asian communities would rather let murders go unchallenged in the name of so-called honour. Some defended what had been done – but would never talk about it on the record. I exposed and pursued the culture of denial. In doing this story, South Asians grew more emboldened. Soon after this case, I was contacted by a women's group in Derby who had watched my reports. They told equally disturbing stories. They wanted to talk. They wanted to campaign. And they saw television as a way of finding their voice. The result of this story was the slow progress to something now enshrined in UK Law: the Forced Marriage Act 2007[21].

Suddenly, I realised people *did* want to talk about topics which the so-called community leaders wanted to keep hidden. Drug use among young Asians[22], denied by their parents but so prevalent, allowed me to expose the worrying trend of Asian youth cornering the heroin trade[23]. This led to an investigation into organised South Asian criminal gangs[24] and the Metropolitan Police spending £500,000 on looking in depth at the problem. And the result of this project was that it shed light on the radicalisation of vulnerable Muslim youth. All these subsequent stories were because of an investigation into so called "honour killings".

No-go zones

My job as a journalist is to be in the front row as history unfolds and report it. I should report events truthfully no matter how uncomfortable. And while you seek out the truth remember the lesson of unintended consequences. For me, this lesson began with a telephone conference call in February 2001. A colleague said that race attacks were at record highs in Oldham. No-one took any notice. When we talk about racial attacks, it is usually about black or Asian people being targeted by white people. In this case 60 per cent of victims recorded by the police were white. It became known as the "Oldham No-Go Zone" story. Why? Well, after six weeks of investigations my producer, Naresh Puri, and I were told by the police that South Asian vigilantes were roaming parts of Oldham. When we got there and saw things for ourselves, we found a group of thirty South Asian youths who openly admitted they were trying to create no-go zones for white people[25].

This story made me question myself. What is my role as a journalist? What is my role as someone from the South Asian communities who knows the implications of the story he is doing? What is the role of being responsible and ethical and yet being true to the ideals which, in the past, have uncovered unpalatable and inconvenient truths? And are they mutually exclusive? Isn't the job of journalists to witness and to write the first draft of history? What if I were witnessing it and realised it could cause potential conflict? What should I do? It is an ethical dilemma. As Martin Bell so eloquently argues, was I practising the "journalism of attachment"?[26] Bell was talking about his fearless reporting in Bosnia when he wrote:

> By this I mean a journalism which cares as well as knows; that is aware of its responsibilities; that will not stand by neutrally between good and evil, right and wrong, victim and oppressor. This is not to back one side or faction or people against another. It is to make the point that we in the press, especially in television, which is its most

powerful division, do not stand apart from the world. We are part of it. We exercise a certain influence, and we have to know that.

In Oldham, I remember urging the young men *not* to talk to us. If they did, I warned, the whole media would descend on them. I did this because I wanted to give them a chance to think. I did this so no-one could accuse me of cajoling them to talk to me by using my colour and cultural links. I explained what could happen and then let them make up their minds. Was this responsible journalism or had I crossed the line from impartiality to partiality? I like to think, ten years on, that it was because I was trying, in my small way, to prevent what I knew would happen in the days, weeks and months to come.

The police tried to discredit us at first. One local superintendent told one reporter at a news conference that we must have spoken to the only literate Asians in Oldham[27]. Six weeks later Oldham erupted in flames. Over several weeks I charted the rise in racial tensions. For this, a Greater Manchester Police spokesman, spitting as he spoke, veins sticking out of his neck, said they wanted to arrest me for incitement to racial hatred. Fortunately, I had specifically asked the BBC lawyers to consider whether any of my pieces did incite hatred because I guessed what was to come. Unintended consequences. And there were to be more unintended consequences. One BBC lifer took me to one side and asked me whether I had made it all up. Another later told the newspapers I was the most hated Asian in the BBC. I had to face two BBC internal editorial policy boards and a Guardian Festival to defend my journalism. Unintended consequences.

As a result of this investigation we uncovered disturbing evidence that in villages, towns and cities across Britain we were living parallel lives[28], running along the fault lines of race. We knew it happened but no-one spoke about it for fear of being called racist. This exposition was the unpicking of a festering scab. In 2005, four years later, the man who runs the Equality and Human Rights Commission, Trevor Phillips[29], told us we were "sleep walking our way to segregation". And there was another unintended consequence of our story – but this time more positive. Out of the flames of disturbance rose the phoenix of social cohesion[30]. In Oldham, more than a decade after the riots, segregated schools are being shut down and new integrated schools are being opened. We will not know until after 2012[31], when the first such school opens its doors, whether this social engineering experiment works. Well, from my vantage point, it is worth trying something rather than twiddling your thumbs and doing nothing while your town burns.

When the government drew breath and ordered three separate inquiries into the Northern riots of 2001, its experts concluded that they were caused by social deprivation. Sadly I don't think we got anywhere near the truth in those enquiries. My hunch is that we only picked up on a scintilla of the real problems affecting white and non-white Britons, even today.

So what?

So what am I saying? The need for investigative journalists has never been greater. Investigative journalists need to be fearless. They need to challenge assumptions, so-called facts and authority. Investigative journalists need to engage truly with so called hard to reach communities. They need to put aside fears of being called racist or sounding stupid by asking the most obvious questions and understanding their subject matter. And investigative journalists need to know that no story is off limits or taboo – as long as we shield ourselves with the cloak of accuracy, fairness, balance and impartiality…and context. They need to know there may well be unintended consequences to their stories – but that should not stop their digging for the truth no matter how unpalatable or inconvenient. They need to know they can be a force for change and a force for good.

The need for investigative journalists has never been greater. My sense is that towing the police line by the media is happening more and more today because of the demands of the 24/7 news cycle and getting rid of good journalists. The big danger is that the curiosity appears to be subsiding and instead we accept at face value everything people in uniform tell us. We can see this with terror raids. The media is there and has access to so-called facts. But it is never there to report how the overwhelming majority of cases end up with the suspect being released. Equally, we have seen an erosion in a suspect's rights – trial by media – as contempt laws are being pushed further and further[32]. The coverage of the Joanna Yeates[33] murder at Christmas 2010 is just one in a litany of cases. And woe betide anyone who does not do as the police say.

The banning of ITV national news from a press conference [34] on this murder is a low point in media relations. We are, in the UK, in hand-to-hand combat with the law and the freedom of expression. The banning of ITV News was, in my view, the heavy hand of the law, flexing their mighty muscles and declaring: "You may think you're influential but we're the ones in charge." It is just a few degrees of separation from the Libyan thugs who conspired to stop an alleged rape victim from speaking to the press in Tripoli.[35]

The need for investigative journalists has never been greater. My investigation into the police's handling of Operation Helios exposed how some forces of law and order appear to become "untouchable". When you spend so much time, effort and money you are under immense pressure to produce a result, any result, no matter how wrong or how stupid or how illogical. The anti-corruption squad started off with thirty allegations against Dizaei. These got whittled down to just two. That fact alone speaks volumes and the warning bells should have sounded loudly but they didn't.

If I were a news editor and this were my team, I hope alarm bells would have rung. I would have been awfully suspicious I didn't have a story. It's what Kevin Marsh[36], former Editor of the *Today* programme, describes as: "The ability to grasp the big truths – with the humility to let them go again when the facts don't fit." Or, if it looks too good to be true then it probably is.

Notes

[1] Toxteth riots remembered 4 July, 2001. Available online at http://news.bbc.co.uk/1/hi/uk/1419981.stm, accessed on 1 April 2011

[2] The legacy of the Brixton riots, by Cindi John, 5 April 2006. Available online at http://news.bbc.co.uk/1/hi/uk/4854556.stm, accessed on 1 April 2011

[3] Broadwater Farm – 20 Years On, 30 September 2005. Available online at http://www.bbc.co.uk/london/content/articles/2005/09/30/kurt_broadwaterfarm_feature.shtml, accessed on 1 April 2011

[4] Q and A: The *Scarman Report*, 27 April 2004. Available online at http://news.bbc.co.uk/1/hi/programmes/bbc_parliament/3631579.stm, accessed on 21 February 2011

[5] Sir William Macpherson's Inquiry into the Matters Arising from the Death of Stephen Lawrence on 22 April 1993 to date, in order particularly to Identify Lessons to be Learned for the Investigation and Prosecution of Racially Motivated Crimes. http://news.bbc.co.uk/hi/english/static/special_report/1999/02/99/ste phen_lawrence/report/#Proposals for the Inquiry, accessed on 1 April 2011

[6] Keeble, R. (2009) *Ethics for Journalists*, second edition. London: Routledge

[7] Mugging: criminal or political offence? London's police finally launched Eagle Eye yesterday. Nicholas Timmins assesses whether the controversy will have been justified, by Nicholas Timmins, 4 August 1995. Available online at http://www.independent.co.uk/news/uk/mugging-criminal-or-political-offence-1594666.html, accessed on 20 February 2011

[8] Blacks stopped more often by "racist" police, 15 October 1998. Available online at http://news.bbc.co.uk/1/hi/uk/194290.stm, accessed on 20 February 2011

[9] Police stop and search figures up, 8 July 2008. Available online at http://news.bbc.co.uk/1/hi/uk/7495075.stm, accessed on 2 February 2011

[10] *A Summary of the Stephen Lawrence Inquiry (Cm 4262-I)*. Report of an Inquiry by Sir William Macpherson of Cluny Presented to Parliament by the Home Secretary February 1999: "The collective failure of an organisation to provide an appropriate and professional service to people because of their colour, culture, or ethnic origin. It can be seen or detected in processes, attitudes and behaviour which amount to discrimination through unwitting prejudice, ignorance, thoughtlessness and racist stereotyping which disadvantage minority ethnic people." Available online at http://www.law.cf.ac.uk/tlru/Lawrence.pdf, accessed on 20 February 2011

[11] ibid

[12] Dizaei, A, and Phillips, T. (2007) *Not One of Us*, London: Serpent's Tail

[13] Final Report of the Morris Inquiry: The Case for Change, 14 December 2004. Available online at www.mpa.gov.uk/downloads/scrutinites/morris/morris-report.pdf accessed on 1 April 2011

[14] Condon's "crusade" against corrupt police, 15 December 1998. Available online at http://cdnedge.bbc.co.uk/1/hi/uk/235284.stm, accessed on 1 April 2011

[15] Met Commander Ali Dizaei jailed for corruption, 8 February 2010. Available online at http://news.bbc.co.uk/1/hi/england/london/8504308.stm, accessed on 1 April 2011

[16] Ali Dizaei hopes to return to police after appeal, 16 May 2011. Available online at http://www.bbc.co.uk/news/uk-england-london-13409222, accessed 31 May 2011

[17] Key witness 'lied' in ex-Met commander Ali Dizaei case, 22 March 2011. http://www.bbc.co.uk/news/uk-england-london-12816843, accessed on 1 April 2011

[18] Race war at the Met: We reveal what's REALLY going on at Scotland Yard, by Richard Pendlebury and Stephen Wright, 28 June 2008. Available online at http://www.dailymail.co.uk/news/article-1030074/Race-war-Met-We-reveal-whats-REALLY-going-Scotland-Yard.html#ixzz1IJGalrWP, accessed on 1 April 2011

[19] Life for "honour" killing of pregnant teenager by mother and brother, by Sarah Hall, 26 May 1999. Available online at http://www.guardian.co.uk/uk/1999/may/26/sarahhall, accessed on 1 April 2011

[20] Covey, S.R. (2004) *The Seven Habits of Highly Effective People.* London: Free Press

[21] Forced Marriage (Civil Protection) Act 2007. Available online at http://www.legislation.gov.uk/ukpga/2007/20/contents, accessed on 1 April 2011

[22] Patel, K. and Wibberley, C. (2002) Young Asians and drug use, *Journal of Child Health Care*, Vol. 6, No. 1 pp 51-59

[23] Asian Gangs Turn to Heroin Trade, by Barnie Choudhury, 21 January 2003. Available online at http://www.bbc.co.uk/radio4/today/reports/archive/features/heroin.shtml, accessed on 21 February 2011

[24] Scotland Yard tackles Asian crime gangs, by Barnie Choudhury, 15 June 2004. Available online at http://news.bbc.co.uk/1/hi/uk/3808165.stm, accessed on 1 April 2011

[25] Asian Vigilantes, by Barnie Choudhury, 19 April 2001. Available online at http://www.bbc.co.uk/radio4/today/reports/archive/politics/oldham1.shtml, accessed on 21 February 2011

[26] The journalism of attachment, by Martin Bell. See
http://books.google.co.uk/books?id=cvzcLqMcv_gC&pg=PA15&lpg=
PA15&dq=martin+bell+Bystanders+No+More&source=bl&ots=WP7j
CAnm3C&sig=jdH5icGMRuXuUIvWPqCk43iZNQM&hl=en&ei=21K
WTYKpFMSYhQev5vToCA&sa=X&oi=book_result&ct=result&resnu
m=2&ved=0CB4Q6AEwAQ#v=onepage&q&f=false, accessed on 1
April 2011

[27] "No go for whites" in race hotspot: Community leaders in Oldham
dispute police claims over attacks by Asian gangs, by Jeevan Vasagar ,
David Ward , Abigail Etim and Matt Keating, 20 April 2001. Available
online at http://www.guardian.co.uk/uk/2001/apr/20/race.world,
accessed on 1 April 2011

[28] Community pride not prejudice – making diversity work in Bradford,
Sir Herman Ouseley. *The Ouseley Report*, 12 July 2001. Available online at
http://resources.cohesioninstitute.org.uk/Publications/Documents/Doc
ument/Default.aspx?recordId=98, accessed on 21 February 2011

[29] Analysis: Segregated Britain? by Dominic Casciani, 22 September 2005.
Available online at http://news.bbc.co.uk/1/hi/uk/4270010.stm,
accessed on 21 February 2011

[30] *Summary Report on Community Cohesion Initiatives in Oldham Primary Schools*,
Maureen Haddock, June 2003. Available online at
http://www.oldham.gov.uk/oldham_schools_cohesion_report.pdf,
accessed on 21 February 2011

[31] Oldham to merge and reopen segregated schools nearly a decade after
race riots, by Nicola Woolcock, 17 April 2010. Available online at
http://www.timesonline.co.uk/tol/life_and_style/education/article71004
38.ece, accessed on 21 February 2011

[32] All students of journalism should read the excellent polemic by Ceri
Thomas, the current editor of Radio 4's *Today* programme: Contempt: An
Editor's View, 8 April 2008. Available online at
http://www.bbc.co.uk/journalism/law/contempt-today/, accessed on 8
March 2011

[33] Jo Yeates murder inquiry: 32-year-old man arrested, 20 January 2011.
Available online at http://www.bbc.co.uk/news/uk-england-bristol-
12238262, accessed on 1 April 2011.

[34] ITV News banned from Joanna Yeates press conference, by Josh
Halliday, 5 January 2011. Available online at
http://www.guardian.co.uk/media/2011/jan/05/itv-news-joanna-yeates-
investigation, accessed on 1 April 2011

[35] Journalists Try to Aid Libyan Woman Accusing Qaddafi Forces of Rape, by Lana Boone, 27 March 2011. Available online at http://www.1stcasualty.com/?p=1289, accessed on 1 April 2011

[36] What makes a good journalist? Speech given to the Society of Editors, 19 October 2004. Available online at http://www.bbc.co.uk/pressoffice/speeches/stories/marsh_editors.shtml, accessed on 21 January 2011

Note on the author

Barnie Choudhury has been a broadcaster for thirty years and a BBC News Correspondent for national television and radio. He has won several awards for his journalism, especially around Black Minority Ethnic communities, social cohesion and the criminal justice system. He is a Principal Lecturer in journalism at the University of Lincoln where he leads the television news department. His specialisms include racial diversity, home affairs and social affairs. He runs his own production company where he provides media training, shows leaders how to present in the most effective way as well as making radio features, documentaries and television films. He also helps to run a community radio station, is a Lay Advisor for the Department of Health's Equality and Diversity Council as part of its communications group and the Chair of AWAAZ, a South Asian Mental Health charity.

Match of the Decade? Andrew Jennings V. Sepp Blatter: A Classic Piece of Investigative Journalism

John Mair looks at Andrew Jennings' decade-long campaign to strip away the layers of onions of untruth protecting the "corrupt" rulers of world football

FIFA was brought to its knees in May 2011 by the work of one journalist: Andrew Jennings. His decade-long campaign against what he sees as a deeply corrupt organisation nearly toppled President Sepp Blatter from his 27-year rule at the Zurich headquarters of football's world governing body. Instead, the scalps of Fifa Vice-President Jack Warner (a long-time target of Jennings) and would-be President Mohammed Bin Hamann were offered up as sacrificial lambs. They were suspended. Blatter has survived – for now.

Jennings is a tenacious investigative journalist: relentless, cussed, stubborn, persistent – and he usually gets his man (or woman). First the sniff of a story; then dig, dig. dig until he gets results. If it takes a decade then so be it. Jennings almost solo forced the IOC (the International Olympic Committee) to reform and drive out corrupt practices including blatant bribes from potential host cities sought and given to IOC members. Today, the IOC can hold their heads high as being near transparent. That is not the case with FIFA.

Jennings learns the craft from the masters

Jennings' tenacity comes from more than four decades of being at the legal cutting edge of investigative journalism: always a heartbeat or a mistake away from a very expensive libel writ. He cut his teeth, like so many broadcast journalists, in newspapers helping out the *Sunday Times'* "Insight" team in their classic period in the 1970s (see Phillip Knightley in this volume). From there to working for the then doyen of broadcast investigations Roger Cook and his *Checkpoint* programme on BBC's Radio Four. Among his fellow researchers was John Stonborough who has since turned gamekeeper from poacher and now makes a living trying to stymie investigations but still retains a high regard for Jennings.

He says: "Andrew Jennings and I worked together on the BBC Radio *Checkpoint* programme in the eighties. I have followed his subsequent career with interest." He continues: "Single-handedly Andrew has taken on the biggest corruption stories in recent years: police corruption, Olympic corruption and FIFA corruption. He has faced down merciless resistance, dangerous people who could kill him, coped for years with the mockery of colleagues, as much for his dishevelled shambling style as anything. They are not laughing now." Jennings' friend and former *World in Action* colleague Paul Lashmar (now a journalism "hackademic" at Brunel University) is as much a fan too, saying: "He has no ambition but to do good journalism and get the baddies. Never been a hint of wanting to have a career."

From radio to television for Jennings and to *Watchdog*, then a strand on the BBC One tea-time programme *Nationwide* in 1982 where he teamed up with producers Vyv Simson and Nick Hayes (to declare an interest, I worked in the same team). Jennings and his producer's relationship is central to his work. Mutual trust is vital. It can break down inside and out. In 1986, the BBC refused to broadcast his and Simson's documentary about corruption in Scotland Yard; Jennings reacted by resigning, Simson too. The documentary was later aired by Granada's *World In Action* and the research material was transformed into his (and Simson and Paul Lashmar's) first book, *Scotland Yard's Cocaine Connection*, in 1991.

Jennings had learned the importance of the dramatic "doorstep" (stopping a villain or target in the street or another public space) from the master Roger Cook. He honed it on *Watchdog* and it reached a zenith when the controversial policeman DCI Tony Lundy was out training for a marathon while on sick leave from the Met: Jennings simply intercepted him and attempted an interview while running alongside the resolutely silent Lundy. Jennings and his producer, Simson, produced some of their finest work on *World In Action*, especially on the near-open corruption in the International Olympic Committee. Their programmes and book, *The Lords of the Rings: Power, Money and Drugs in the Modern Olympics*, in 1992, heaped ordure on the organisation and forced change. Jennings had found a world famous organisation to pull apart. The IOC became almost an obsession for him for that decade.

The first book was followed up by two others: *The New Lords of the Rings* in 1996 and *The Great Olympic Swindle* in 2000. Jennings laid out his stall in an interview in 2008 with Steve Amoia, of Soccerlens: "There's always two stories at these big international sports organisations like the IOC and FIFA. There is the story about themselves, how wonderful they are, how they care about the athletes, and then you find out about the kickbacks, find out about the immoral activities." His *métier* was ferreting out the latter.

Sport the new investigative frontier

Jennings was now firmly set on a path of serious sports investigation. His was not to be the conventional sports journalism route. Lashmar comments on the Jennings' view of sports hacks: "He holds sport journalists generally in contempt though he speaks well of a few." The template was established. Find, investigate, get a mole or more, investigate more, co-operate and build a community of journalists with similar interests; publish and watch the results. The IOC ancient regime crumbled under the Jennings spotlight. FIFA – the Federation International of Football Associations – was next to come under the Jennings' microscope. His view of the history of FIFA: "There is no question since Joao Havelange, the Brazilian, took over, in 1974, corruption immediately followed. Before him, there was the Englishman, Sir Stanley Rous. Now, I am not being patriotic about it, but Stan Rous was clean. He may have been a bit of a bumbling old fool, but he would never take a bribe. What you need to know for any World Cup bid, there is no accountability nor transparency. Partly because they get away with it, and frankly, the coverage of journalists is not as good as it could be. Money has gone through Caribbean banks, or accounts in Lichtenstein."

Jack Warner likes a "bung"

Intent was signalled by his programme, *The Beautiful Bung: Corruption and the World Cup in 2006*, on the BBC's flagship investigative show *Panorama*., Jennings investigated several allegations of bribery within FIFA, including million-dollar bribes to secure marketing rights for company ISL along with vote-buying (to secure the position of FIFA President Sepp Blatter) and bribery and graft attributed to others in FIFA. Jennings revealed the previously secret machinations of Jack Warner, the seeming President for life of Concacaf; the Caribbean and Central American football umbrella body. Warner used football and FIFA as a cash machine, milking it for personal gain through the unfair deals he made with Trinidad and Tobago national players, through thinly disguised requests for bribes to potential host countries for the World Cup and through deals made by his son's firm on ticketing and travel for the 2002 World Cup. To put it in layman's terms, Warner used his FIFA position to be "on the take".

Jennings gave this ventilation worldwide. He does not mince his words about Warner in the 2008 SoccerLens interview: "For the Under-17 Youth World Cup in Trinidad and Tobago in 2001, he set up a company to initiate construction; he got tickets, this was all for 17-year-olds, the next generation of stars. There were World Cup tickets every which way, there was an exclusive travel company, high-priced tickets for Confederation officials. Jack has gone from a not-very-well-paid teacher to the top man in Trinidad."

In addition to his Concacaf role, Warner is also a politician in his native Trinidad and Tobago and is the current Minister of Public Works and Transport and *de facto* deputy prime minister. He is no fan of Jennings and his work, once berating him during a doorstep. As Jennings recalled: "Warner said to me: 'I would spit on you but I would not denigrate my spit. You are garbage'" (Soccerlens 2008). To some in Trinidad, Warner is a hero, to others Jennings is for having exposed him and his financial machinations.

So to President Blatter

The FIFA President, Sepp Blatter, was always in his line of fire. Jennings on his nemesis: "Sepp Blatter really never had a real job. Like a rock star.

And he'll never have a real job again. Blatter studied Business Administration in Lausanne...He did get a real job for about a year with the Swiss Tourist Board. Then he got a job with a Swiss watch firm as a PR man. In 1974, just after the Winter Olympic Games, he was recruited by FIFA. He has never worked anywhere else. He was a technical man, then was in marketing, then became General Secretary and worked with Joao Havelange, from Brazil, whom he deposed in 1998. He then became President in a rigged election" (Soccerlens 2008).

Paul Lashmar comments on Jennings: "He finds a corruption-riddled organisation and sticks with it for the long haul. A decade if necessary. That way he builds up relationships and trusts and gets hold of killer documents and interviews. But it is not a solo effort. There is his producer in television and Jennings has also built up a network round the Play the Game organisation" (see www.playthegrame.org). Lashmar adds: "He has been one of the first journalists to build an international network of like-minded journalists all looking at the same story. They share the work and then the success. He funds his own investigations really."

Like many great journalists Andrew Jennings has curiosity and mischief in equal measure and he makes his luck. In the case of FIFA, the liquidation of the sports promotion company, ISL, in 2001 meant a treasure-trove of FIFA documents became available once the liquidator was on board the Jennings train. And he has used them well since.

Chasing a host: doorstepping Blatter
Good investigative journalism, if effective, does not win friends in high places. Blatter was now on the Jennings radar and in 2005 he was banned from all FIFA press conferences. He still is. Any questions which he has for Sepp Blatter or other FIFA officials have to be asked through a surrogate or in the rather bizarre setting of a series of Jennings doorsteps of Blatter. Jennings comments on one of his many Blatter doorsteps: "If you go up to someone on a public highway, if you behave properly, don't touch them, you can approach them to ask things. It's a skill I have developed over the years. So I had a much-traveled crew and waited for Blatter outside of FIFA House in Zurich, as they say in English slang, like a ferret out of a drain pipe."

They have become a double act In the words of Simon Chadwick, Professor of the Business of Sport at Coventry University: "Andrew

Jennings is a wailing, worthy and entirely appropriate adversary for Blatter." Paul Lashmar comments on how Andrew Jennings has evolved as a journalist: "His writing style has become much more mellow and subtle since the IOC investigation. He has also become more adept at using dry humour to undermine his targets. Look at his repeated doorstepping of Blatter."

As Lashmar indicates, Andrew Jennings is ever aware of the simplicity of the television film. His producers over the years have made sure of that. A project of the scale of FIFA generates huge amounts of background research. Little is used on air. Better to turn it into a book as he did with his 2006 book *FOUL! The Secret World of FIFA: Bribes, Vote-Rigging and Ticket Scandals*. The next year he was back to *Panorama* on screen and the 2007 programme on links between FIFA and Lord Sebastian Coe who led the successful bid for London to stage the Olympics in 2012.

Did Jennings and *Panorama* lose England the right to stage the 1918 World Cup?

The most high profile Jennings' investigation of all – *FIFA'S Dirty Secrets* – was aired on the BBC's *Panorama* programme on 29 November 2010, just three days before FIFA decided on the host country for the 2018 World Cup. England was in the running, had been lobbying and schmoozing the 24 delegates who decided for months and years (including England playing a bizarre international in Warner's Trinidad in June 2008 to curry favour there). The tabloids indulged in patriotic predictions: "Football's coming home to the land of its birth," they cried. Hopes were high: a superstar level delegation of Prince William, David Cameron and David Beckham were sent to seal the "deals" made. But, sadly, the "deals" were all too hollow. Jack Warner was not the only double crosser amongst the 22 high and mighty executives in FIFA. Many promised votes simply melted away. England's bid garnered just two votes – one from their own delegate. Russia won as had been predicted by Football Association Chairman Lord (David) Triesman during an undercover sting by the *Mail on Sunday* in May 2010. Triesman had to fall on his sword, even though he was perfectly correct. He repeated many of his charges in the open to a House of Lords Committee in May 2011 (though these were later rejected by FIFA).

Much heat and noise surrounded the Jennings allegations that Ricardo Teixeira, President of Brazil's Football Federation (CBF) and of the 2014

World Cup Organising Committee, Nicolás Léoz, of Paraguay, President of the South American Football Confederation (CONMEBOL), and Issa Hayatou from Cameroon, President of the Confederation of African Football (CAF), all accepted bribes from a television marketing firm ISL. Once again this exclusive was based on insider knowledge and insider documents. The tabloids accused the BBC and Jennings of costing England the chance to stage the World Cup. John Stonborough comments: "People who say he cost us the World Cup, are talking crap, we never were about to get it and only thanks to Andrew we know why."

The BBC had faced much pressure-from the highest levels of government not to transmit or not to transmit in that slot. They firmly resisted. John Stonborough adds: "I shall never forget Jennings doing a Columbo outside the *uber*-swanky Baur au Lac Hotel in Zurich, shouting questions at the FIFA high command as security goons tried to hustle him away. It was the finest television theatre: Peter Falk with a rasping English accent. The set-piece, old school doorstep, never intended to glean an answer, merely to shock and embarrass his prey."

FIFA in deep crisis, May 2011

After the votes for 2018 and 2022 venues, it all seemed to be over. Blatter was in control. The *dénouement* of that came not in the expected selection of Russia to host the Cup in 2018 and the very unexpected choice of Qatar in 2022 (which FIFA General Secretary Jerome Valcke later alleged they had bought) but in the fall-out six months later over the election of the new FIFA President

Life mirrored art and the Jennings narrative. Three days before that Presidential election, Jack Warner and Mohamed Bin Hamman (the head of the Qatar FA) were called before a FIFA Ethics Committee – surely an oxymoron – to answer charges of having bribed Concacaf delegates a few weeks before to the tune of $40,000US each to vote for Bin Hamman in the election. They were both suspended. Blatter was also called to the committee but not surprisingly they found no case. Three days later, on 1 June, Blatter's was the only name on the ballot paper. He was elected unopposed by 186 out of the 203 "votes" cast. British Prime Minister David Cameron called it "a farce". He was wrong. It was a tragedy. Blatter was heading an almost completely discredited world governing body. Andrew Jennings' work over a decade had put FIFA firmly in the doghouse.

Lessons from the new master?

So, just what does the Jennings/Blatter decade long marathon tussle tell us about how to make an investigative classic?

Firstly, you have to have incredible stamina, stubbornness and sheer cussedness to stick at it until you get results. Many would have put off by the FIFA/FA incoming fire. Not Jennings. His former *Checkpoint* colleague John Stonborough comments: "Andy is arguably Britain's finest investigative reporter. I don't think he would agree with my opinion of his status as a (superb) journalist – his obsessiveness, his self-doubt would never let him believe it, not until the next exposé is in the can or the one after that."

Secondly, you need an outlet and a powerful backer. The BBC with the might of its brand and gold standard journalistic reputation has stood full-square behind Jennings on his FIFA revelations. No doubt there have been full and firm discussions before transmission with lawyers and programme editors but once on air the BBC has backed the story to the hilt. The FIFA story would have died or been marginalised without the Corporation giving it airtime-worldwide.

Thirdly, you need to stick at it and show results. That way you build up contacts who trust you and reveal more and more to you. Paul Lashmar stresses: "He doesn't really do it for the money – as far as I am aware, he doesn't have any assets. This makes him a much harder target for lawyers." Others, though, such as Professor Simon Chadwick, are more sceptical on the Jennings' effect: "He has told a story that needed to be told but he seems somewhat stuck in a loop. In football terms, nice build-up work in midfield but he now needs to put the ball in the back of the net by going one step further and overthrowing those he seeks to topple."

Fourthly, cultivate your sources but also respect them and protect them in all circumstances. "In forty years in this business, I've never let a source down. No source has ever been detected. I know all the tricks of the trade to disguise where I get stuff from. Young journalists or anyone who wants to investigate corruption, know that there are good people with mortgages, bills to pay. If you get them to say: 'This isn't right, help me' and they will help" (Soccerlens 2008).

Fifthly, courage helps. Andrew Jennings is brave. Not many would take on such worldwide brands as the IOC and FIFA or the Chechen warlords as he did for *World in Action*. Paul Lashmar: "He is fearless – I know I have been with him in some very dodgy situations."

So, to get to the kernel of the truth about what you see as a corrupt organisation you need stamina, trusted sources, luck, a backer with deep pockets, a moral compass and a modicum of investigative skills. Andrew Jennings has those aplenty. Sepp Blatter must wish his gaze had never landed on FIFA. Jennings has given him deserved nightmares. He may yet topple him. Investigative journalism works.

Note on the author
John Mair is a senior lecturer in broadcasting at Coventry University. He is the inventor of the Coventry Conversations and co-editor with Professor Richard Lance Keeble of this and four other books. He is a former BBC, ITV and Channel Four producer and worked with Andrew Jennings on *Nationwide/Watchdog* in 1992.

"Dynamic Television" and the Big Society

Peter Hill argues that "dynamic television" suffered its death blows at the BBC when the Head of Sport and then the Head of Comedy began to influence the work of investigative journalists. And it was buried in late 1987 when John Birt took over control of BBC Current Affairs

In his inaugural address in 1961, President Kennedy gave the watchword for his presidency: "Ask not what your country can do for you – ask what you can do for your country."

The phrase appealed to the entire post-war generation, both in the USA and the UK. Young people, inspired by such thoughts, set up many of the non-governmental agencies we now take for granted – such as Shelter, the Child Poverty Action Group and the Samaritans. Others turned to the new medium – television. I joined the BBC at that time.

Something similar is happening today. On 19 July 2010, four months after taking office, David Cameron spoke of his innovative idea – the "Big

Society". "The Big Society is about a huge culture change...where people, in their everyday lives, in their homes, in their neighbourhoods, in their workplace...don't always turn to officials, local authorities or central government for answers to the problems they face ...but instead feel both free and powerful enough to help themselves and their own communities."

For television producers, "helping communities...in the workplace" can only be done by shaping the content of their programmes. Such was certainly so after Kennedy's speech; will Cameron's appeal to altruism have a similar effect?

Drawing lessons from history is never easy, for societies and values change over the years. Further, such conclusions are always based on personal experiences. I can only write about what I witnessed within the BBC Current Affairs department during the three decades when I worked there. But here is what happened then. It is for the reader to judge if it might again happen now.

When newcomers ousted the old guard at the BBC
In the early sixties the creation of BBC2 doubled the staff of BBC TV. This had important consequences. Most of the new employees were in their early twenties. The executives above them came from a post-war era, when the BBC was still in many ways an arm of the civil service – as it had been during the war. The newcomers soon outnumbered the old guard. They had little or no television experience and so tended to experiment. The increase in output forced them into new areas of subject-matter.

I worked on a weekly programme called *Man Alive* which specialised in social issues. We reported on subjects which our viewers may never have even thought about before – lesbianism, illiteracy, extreme poverty, alcoholism...if anyone suffered from it, we filmed it.

Man Alive was run by Desmond Wilcox. He had a clear vision of its aims: "We are the oil on the wheels of democracy." He believed the programme had a cathartic effect on the interviewees – and on its viewers with similar problems. He was doing a job that the social services were not doing. His programme helped create the caring society.

Man Alive was not alone in bringing about change. *Cathy Come Home*, transmitted by BBC drama in 1966, highlighted the problems of a young couple living in poverty. It caused a storm – and reforms were introduced as a result. At the same time, *That Was the Week That Was*, a light-hearted entertainment show with David Frost, was persuading us all to look at political affairs with a raised eyebrow.

As *Cathy Come Home* hit the headlines, BBC 1 also transmitted an edition of *Panorama* about the case of James Hanratty, who had been executed for murder. There had been occasional programmes on miscarriages of justice before this, mainly presented by Ludovic Kennedy. They had helped bring about the abolition of the death penalty. However, John Morgan's report contained two important new elements. He interviewed key witnesses at Hanratty's trial, and he tested timing evidence by reconstructing particular journeys. Morgan was "doing somebody else's job". He was doing what the police and the legal system should have been doing.

"Doing somebody else's job" became a standard definition for the word "investigation" within the BBC. It was also called, in some circles, "dynamic television" because its aim was usually to embarrass governmental agencies into working as they should.

We see few such programmes today. However, when members of the public do not "turn to officials, local authorities or central government for answers to the problems they face" they invariably turn to television for help. "Finding answers to problems" through television means investigating the problem – usually to "demonstrate a need".

Growth of investigations in the sixties and seventies
There were other factors behind the growth of investigative television in the sixties and seventies. Just as today, with the theories about the causes of the wars in Iraq and elsewhere, the sixties were dominated by the conspiracy theories surrounding the death of President Kennedy. In Britain, there was a similar rash of theories about the Suez campaign of 1956. Had the top three politicians in the country really agreed to go to war without telling us? There was a feeling that governments were not telling the whole truth – and it was the job of journalists to correct this.

The British government quickly perceived what was happening in television. Harold Wilson regularly tried to gain control over political programmes. He was the first Prime Minister to blackmail the BBC by refusing to be interviewed. Many politicians, most of whom had experienced the BBC during the Second World War, thought that the government should ultimately decide BBC editorial policy.

Harold Wilson invented tactics which have since become common. The worst outburst came after a programme called *Yesterday's Men* which took a more than frank look at the government that had been defeated by the Conservatives in 1970. Such was the intensity of these attacks that it was not surprising to hear in the BBC that the politicians involved were not acting reasonably – and must have something to hide.

This was the general atmosphere when Watergate broke – and the war in Vietnam reached its peak. Many Americans, raised on the Monroe doctrine and isolationism, were politically opposed to US involvement in Vietnam. Moreover, young men who had been born during the Second World War disliked being drafted into another war.

Vietnam was filmed as no war before it had been filmed. Journalists worked right at the front. They filmed the action as it happened, blood, guts and all. Many memorable images came out of this – the girl who had been burned with napalm, the Viet Cong soldier shot in the head for the camera to film, the slow pan to the ground as a cameraman died whilst still filming. Such images brought the war into the living rooms of America and played on their emotions. American parents saw the hell that their children had been drafted into.

How Vietnam increased the power of TV networks in the US
However, this horror gave the TV networks in the USA immense power. When the US troops were finally pulled out, it was largely attributed to the determination of just three men – the heads of NBC, ABC and CBS. It was power as great as any President's, and which television should never have. But it came at a time when the President was also seriously wounded by the Watergate scandal.

In Britain, television producers, bruised by the political attacks on them, watched in amazement as investigative journalists in America brought down President Nixon. This was power, indeed. Investigations became the programmes that editors wanted.

Over the next decade a series of categories developed for such programmes inside the BBC Current Affairs department. The essentials were that someone (the victim) was suffering – and, therefore, that the person causing this suffering (the target) should be exposed. The conclusion was that someone who was being paid to stop such outrages was not doing the job properly.

The lowest category of investigation was typically the "conman" type of exposé. Someone was tricked into handing money over to a conman; they complained to us, we told their story – and approached the trickster for an explanation. Trading standards offices were only just springing up – television was demonstrating the need for them.

The second category of investigation was the "loophole in the law". Such programmes identified an area of law were there was a serious failing – and pointed this out. I can perhaps explain this strand best by quoting an example from my own work.

In 1977, I learned from a police contact that several bags of pornographic photographs had been found in a raid – all involving children. The police did not know what to do because there was no law on child pornography. We examined the photographs, tracked down some of the locations, discovered the perpetrators and exposed the scandal.

The initial government reaction was that the problem did not exist – because Scotland Yard had no figures for child pornography. It was claimed that the photographs had been taken abroad. We drew their attention to the British television sets and the three pin plugs in some of the shots. We pointed out that Scotland Yard had no figures because they had no child pornography squad. That was because there was no law on child pornography. The Protection of Children Act of 1978 was then passed as a Private Members Bill.

Exposing the law-breakers
The third category of investigation was the most serious. Here we identified a breach of the law by someone, exposed it, and put enough

evidence into the public domain for the police or some other official body such as the Inland Revenue to lay charges.

As these investigative programmes developed, so too did the internal legal involvement in them. All investigations had a legal background to a certain extent. In the lower categories, it may only have been a threat of a writ of defamation. The "right of reply" became so common that it was considered mandatory in all categories of investigation. However, in other investigations there was also copyright, contempt of court, trespass, harassment and privacy to consider. Category three investigations might even include a potential breach of the Official Secrets Act. Further, BBC internal rules – particularly about surreptitious photography and recording – were far stronger than the general law of the land, so these had to be taken into account as well.

The former practice of merely asking a lawyer to watch a programme and pronounce on any possible defamation writs was abandoned. Lawyers became involved from the very start of an investigation. They sometimes drafted scripts. In some programmes, witnesses (as they were now called) were asked to sign sworn statements before their interview was filmed. We began to record all conversations with people involved. We prepared for trouble after transmission.

This approach introduced a new element into programming that few outside the investigators really understood. Defence of the BBC became as important as the programme itself. The content of programmes became somewhat incidental within the context of the overall operation. We had to do everything necessary during the making of the programme to ensure that the integrity of the BBC and of the programme itself could not be damaged after transmission.

Trying to "make a difference"

The common thrust throughout all investigations was the same: to uphold the standards that the government laid down – but which some people were not adhering to. It was "doing the job for them". It was "dynamic television". It helped get things done. We tried to "make a difference" and make life better.

This might mean, for example, looking at the immigration authorities and investigating white slaving – or investigating building contracts in a local council. However, because of the many rumours circulating about police corruption in the seventies, the body frequently under scrutiny was the police. It was this kind of thinking that led me towards *Rough Justice* which I created in 1979. There were programmes about miscarriages of justice before it, but none with the intensity of investigation which my team and I brought to this project. The genesis was simple. In late 1978 I began to work with Ludovic Kennedy on a weekly interview. It was during the many meetings I had with him that his wisdom and my investigative experience came together.

Ludo had made several programmes on the subject – in particular, the cases of Timothy Evans and the Luton Post Office murder. However, he was not an investigative journalist of the type which had sprung up since Watergate. I saw the idea in a wider context. It was doing "somebody else's job" – the job of the Home Office civil servants who looked at suspicious cases.

Ludovic Kennedy pointed me to the legal reform group Justice. It mainly comprised lawyers who gathered research and published reports on various legal reforms. They did this unpaid and in their spare time. They were already doing the job of the Home Office officials for them, though in a rather amateurish manner. I decided to cooperate with them.

When I first visited the Justice offices I was surprised and pleased to see the amount of documentation they held on suspect cases. This was largely the work of the indomitable Secretary of Justice, Tom Sargant. He had the evidence, we had the technique. It made for a powerful partnership. We did the job that others were being paid huge salaries to do.

Attracting powerful enemies

We attracted powerful enemies. These included the police generally – as well the specific officers who had investigated the cases we looked at. Judges hated the idea that the system was not perfect. We would also often detect animosity among solicitors and barristers who had conducted cases which we looked at. They feared criticism. Further, we found that there was animosity from people who lived near where crimes had taken place. They had suffered severe pressure during the original police investigations and they were pleased when someone was convicted for the crime. That relieved the pressure and allowed them to retreat to their normal quiet lives. We introduced the idea that a murderer might still live among them.

The "operation" that this programme became, meant that we needed to introduce even more rules for ourselves. I decided that no *Rough Justice* programme would openly criticise any person involved in the legal process which had resulted in a suspected miscarriage of justice. We often saw mistakes in a judge's summing-up – no such instances were mentioned in our programmes. We discovered poor, indeed criminal, police practice. No such instance was ever mentioned. If we proved that an innocent man was in prison, *no one was to blame*. It was just an unfortunate accident.

We also worked to bolster our defences. We organised meetings with very senior retired judges, several of whom were Law Lords. With them, we discussed the nature of our programmes and our intentions in making them. Every programme had a senior retired judge behind it, examining our evidence and guiding our research. Eventually, I even managed to set up a "back channel" to the Home Office in order to discuss the progress of our cases and learn of their prospects.

None of this was done because we doubted our abilities to research properly such programmes. We did it all in order to protect the integrity of the BBC and our programmes after transmission. This evolved into what I termed the "pledge".

Doing the job social services fail to do

The "pledge" meant that if we took up a case, we would follow it up as far as we could. The timing of the programme was irrelevant to this. Thus, when we made the second series of *Rough Justice*, we included a report on the progress of the cases in the first series. When we had a convict released, we followed him through his first few months of freedom. This was not because we were particularly interesting in what he did, but because our support while filming helped to set him up in society. We did the job that social services failed to do. Although I left *Rough Justice* in 1986, I am still working on one of the cases – because of "the pledge".

The BBC ceased making *Rough Justice* programmes a quarter of a century after I made the first. But, in fact, I considered our job was done after our second series in 1983. After all, we had merely tried to demonstrate to the British public that innocent people were in our jails and that there was a need for a body to consider such cases. Surely, by 1986, this was clear. Yet no government agency stepped in – until a decade later.

As we moved through the eighties, I realised that *Rough Justice* had, in fact, come some five years too late. Everything slowed down, as the Thatcher government tightened its grip on the BBC. One of the consequences of this was that non-journalists were put in charge of journalistic output. The Controller of BBC 1 had, almost traditionally, been chosen from the Current Affairs department. But as the government increasingly piled on the pressure about the BBC's political output, it was thought wise to change that policy.

For most of my tenure of *Rough Justice*, the BBC 1 Controller was a former head of the Sports department. He knew little of our rules of journalism. His concern was largely viewing figures. *Rough Justice* won massive audiences. I believe that one edition still holds the record for a serious Current Affairs programme. It was also winning awards. This naturally pleased Controller One. So, when I suggested we change things, I was told to get on with doing what I had made into such a success.

BBC emphasis shifts to entertainment

By the mid-eighties, this change in the type of person at the top had more or less killed "dynamic television". When Bill Cotton, a former head of comedy, became Controller One, things were particularly bad. He saw nothing but trouble in what we in Current Affairs were doing. The BBC Charter stated that our mission was to inform, educate and entertain. That was why the various departments of the BBC had been created. Current Affairs had always considered that information was our contribution to the BBC's Charter commitment. But the general emphasis was moving to entertainment, not information. We were told that "campaigning television" was not in our remit. It followed that we should not make programmes which "oiled the wheels of democracy" – for they caused trouble in negotiations over the licence fee.

Rough Justice lingered through the nineties because it had touched a raw nerve. If the innocent people it covered had been thrown into prison – who was safe? The government eventually saw the light – and, some fifteen years after I made the first programme, the Criminal Case Review

Commission was created to deal with the problem. The Home Office civil servants who had failed to do their job properly were ousted.

I should add that *Rough Justice* was not alone. Other investigative journalists were working in the same field with similar principles behind their programme-making. *Rough Justice* faded as the Thatcher government took increasing hold on the BBC. It was producers and reporters – particularly in Granada and Yorkshire Television – who made the final push. They had worked on the Irish cases, the Guildford Four and the Birmingham Six. When the convictions of those ten people were overturned the change really started to happen. Mention too must be made of the Paul Foot, Chris Mullin MP, Robert Kee and Bob Woffinden whose books and articles added greatly to the impact of the television programmes.

If "dynamic television" had suffered its death blows when the Head of Sport and then the Head of Comedy began to influence our output, it was buried in late 1987 when John Birt took over control of BBC Current Affairs. Birt's "blue-sky" thinking had one sentence written in its clouds – everything the BBC Current Affairs had done in the past was wrong.

The impact of Birt

Birt's arrival coincided with the BBC switching from typewriters to computers. This innovation was fortunate for Birt – it increased his ability to interfere with programme-making. His interventions produced great tensions with seasoned producers. With one particular edition of *Panorama*, a desperate producer and reporter locked Birt out of the edit suite because the transmission deadline was in jeopardy. Birt's desire to put his own stamp on the output, combined with the ability of his lieutenants to read from their offices what producers and reporters were writing on their computers, moved the Current Affairs department into a more *dirigiste* system.

Such intervention from the top level had been almost non-existent in the BBC before Birt's arrival. An "empire" system had been created during the sixties in which trust was the essential element of the management structure. Departmental heads ensured that programmes were fair and balanced, not the Director General. Of all the balances, political balance was the most important – and investigations were often said to be in that category by those in government agencies who felt their heat.

The BBC's strategy on political balance had evolved in response to the attacks made on programmes by the Wilson government. Ministers had begun demanding a set amount of time within any proposed programme, and even a requirement that they should not be involved in any discussion, but merely questioned at the end of the programme. The absence of a government voice, it was said, would inevitably lead to unbalanced programming. Such demands seem to be returning to pre-programme negotiations.

The BBC's response to this blackmail in the sixties and seventies was a policy that political balance was to be achieved over a series of programmes, not necessarily within any single programme. Such matters were dealt with at producer or editor level who knew best what was going on. The Director General only became involved if a matter of principle had to be decided.

Strangling investigations

With investigations, this meant that when the Director General was told of a programme by a departmental head, his usual response was to ask the head of the legal department if the programme was fair and balanced – and above all, safe. The system John Birt introduced to achieve "balance" tightened the control. It generally strangled investigations. People who knew little of the law, and even less of the intricacies of an investigation, made fundamental decisions about how programmes were to be edited. "Weasel words" became common. The lack of investigative expertise in higher management made investigative producers very vulnerable.

John Birt also introduced important structural changes within the BBC legal department. The "checking" lawyers who watched the programmes had always been responsible for any later litigation. But now a team of "litigation lawyers" handled any writs. Tensions between these two departments were such that the "checking" lawyers soon ensured that nothing was transmitted that might possibly attract a writ. In this way they did not suffer the criticism of the litigation lawyers; but it meant the end of investigating programmes.

A whole generation of producers and reporters has joined the BBC since this major change in administrative structure. No one remembers "dynamic television" at all. Current Affairs does not even exist as it did – it was amalgamated into News, where subjects are generally taken from the Press Association morning list, and producers and reporters then assigned to them.

The relationship between the BBC and the government has also changed. Since the controversies of the eighties, the BBC has largely "come to heel". Programmes publicised as "investigations", with some notable exceptions such as those of Donald McIntyre, and the occasional *Panorama*, are usually made in cooperation with some governmental institution. The police, the Inland Revenue, Customs and Excise, Social Services and others benefit from the publicity such programmes give them. The "raised eyebrow" is no longer a part of the face of the BBC. No one "does somebody else's job".

How playing on emotions can easily become propaganda
The idea of using television to make a better world exists in one burgeoning area of BBC output – the Red Nose Day and the Children in Need evenings. The idea came from the United States where the Jerry Lewis telethons began in the mid-sixties. They have raised millions of dollars for worthy causes. However, the approach of such programmes is not to inform "to demonstrate a need". Just as the heads of the three main American broadcasters during the Vietnam War used the emotional effect of television to bring about change, these telethons use the emotional possibilities of television to persuade viewers to give cash to a worthy cause. Playing on emotions rather than simply presenting information is dangerous, for it can easily become propaganda.

Two systems of originating programmes have emerged from the Birtist revolution. Neither promotes the production of investigative programmes. Inside the BBC, producers appear to work almost as they did in the seventies and eighties. However, the system by which programme subjects are chosen is far more editor-led than it was three decades ago. The ability of producers to choose their subjects – and their responsibility for the final programme – is far less than it was.

Alongside this internal system is the external commissioning system. The problem, with this is that independent production companies die if they do not get commissioned, so they tend to do whatever they are asked – and they are asked to do things by someone who knows very little about the subject of the programme. The BBC Editor demands a certain level of content – and the commissioned producer is supposed to find it, even if such is impossible. It is a wonder that some bright and enthusiastic producers occasionally manage to overcome the problems with these two commissioning systems.

Mr. Cameron may be dismayed to learn that in the television workplace the workers do not "feel both free and powerful enough to help themselves and their own communities". The system of originating programmes will need to be changed if such is to be achieved.

Moreover, if the Prime Minister seriously wishes to create what he calls the "Big Society", he should be looking to intelligent people such as those in television to help him. But he cannot do it by persuading them to transmit government propaganda. *Dirigisme* does not promote altruism. If management structures in terrestrial television cannot be changed to encourage such output, a new journalistic outlet, a "gateway" to the public, must be found.

Such gateways still exist in print journalism, though they seem not to be appreciated. Where was the praise for the *Daily Telegraph* journalists in 2010 when they exposed the MPs expenses scandal? And why was it left to print journalists to do this job when television budgets are so much greater than theirs?

Ironically, the BBC – an organisation entirely paid for by the public – merely followed these events. It never got ahead of the print journalists. The reason is simple, the *Telegraph* was doing "someone else's job" – the job of the House of Commons rules office and the job of the police. "Doing someone else's job" is no longer a part of the BBC's remit.

David Cameron may look to history and the creation of non-governmental organisations to support his view that people outside government can contribute to improvements in our society. He says that creating the Big Society means that we should not "always turn to officials, local authorities or central government for answers to the problems". Being of a later generation, he may be unaware that many journalists in the past have felt free and powerful enough to help the community without turning to officials and central government.

In the early seventies, *The Sunday Times* did this famously with their "Insight" team's investigation of Thalidomide. That was just one of their many important investigations which made society better, more just, more open, less discriminatory. Many television journalists in the past have used their job to help promote similar improvements in the way we live. Today their chairs are occupied by people of equal intelligence and enthusiasm – but with less power and, sadly, less experience of how to carry on the good work.

If we wish to encourage investigative journalism back into television, we cannot expect any of the major broadcasting organisations to change their ways. They have been badly burned in the past. However, the past quarter of a century has seen the birth of a big new "gateway" – the internet. It could point to a rebirth of investigative journalism – if certain obstacles can be overcome.

Why journalists must operate between the community and the authorities

Firstly, investigative journalists will have to demonstrate that there is a need for their work. One aspect of the investigative journalism of the sixties and seventies is certainly needed today. Many people are afraid to talk to the police – fearing they may suffer as a consequence. We are currently being asked to report to the police any suspicious behaviour in the Muslim community: many might think it foolish to do so. Journalists can become useful "middleman" between the community and the authorities.

However, demonstrating a need is not enough. Investigative journalists must be experienced and reliable – and they will need money and legal advice. *Pro-bono* lawyers might well be found, but funding is a more difficult problem. Most funding organisations wish to control output, and that could not be a part of any deal.

One suggestion is that the terrestrial broadcasters organise a *pro bono* system, similar to those within the legal system, loaning personnel and even equipment when it is not being used for other programming. This may seem far-fetched, but an advantage would be that the broadcasters could transmit the *pro-bono* programmes if they wished. The BBC has done something similar in the past with Open University output.

Some minor investigative efforts are already on the internet. One is the Bureau of Investigative Journalism which publishes exposés. Others are libraries of programmes. The audiences for these are small, but the programmes are always available, so the number of viewers increases week on week. As viewing habits slowly change from watching live transmissions to choosing programmes from "video on demand" libraries – such websites might become popular.

A rebirth of dynamic investigative journalism using the internet would certainly be, as David Cameron would have it, "something different and bold", but we are many years away from anything of any great benefit to society as the investigative programmes of the seventies were.

Note on the author
Peter Hill worked for the BBC TV Current Affairs department for thirty years and became one of their leading investigating journalists. In particular, he created the *Rough Justice* series investigating miscarriages of justice, which eventually helped to create the Criminal Case Review Commission. He always projected the image of being a maverick – to gain greater control over his output. He believes that investigations suffer from the intrusion of senior management who do not understand the rules of investigations.

The Ethics of Going Undercover

"Yes, I had gone a bit native. Yes, I had grown fond of some of my targets. But I hadn't let it interfere with how I did my job." BBC undercover reporter Mark Daly talks frankly about the many tricky ethical dilemmas he faced while filming his Bafta-winning investigative programme, *The Secret Policeman*

There's nothing wrong with invading someone's privacy, telling a pack of lies about who you really are and covertly recording every move they make all in the name of the public interest is there? Well, yes actually. There can be an endless number of things wrong with that, depending on the subject matter. And this is why undercover reporting is one of the most closely regulated journalistic endeavours in the BBC.

Good undercover footage is always exciting. By its very nature it affords you glimpses of worlds you are not supposed to see. But it should never be voyeuristic or gratuitous and must always be the very last resort for the journalist. There are rules and there are ethics. The rules can be hard and fast, but the ethics should never be fast and loose.

In this chapter I will explore the ethics behind undercover reporting, based principally on my own experience. If one wishes to view it as a kind of useful ethical pamphlet for the undercover operative, then it will have fulfilled some purpose.

I have been a reporter for around 14 years; at the BBC for the past nine and various newspapers before that. In that time I have covered probably hundreds of stories, been undercover less than a dozen times, and only once for a significant period. During my career I have been undercover as a drug user and drug dealer. I have played roles trying to catch out dodgy businessmen, witch doctors and suspected murderers. I have also been a policeman for the 2003 *The Secret Policeman* documentary which has given me a perspective on long-term, deep cover which does not come with any of the more transient roles I was previously or since involved in. My job was to investigate racism, and I was in uniform, filming covertly, for more than seven months before I was discovered and arrested. Not even my closest family knew what I was doing.

Ethical issues as pertinent as ever
I shall try to explain briefly the background to my investigation and, while the events took place in 2003, the ethical issues of going undercover remain as pertinent as ever.

Undercover must never be a fishing expedition – you must know, or at least have very good reason to suspect, that whatever it is you are looking for is actually there, it's called *prima facie*. With my project, the Stephen Lawrence Inquiry's devastating assessment of the police was still raw, and in 2002 the then-Chief Constable of Greater Manchester Police (GMP), Sir David Wilmot, admitted his own force was institutionally racist. GMP's statistics in recruitment and retention of Black Minority Ethnic (BME) officers in the early 2000s bore this out. We also obtained significant anecdotal evidence about the problems within the GMP from serving and ex-officers.

In addition, there was also a report about the problems being faced by BMEs within the force which had been undertaken by a local university. This was good *prima facie* evidence and the BBC had good reason to suspect racism. But the only way to establish if such behaviour was manifest was to infiltrate covertly the GMP with an undercover reporter becoming a police officer. Asking questions openly as a journalist simply would not have uncovered the truth.

In 2002, a decision was taken at the highest level within the BBC to begin an intrusive investigation. Along with this decision came issues of how the BBC, as a national institution as well as myself as the undercover reporter, would conform and adhere to an ethical framework for the investigation.

In addition to the BBC editorial guidelines, my production team and I had set my own rules of engagement. I would be no *agent provocateur*; I would never be racist myself. I was not allowed to make racist comments or incite anyone to say or do anything which they would not have otherwise said or done. But I could laugh at their jokes and behave like a "dumb apprentice". I said I was eager to hear other people's views in order to form my own. I had to gain their confidence whilst not being critical. Essentially my job was to blend in to the extent that my colleagues would feel comfortable enough to be themselves. There should never be any grounds to be accused of entrapment.

We knew this investigation would come under significant scrutiny from the police and the media – and rightly so. My behaviour had to be demonstrably ethically and morally sound. There were other rules too, some unwritten: I should never become romantically involved with anyone, since that would compromise me and the investigation. I am aware of undercover police officers (and other journalists for that matter) who have fallen into that trap and jeopardised the project. Cover stories of wives and partners can be used to prevent those situations developing.

A real concern of mine was whether I would actually find any racist behaviour. Over time, I felt this concern could pose a real dilemma for the undercover reporter: Is it OK to actually *want* to find criminality, or in my case, racism? Well, I'm not sure of the answer to that, but I reckon it is part of human nature to want to be successful. And if a project is to be successful, then it follows that the reporter needs to find something. If they don't, then perhaps the *prima facie* background work has not been done properly and the job should not have been embarked upon in the first place. We knew what we were looking for and we strongly suspected that racism existed, but the desire to prove it would not, and should not influence how I would do my job. If I got rumbled on the first day of the investigation because I had left a wire hanging out my trousers, then while it would be very embarrassing, at least the BBC would be able to justify the intrusion because the preparatory work had been done.

Crucial role of the "second chair"

What can never be justified is putting the desire to get the evidence ahead of everything else. The priority must be to do the job correctly and ethically. The story, if it's there, will follow; if it has been gathered correctly, then this will stand you in good stead, and protect you when it feels as if they are coming after you at 100 miles an hour. I shot 180 hours of material, and had a "second chair" producer watch every second of it. The second chair is entirely independent: separate from the production team and is tasked with the sole aim of maintaining the high ethical and legal standards of the BBC. In my case, he had only one concern about my behaviour throughout those tapes, and to ensure transparency, we made sure that part was included in the film to allow the viewers to make up their own minds.

The desire to succeed should never cloud your view, no matter what pressure you are under. There have been times during my early career, when I was under pressure from a senior colleague to ditch the rules and make covert remarks to targets in order to entice them into a comment or action. I never did it, and got the story anyway. Those journalists don't stay in the business long.

The undercover operative will often be a witness to criminal or anti-social behaviour. It's probably why you are there. But what happens when it gets out of control? What do you do? Well, it depends. A useful tool for the undercover operative is to role-play as many situations as you can envisage before going in. One of the scenarios I imagined concerned what I would do if I was witnessing a racist assault by another officer. What should I do? Well, the answer was to try and film as best I could the incident as it unfolded, and in doing so capture the evidence of a racial assault – and then intervene before it got out of control.

I never had to make that call, as the scenario never emerged. But in the recent *Panorama Undercover Care: the Abuse Exposed* (2011), the reporter witnessed persistent abuse of vulnerable patients in residential care by out-of-control staff. Some viewers might have expected the BBC reporter to intervene. He did not, and by doing so, captured, in my opinion, the most dramatic and shocking undercover footage seen for many years. By not intervening, and attempting to stop the abusers in their tracks, it is likely that the film was more powerful and will, therefore, have more long-lasting consequences. However, it was undoubtedly very difficult for the reporter (as it was the viewer) to stand by and watch the abuse escalate as it did.

As an undercover journalist and an operational police officer, the two roles were, initially, entirely separate. Later, they would begin to fuse, and there would be many internal and ethical conflicts to deal with. But first things first, I had to make sure I could cut it as a cop. I took to it easily and made friends with some of my colleagues quickly. I actually really enjoyed the training, and laterally, the on-the-beat job.

When you become friends with your "targets" the dilemmas multiply

Cliques had formed early on and I was in such a group where racist abuse terms such as "Paki" and "nigger" were commonplace for these PCs. The idea that white and Asian members of the public should be treated differently because of their colour was not only acceptable for some, but preferable. I had become a friend to these men. They trusted me with their views. And they believed I was one of them. I was able to do this, not by being a leader, but a follower. I acquiesced, and sometimes asked questions.

I developed several hypothetical tests that I would use to test just how racist my colleagues were. One of them was called the "jaguar test". What would they do if they saw an Asian driving a Jaguar? This is a short selection of some of the answers I encountered:

PC Pulling: "Have him, he's coming over the road….A dog that's born in a barn is still a dog, a Paki born is still a fucking Paki."

PC Hall: "I'll stop him 'cos he's a Paki. Sad innit but I would. He's a Paki and I'm stopping him 'cos I'm fucking English" (*The Secret Policeman*, 2003).

Some of the racist comments I had recorded were made whilst the officer was drinking. I knew this would be an issue, so it was decided that none of the comments made in those circumstances would ever be broadcast unless I had noted or recorded similar comments from that same person at a point where no alcohol was involved. This posed another ethical challenge: if I was going to be one of the boys, which I plainly had to be, I would have to be involved in my fair share of rounds, which would often involve drinking shots. There was, in my experience, a particularly macho culture in the service – even at training school, which involved a good deal of drinking, among other things. But there were very few social occasions when I would not be fully rigged up with the undercover recording equipment, so I had to remain alert. A couple of pints were OK, but when it got to drinking multiple shots of tequila, I learned to go to the toilet and quietly make myself sick.

As best I could, I stuck to the truth about my life, allowing fewer chances for any slip-ups. My professional background was false obviously, but I kept the rest reasonably accurate. For me, being undercover in the police was not that difficult. I was busy and sleep deprived, but kept going by the adrenaline and the genuine belief that I was doing something important. An average day for an undercover operative can often much longer than those of the community he (or she) is infiltrating. When my colleagues went to bed, my other job – the journalist – would start. I would have to start logging all my material and writing up my diary and often be up until two or three o'clock in the morning and back up on duty at 7.30 am. I became an expert at napping. For any extra breaks I would slip way and steal fifteen minutes' sleep.

Dealing with the problem of personal preferences

No matter what my personal preferences were within my group of colleagues, I would go through my covert "process" with everyone to try to discern whether or not they were racist. It wasn't difficult, I would play dumb, and just ask general questions, based either on something that happened in class that day in race relations training, or perhaps linking it to some current affairs event – such as the anniversary of Stephen Lawrence's murder. What was difficult, was when I would get answers I didn't want to hear, particularly from someone I had grown to like. This is the hardest part of the job, the part which you cannot prepare for. As soon as it became clear that someone was displaying racist tendencies – that was it, they had to be recorded in my diary or on film. And in an ideal world, all the people we identified in the programme as being racist would have been people I didn't care much for. That wasn't the case.

There could be no excuse for people ever behaving like that, never mind in a police officer's uniform. Therefore, I should have been contemptuous about the people who had uttered such things. But it didn't always work like that. I run the risk here of sounding like I turned "native", which I suppose I did, a bit, but this is a key ethical issue, as well being an important discipline for long term undercover work. For me to become close enough to colleagues and go through my "process" with them, bonds had to be formed.

Now, it is true that some of the racist men I met had very little about their character that was in any way redeemable. I am thinking here of PC Pulling and one or two others who displayed a level of racism and contempt for ethnic minorities which really was beyond belief. It was hard work hanging around with PC Pulling in one way, but in another, he was the easiest to spend time with, because there was no internal conflict. He didn't deserve to wear the uniform and, therefore, I would lose no sleep over my role in him being sacked. It became clear that several people were going to lose their jobs but I did not dislike all of these people. In fact, I had become very close to some. How does this happen? And how does one deal with it? Well, dealing with it is one aspect, but the most important thing is to stay focused, and do the job as best you can – without emotion. That however, is easier said than done.

PC Andy Hall, was one of the men that I spent most time with and who was also a racist. I would only hear him being racist occasionally. I diarised and recorded that; filed it away in my notes, and put it to the back of my mind. The rest of the time he was a model friend and colleague; charming and funny and so that is what I focused on. The problem with that strategy though, is that it's easy to get confused. What I ended up having to do was to make a kind of compromise with myself, where I agreed that I would deal with the emotional ramifications of what I was doing, somewhere further down the line.

There were occasions when I was really willing someone not to be a racist because I was fond of them, and then they would come out with something repulsive. This happened notably with my colleague and friend PC Carl Jones. One day, when I was supposed to be filming PC Hall, Jones started talking about "Black Added Tax". This was a reference to his previous job at a garage. My heart sank, thinking: "Not you, Carl." I switched on, knowing he would lose his job and would be disgraced. He turned out to be one of the most racist probationer officers, yet somehow, I still regretted his inclusion in the programme.

Did I betray him and PC Hall and the others? Well simply, yes. Even though they were racist, and I hated that part of them, some of the lines had become blurred. We had lived in each other's pockets for months, and it hurt to betray them. But that's where it's crucial to have some kind of ethical code. Why am I here? Why am I doing this? Is it worth it? The answer was yes. It was worth it. This helped me to rationalise my feelings, which I knew to be at least partly irrational, and get on with the every day demands of having two pretty stressful jobs at once.

Putting all the emotion and complex material to the back of my mind

I actually did not want to come out, as I wanted to put off for as long as possible the moment where all my colleagues would learn that I had betrayed them. Yes, I had gone a bit native. Yes, I had grown fond of some of my targets. But I hadn't let it interfere with how I did my job. I had tried to put all that complex and emotional stuff to the back of my mind – and comprehensively turned my colleagues over. And the time was now approaching where they would find out, and they – as well as I – would have to deal with it.

There were also the other guys, the guys who were not racist, and to whom I had grown close. What would they think? I just hoped that they would understand one day.

The issue was taken out of my hands in any case, and one day in August I was intercepted on my way to begin a shift and arrested on suspicion of obtaining pecuniary advantage by deception. I was taken to my local police station near the production flat in Didsbury, Manchester, questioned and kept in overnight. I knew all my tapes were safe, as I had only a few hours previously made my final crucial handover to my producer.

Sitting in my stinking cell that night, my thoughts were with my police colleagues, who would be having the news broken to them. Eight weeks later we broadcast *The Secret Policeman* to a national outcry. Ten officers were sacked, 12 disciplined and several police teachers removed from post. Sweeping changes were made to police training.

It could have gone very wrong but it didn't because we stuck to our own rules of engagement, and not once did I do anything of which I was ashamed. There were things I regretted, of course, because of the consequences for those involved. But to walk away from something as draining as seven months in a double life (relatively) emotionally unscathed as I did, one would have to be satisfied, that no matter the outcome, what had been done was done in the public interest, and most importantly, was done ethically.

Note on the author

Mark Daly, 36, is an award-winning investigative journalist for the BBC. He was the undercover reporter behind the BBC's 2003 Bafta winning *Secret Policeman* programme, which exposed racism in the police. During his nine years at the BBC, he has also investigated and made programmes about the Stephen Lawrence case, the Glasgow terror attack, the banking crisis and many others. He has also worked for the BBC's *Rough Justice* programme, researching and presenting a film *Rough Justice: Murder Without a Trace* in 2005 which led directly to the release of a man wrongly imprisoned for murder. He started his journalism career in newspapers in 1997 and worked for the *Scotsman* and the *Daily Record* until moving to the BBC in 2002. His journalism awards include a Bafta, two Royal Television Society awards, several programme awards and Scottish Young Journalist of the Year. He is currently the investigations correspondent at BBC Scotland and regularly reports for *Panorama*.

Section 2. Alive and Well Internationally

Signs of Life: Investigative Journalism Beyond Britain

John Mair

If domestic investigations are expensive, foreign ones even more so. But yet they too survive. Eamonn Matthews is one of the inventors and executive producer of the long-running Channel Four series *Unreported World* which for twenty weeks every year reveals stories from afar that deserve an airing but have not had one. Matthews argues that the best way to tell good stories on television is to remember the medium you are using. Television to him is more than radio with pictures.

Headlines about the WikiLeaks Cables tended to concentrate on the current or recent theatres of war – Iraq and Afghanistan. Paul Lashmar, a veteran investigator turned "hackademic", argues those headlines ignored the real revelations from the cables – the Pakistan story.

Shez Baz Kahn, a former journalist with the *Dawn* newspaper in Pakistan, examines the enormous pressures facing investigative journalists in the country on the frontline in the "war on terror". He concludes: "Like the state of Pakistan, journalism is at crossroads in this country. Every effort is being made to gag the press and keep the people in the darkness.

Investigative reporters are either killed or harassed to the point where they start censoring themselves in order to stay alive. Good journalism can thrive in Pakistan only if the powerful Pakistan army demarcated its boundaries by letting an accountable and media-friendly democratic government and culture flourish in this county in the coming years."

David Cay Johnston is a Pulitzer Prize winner in 2001 for his work on uncovering loopholes and inequities in the US tax code. He has just been made a columnist at Reuters. Cay Johnston looks at the state of investigative journalism in the USA today and comments: "For investigative reporting this is the best of times; this is the worst of times; it is the age of data-driven exposés; it is the epoch of gullible belief, at least in America."

Stephen Engelberg is Managing Editor of Pro-Publica, a not-for-profit American organisation which investigates and reports to the public on a wide variety of issues. Here, in a special interview for the conference, he talks on how to keep your distance from your paymasters and maintain your integrity.

Paul Kenyon is a multi-award-winning investigative journalist. His work – mainly on *Panorama* – is not easy, often featuring investigations over months and over continents like the one of which he describes the making. "Chocolate: the Bitter Truth" transmitted in April 2010. Here, he takes us through that production in a simple ten-point guide. Alas, making the programme in the UK, Africa and elsewhere was not that simple.

China and investigative journalism are not words that normally appear in the same sentence. Yet the next two contributors find reason for hope there. Homson Shao, from the second largest media university in China – the Zheijiang University of Media and Communication – argues that journalism plays the part of a licensed opposition in the PRC. Professor Hugo De Burgh, an old China hand and the Director of the China Media Centre at the University of Westminster, argues that investigative journalism in China is seen essentially as helping to promote good government, the welfare of the people and institution-building. He concludes that investigative journalism in China is more supervisory than adversarial.

How to Get Investigative Documentaries on Television

Eamonn Matthews identifies some basic rules that make for compelling investigative journalism on television. He concludes: "Of course, rules exist to be broken. However, if you break these suggestions you need to be able to explain why you are breaking them and why the end result will be improved."

Television commissioning editors are desperate for scoops that will bring acclaim, notice and audience to their channels. They are hungry for fresh stories that will spark headlines and draw in fresh viewers. It's a great time to be a journalist pitching investigative documentaries.

Yet I'm puzzled that I often meet fantastic journalists who believe fervently that television is set against investigations. They list wonderful stories that have been rejected, and portray a Britain of dumbed down television that has no room for journalistic sleuthing. Of course, any TV listings guide will show they are wrong.

I think in many cases they would get their ideas accepted if they had a better understanding of the language of television, its demands and its power. It doesn't help that sometimes journalists have a wilful disdain for understanding the language of television. They believe that the story is all, and everything else is flummery. That makes no sense. The story is important, but these same journalists would never rage against a newspaper editor who required their scoop to be written in clear, vigorous writing in grammatically correct English.

Some rules for making worthwhile television

I think that to make worthwhile television there are some rules that by and large have to be followed. It follows from this that to convince a commissioning editor that a film should be made, journalists need to demonstrate they understand these rules and can meet the demands they impose.

1. Narrative

There must be a narrative, by which I mean cause and event must relentlessly follow each other, from start to finish. A documentary has to tell a story which unfolds in a compelling way, with the viewer desperate to know what happens next. Television is a hugely powerful medium but it is a limited one, and an unforgiving one. You can't turn back a page, or click back to the previous page. There are no second chances. It is a medium that has to hold its audience every second. Viewers are holding remote controls with their fingers poised. And they're gone if your grip on their attention falters for even half a second. Narrative is all.

From the start anyone carrying out an investigation needs to think about the range of revelation needed to construct a narrative that will drive the film forward. Let's say you obtain evidence that proves a politician has been fiddling his or her expenses. That single revelation that will make the front page in a newspaper but it will only sustain a television narrative for a few minutes.

However, a few moments thought shows how you can build up a narrative. Who approved the expenses? Why? Did officials know the expenses were corrupt? Did they try and hide that fact? Were other politicians involved in a cover up? Why? As soon as you start asking those questions you start to shape a narrative, and simultaneously increase the power of your journalism because each of those questions are themselves important investigative targets.

The thousands of US cables that have found their way on to WikiLeaks are worth thinking about in terms of narrative. While the cables have filled newspapers day after day, they have received very little coverage in television documentaries. This is because on the whole the cables are pieces of unrelated information that do not form a natural narrative. Effective television programmes cannot be constructed around a washing line of unrelated nuggets of information.

The cables dealing with civilian casualties in the aftermath of the invasion of Iraq were an exception in that they lent themselves to a powerful piece of story telling because they dealt with the original incidents and the subsequent investigations. Guess what? A documentary was quickly made.

Constructing a narrative also forces a journalist to work out what is important and what isn't because facts that don't have consequences can't be placed in a narrative. There are wonderful journalists who hate throwing out facts in this way. For them all information is wonderful and to be treasured equally. Television is not the medium for people who want to operate like that. Television needs journalists to work out what information drives a story forward and then to focus ruthlessly on these areas. This makes for better journalism, because it focuses investigative time on first order questions. It's pointless knowing the colour of the car your corrupt politician purchased if you haven't established it was bought corruptly.

2. Actuality
Documentaries need pictures of real events that tell the narrative before any script is added. It is vital to realise that in television, it is rarely enough for investigative journalists to reveal wrong doing: they need to have footage of that wrong doing. "Show me, don't tell me."

Newspaper and web journalists can write about abstract issues. Television demands to see something concrete happening. I have heard journalists deplore this as the "tyranny of television". I think this is missing the entire point of the medium. Television's greatest strength is taking viewers to places they can't go and showing them what is actually happening. That's its purpose.

Journalism on television means taking a camera inside tough and difficult situations and showing the reality of what you are revealing. It can entail journalists getting their hands on CCTV footage, or mobile phone footage, or police or security service surveillance footage.

Increasingly it means secret filming with hidden cameras. You might get hold of documents showing a hospital is the worst in Britain; you might then painstakingly construct a television narrative around these revelations, plotting the story of how patients risk death. You then need to convince a commissioning editor that you will be able to film the ill treatment actually happening. Hospitals, schools, police stations, dental surgeries and care homes have all been exposed in recent years to shocking effect. Powerful films have documented old people starving in care homes, policemen refusing to answer emergency calls, and pupils beating up school teachers in failing schools.

Gathering this type of actuality creates more powerful journalism. It provides incontrovertible on-screen proof of wrong doing. It creates programmes built on objective truth rather than massaged reality.

Now you can construct television investigations around reporter pieces to camera and moodily shot documents, but you will have a hard time convincing a commissioning editor that the film should be made, and a harder time convincing the audience to watch. A programme like this could be broadcast on radio, or the documents posted on the internet but it is not utilising the power of television as a medium, and so pitching this approach to a commissioner is like pitching a book to a publisher and telling them you will write it badly.

3. Characters

Television programmes should be built around characters. I have mentioned that television is about taking viewers to places they can't get to, and showing them the reality of those closed worlds. It's also about letting viewers meet other people whose experiences and suffering they can relate to through a common bond of humanity. It's not enough to meet them as "talking heads". We need to enter their lives. Television is uniquely equipped to do this, and commissioning editors will expect it to happen.

So just as an investigation into a failing hospital needs to show the actuality of neglect and failure, it also must allow viewers to meet those who are enduring abuse. It must make viewers think – what would I feel if I were that person? Developing characters in this way helps hold an audience. It also makes for stronger journalism. An eminent newspaper columnist once wrote of a programme I had made that it was too emotionally powerful and would hinder politicians from taking logical decisions.

I instinctively distrust this plea for desiccated story telling. The emotional response we feel to characters is also part of understanding the complexities of a situation. It's right that we ask: how would I feel if this happened to me? To my parents? To my children? Indeed, it's often only when we ask these questions we start to understand the implications of a revelation. *The Sunday Times*'s investigation into Thalidomide was so powerful precisely because it showed the devastating effects of corporate avarice on individual parents and children.

4. Interviews

Documentary interviews should be filmed to capture testimony not information. Many journalists spool off a list of potential talking heads when they are asked what will be in a film. That is a quick way of frightening commissioning editors, and stems from a misunderstanding of the purpose of television interviews. Too many people think interviews are conducted to search for information.

When a print journalist interviews someone it's often the first time they have met them and so the interview is a fishing trip, a trawl for information. A television journalist conducting an on-camera interview for a documentary should not be seeking information; they should already know what the person will say through their preliminary research. A television interview is conducted for quite different purposes:

- The first purpose is to get first hand testimony that corroborates or develops the actuality pictures. The reporter is not trawling for information but, like a barrister in court, is seeking to establish key points. If the story is being told properly these moments will be ones of great drama, powering the narrative forward. However they will only occupy a minute or so of screen time.

- The second purpose of interviews is to put revelations to those who should be held to account. Again the reporter needs to be more akin to a barrister than a print journalist seeking information.

5. Script

A script can never compensate for the lack of pictures of real events. Commissioning editors are instinctively wary of journalists who believe that their voice over can make up for deficiencies in the narrative or in characterisation.

When I watch an initial cut of a programme I watch it without any reporter commentary. In a programme that is working the picture actuality and the interviews with key characters will tell much of the story, otherwise it's a radio show with some visual wallpaper laid underneath. If that isn't happening then either the material isn't being edited properly or the wrong material has been filmed. "This is boring but it will be good when there's script on it" is not a statement I have ever found to be true.

The pictures should tell the story so well that the script can exist in another plane that lies beyond basic story telling. Most one hour documentaries have about sixty pieces of commentary, each two or three sentences long. Even in a great film about a quarter of these sentences will still have to be expended on steering the story telling. Those that remain are valuable. They need to provide analysis and context, not information that should be coming vividly from pictures and interviews.

6. The story

It's vital a substantial number of people care about your revelations. In all I have written so far I have assumed there is a scoop at the heart of the documentary programme. However, at some time all journalists become enmeshed in stories which matter to them and no one else.

A journalist who makes a documentary is asking a television audience to watch for half an hour, or more likely an hour, probably in the evening during their leisure time. That's a big ask – far more than the fifteen minutes or so most people spend reading an entire newspaper. So any revelation must be one that affects large numbers of people. There is no point in broadcasting programmes that no one watches, or in arguing that people "ought" to watch something.

So it's easy. Work for months to uncover an amazing revelation that affects millions of people. Keep repeating until you have enough revelations to construct a gripping narrative. Work out how to capture in pictures the wrongdoing you have documented. And then persuade the people affected by your revelations to relive their ordeal in front of a camera.

Of course, rules exist to be broken. However, if you break these suggestions you need to be able to explain why you are breaking them and why the end result will be improved. If you can't, think again before pitching the idea. And even if you think you can, you should probably think again.

Note on the author
Eamonn Matthews is the Managing Director of Quicksilver Media. As a film maker and executive producer he has won many major television awards, including two BAFTAs.

Blonde on Blonde: WikiLeaks Versus the Official Sources

Focusing on the coverage of Pakistan, Paul Lashmar examines the impact of WikiLeaks on investigative journalism in the UK and US

The dramatic release of secret United States government documents by WikiLeaks has been a gift to journalists across the globe providing a treasure trove of inside information and insight into the foreign policy of the US. Equally important is the mass of intelligence about what really goes on behind the scenes in many countries and the activities of a wide range of dubious actors including terrorists, politicians, businessmen or agents of state terror. Journalists are using the material to begin to bring to account the despotic, corrupt and incompetent across scores of countries. The WikiLeaks release is already seen as one of the great stories of the early years of the 21st century.

But what does WikiLeaks tell us about the contemporary state of journalism especially in the UK and US? I would suggest that in a perfectly reported world much of the significant information contained in the leaked US cables should have already been published or broadcast by the media. What the WikiLeaks documents revealed should not have been news but only confirmation of what had already been reported. It's exactly the kind of information that serious journalists are supposed to uncover. That much of it had not reinforces the contention that the commercialisation of the news, prioritising resources for celebrity entertainment and celebrity gossip, has left serious news coverage threadbare[1].

This chapter suggests that the WikiLeaks disclosures will allow academics to develop empirically-based analysis which is vitally important for discussing the role and efficacy of journalists in the modern age. As a case study, the WikiLeaks documents are used here to examine how effectively Pakistan has been reported by the media before May 2011. "It's become clear that Pakistan is a story every bit as important as Afghanistan. You might even say it's the story. Journalists have missed much of it and its worth looking to see why this is," *New Yorker* correspondent Jon Lee Anderson observed in an interview at the beginning of 2011[2].

The alternative narrative

To test an official government narrative the researcher needs access to verifiable and reputable other sources of information which confirm or disprove the official version. Leaked secret reports can provide a very different narrative of the war of terror than the official versions constructed by Western governments and then disseminated to the media.

Testing of the official coalition narrative of the immediate post 9/11 period through the invasions of Afghanistan and Iraq in the period 2001-2005 has been achieved by a wide range of leaks, interviews and writings by participants and freedom of information requests. The unprecedented and unsanctioned release of government documents to WikiLeaks provides a unique opportunity to critique official narratives and build on existing analysis.

Many of the documents so far released by WikiLeaks are focused on the "war on terror". The primary date range of the material is 2003 to early 2010. As the documents are internal US military and diplomatic material they provide little direct critique of the US official position. They do, though, often provide revealing analysis of many of the players in the "war on terror" including of the intention and motives of putative allies.

WikiLeaks documents

WikiLeaks releases in 2010 were in four batches. In April 2010 there had been the startling footage of the US helicopter attack on a group of men in Baghdad dating from 2007. Next came the Iraq war logs and then the Afghanistan war logs both of which consisted of military situation reports from the frontline.

On 28 November 2010, WikiLeaks and the five major newspapers started to publish simultaneously the first 220 of 251,287 leaked confidential – but not top secret – diplomatic cables from 274 US embassies around the world, dated from 28 December 1966 to 28 February 2010. WikiLeaks plans to release the entirety of the cables in phases over several months[3].

Key figures on documents

According to WikiLeaks the cable content breaks down as:
- 15, 652 secret;
- 101,748 confidential;
- 133,887 unclassified;
- Iraq most discussed country – 15,365 (cables coming from Iraq – 6,677);
- Ankara, Turkey had most cables coming from it – 7,918;
- from the Secretary of State's office – 8,017.

According to the US State Department's labelling system, the most frequent subjects discussed, using data from WikiLeaks website, are:[4]
- external political relations – 145,451;
- internal government affairs – 122,896;
- human rights – 55,211;
- economic conditions – 49,044;
- terrorists and terrorism – 28,801;
- UN Security Council – 6,532.

The cables

At the time of writing (May 2011), some 12,600 cables of the batch have been released, just 6 per cent of the total[5]. Some of the key revelations so far include:

- Saudi Arabia put pressure on the US to attack Iran. Other Arab allies also secretly agitated for military action against Tehran.

- Washington is running a secret intelligence campaign targeted at the leadership of the United Nations, including the Secretary General, Ban Ki-moon, and the permanent Security Council representatives from China, Russia, France and the UK.
- Details of the round-the-clock offensive by US government officials, politicians, diplomats and military officers to curb Iran's nuclear ambitions and roll back its advance across the Middle East.
- How Israel regarded 2010 as a "critical year" for tackling Iran's alleged quest for nuclear weapons and warned the United States that time is running out to stop Iran from acquiring a nuclear bomb.
- China is ready to accept Korean unification and is distancing itself from North Korea which it describes as behaving like a "spoiled child". Cables say North Korea's head of state Kim Jong-il is a "flabby old chap" losing his grip and drinking.
- US diplomats have reported suspicions that Italian Prime Minister Silvio Berlusconi could be "profiting personally and handsomely" from secret deals with the Russian Prime Minister, Vladimir Putin. They centre on allegations that the Italian leader has been promised a cut of huge energy contracts.

Some these revelations do reveal a different narrative to that pushed by the White House, State Department, or Pentagon. But most are informative about the subjects and just plain embarrassing for the US to have them in the public domain.

I took as a small-scale, interim, case study of the WikiLeaks material concerning Pakistan, to establish how far the leaks could reveal a parallel narrative of that pushed by both the home countries and Western governments.

Pakistan in the mainstream media

Pakistan has been portrayed as a keystone ally to the US led coalition in the "war on terror". This changed dramatically on 1 May 2011 when a US Special Forces team flew into Pakistan and assassinated Osama bin Laden who was living undercover in a military barracks town not far from Pakistan's capital Islamabad. The world wide impact of this carefully planned operation was enormous. Journalists from all over the world poured into Pakistan.

Bin Laden's death triggered an all consuming media interest in Pakistan. Few believed that no one in the Pakistan government knew that bin Laden had been living, for up to seven years, right in the Pakistan heartland. From that point every aspect on Pakistan's involvement in the "war on terror" was interrogated. The possibility that the Pakistani intelligence service, ISI, was a playing a double game was widely speculated.

This intense focus on Pakistan was in stark contrast to what had gone before. International media coverage of Pakistan had been slight compared to the attention paid to Afghanistan. A number of Western senior journalists have expressed concern that the media was missing the real story and Pakistan was equal if not more important than neighbouring Afghanistan.

Before May 2011 it had been in the US interest to portray Pakistan as far as possible as a viable democratic state dedicated to the elimination of the Taliban and al Qaeda. As the war of Afghanistan has become more problematic with the Taliban and al Qaeda continuing to resist, Pakistan has become more central to fighting the US-led "war on terror". This has required the US to pay a great deal of attention to its ally in terms of diplomacy, resources and political support.

In June 2004, President George W. Bush designated Pakistan as a major non-NATO ally, making it eligible, among other things, to purchase advanced American military technology. US leaders waxed lyrically over its new ally and rushed support whenever Pakistan had need. In October 2005, the then-US Secretary of State, Condoleezza Rice, made a statement where she "promised...that the United States will support the country's earthquake relief efforts and help it rebuild" after the Kashmir earthquake. And in June 2008, President Bush described Pakistan as a "strong ally".

Since Barack Obama became President in January 2009, the US has increased military aid, tying military aid to progress in the fight against militants. This was to help strengthen the government led by President Zardari as well as and civil institutions and the general economy in Pakistan, and put in place an aid programme which was broader in scope than just supporting Pakistan's military.

The Obama administration maintained the public position of friendship with Pakistan set by the George Bush presidency. On 1 December 2009, Obama said: "In the past, we too often defined our relationship with Pakistan narrowly. Those days are over...The Pakistani people must know America will remain a strong supporter of Pakistan's security and prosperity long after the guns have fallen silent, so that the great potential of its people can be unleashed." As recently as October 2010, the White House said President Barack Obama considered Pakistan a strong ally in the fight against extremist forces[6]. And Obama later confirmed he would visit Pakistan in 2011[7].

WikiLeaks and Pakistan: a different narrative

The US documents leaked through WikiLeaks give a very different perspective on Pakistan's allegiances projected by the US official narrative. The ambiguities of the Pakistan's stance on the "war on terror" emerge in the Afghan war logs which contain allegations that Pakistan's Inter-Services Intelligence has been covertly supporting the Taliban. More than 180 intelligence files in the war logs detail accusations that Pakistan's premier spy agency has been supplying, arming and training the insurgency since at least 2004. It has to be said that most of these allegations cannot be confirmed.

At the time of their release, an ISI spokesman said the agency could not comment in detail until it had examined the files, but described the general allegations as "far-fetched and unsubstantiated". Reports describe covert ISI plots to train legions of suicide bombers, smuggle surface-to-air missiles into Afghanistan, assassinate President Hamid Karzai and poison Western beer supplies.

When releasing the material, the *Guardian* was careful to point out: "Much of the intelligence is unverifiable, inconsistent or obviously fabricated, and the most shocking allegations, such as the Karzai plot, are sourced to the National Directorate of Security (NDS), Afghanistan's premier spy agency, which has a history of hostility towards the ISI."

"The vast majority of this is useless," a retired US officer with long experience in the region told the *Guardian*. "There's an Afghan prejudice that wants to see an ISI agent under every rock."[8] But he said the allegations chimed with other US reporting, collected by other agencies and at a higher classification which pointed to ISI complicity with the

Taliban. "People wouldn't be making up these stories if there wasn't something to it. There's always a nugget of truth to every conspiracy theory."[9]

In the spring of 2010, the key finding of a Harvard scholar's report, albeit controversial, for the London School of Economics concluded that the relationship of Pakistan's ISI with the Taliban and the Haqqani group (an independent insurgent group based in North Waziristan) was anchored in official policy — and that it went "beyond contact and coexistence"[10].

The US position on Pakistan rankled in neighbouring India which often perceives Pakistan as the purveyor of state-sponsored terrorism against India's interests. The Indian-based *Asian Age* commented at the time: "However, Pakistan has sought to deflect attention by suggesting that only rogue elements, or some retired personnel of its security apparatus, were mixed up with the jihadist insurgents. Publicly, the West, and the US more specifically, bought this line for reasons of expediency as America believed it simply could not afford to show up Pakistan's falsity as it needed the assistance of the Pakistan Army to pursue its objectives in the Afghan theatre."[11]

Pakistan – according to the cables

Pakistan appears in a good deal of the cable traffic so far released. As one of the most important outstations of the "war on terror" the US Embassy in Islamabad is copied into anything in the world that touches on Pakistan. On the third day of media's WikiLeaks release, along came a batch of significant cables relating to Pakistan:[12]

- US and British diplomats fear that Pakistan's nuclear weapons programme could lead to terrorists obtaining fissile material, or a devastating nuclear exchange with India.

- Also, small teams of US Special Forces have been operating secretly inside Pakistan's tribal areas, with Pakistani government approval. And the US concluded that Pakistani troops were responsible for a spate of extra-judicial killings in the Swat Valley and tribal belt, but decided not to comment publicly.

- The US ambassador to Pakistan said the Pakistani army was covertly sponsoring four major militant groups, including the Afghan Taliban and the Mumbai attackers, Lashkar-e-Taiba (LeT), and "no amount of money" will change the policy. Also, US diplomats discovered hundreds of millions of dollars in aid to Pakistan earmarked for fighting Islamist militants was not used for that purpose.

- Pakistan's army chief, General Ashfaq Kayani, considered pushing President Asif Ali Zardari from office and forcing him into exile to resolve a political dispute.

- Separately, Zardari once told the US Vice-President, Joe Biden, he feared the military "might take me out". He told the Americans his sister would lead if he was assassinated.

- Zardari claimed that the brother of Pakistan's opposition leader, Nawaz Sharif, "tipped off" LeT about impending UN sanctions after the 2008 Mumbai attacks, allowing the group to empty its bank accounts.

Searching through the WikiLeaks produces scores more cables about Pakistan or references to Pakistan. The US cables confirm the US-Pakistan relationship has been fraught. The cables often seethe with frustration over obstruction, incompetence, corruption, patronage and apparent wilful resistance to US influence by the Pakistan government. It is hard to put the problems facing Pakistan more succinctly that one of the leaked US cables from early 2010:

> PAKISTAN continues to face extraordinary challenges on the security and law enforcement front. The country has suffered greater military, law enforcement, and civilian casualties in fighting extremism and terrorism than almost any other country. PAKISTAN's military is currently engaged in combat operations against militant groups in the Malakand Division of North West Frontier Province (NFWP) and six of the seven agencies of the Federally Administered Tribal Areas (FATA) along the Pak-Afghan border. At the same time, PAKISTAN has experienced an alarming increase in terrorist attacks against government and civilian targets in PAKISTAN's major cities, resulting in several hundred deaths in recent months[13].

In addition, the economy of Pakistan has been in an extremely fragile position. A 2008 document from a US-Pakistan economic meeting reveals just one aspect of the depth of the financial problem:

> PAKISTANi Minister of Finance Syed Naveed) Qamar noted that PAKISTAN needs USD 110 billion in infrastructure development in

the energy, mass transport and municipal services sectors. Feasibility studies and a sovereign guarantee fund are needed as well as funding from Overseas Private Investment Corporation (OPIC) and the Export Import Bank in the form of grants[14].

One of the most frank and revealing is entitled "SCENESETTER FOR FBI DIRECTOR MUELLER'S FEBRUARY 24 (2010) VISIT" which contains a wealth of insider and, it has to be said, insightful information about the difficulties of working with the Pakistani government[15].

"Domestic politics is dominated by uncertainty about the fate of President Zardari. He enjoys approval ratings in the 20 per cent range and has repeatedly clashed with key power centers, including the military, politically ambitious Supreme Court Chief Justice Iftikhar Chaudhry, and opposition leader Nawaz Sharif." Perhaps the most telling quotation from this cable is: "In the midst of this difficult security situation, PAKISTAN's civilian government remains weak, ineffectual, and corrupt." The US administration would never have framed Pakistan this way publicly at that time.

Pakistan in danger of becoming "mere satrapy of US"

Simon Tisdall, of the *Guardian*, observed that the leaked US diplomatic cables showed the extraordinary extent to which Pakistan was in danger of becoming "a mere satrapy of imperial Washington": "The US assault on Pakistani sovereignty, which is how these developments are widely viewed in the country, is multipronged. At one end of the spectrum, in the sphere of 'hard power', US Special Forces are increasingly involved, in one way or another, in covert military operations inside Pakistan."

Tisdall said the US hand could be seen at work in Pakistan's complex politics, with the standing and competence of President Asif Ali Zardari seemingly constantly under harsh review. At one point, the military chief, General Kayani, reportedly consults the US ambassador about the possibility of a coup designed, in part, to stop the advance of the opposition leader, Nawaz Sharif. "The clear danger, highlighted by the leaked cables, is that the West's unwinnable war in Afghanistan is spilling over into its weak, ill-led and much put-upon neighbour – and that Pakistan, too, could become a war zone," said Tisdall[16].

US policy and interests required it to pretend publicly that Pakistan was a stable, democratic, lawful and pro-US nation. What has become clear to many observers is that US policy has allowed the deeply entrenched corruption of Pakistan to remain untackled. Pakistan's economic plight is in stark contrast to it neighbours India and China who are pulling their nations out of poverty while in Pakistan the rich grow richer from US largesse as the poor remain in poverty and unemployment.

Coverage of Pakistan has been limited in the UK and US media. Much has had reflected the official UK Foreign Office and US State Department official line. There's been virtually no reporting from the tribal frontier areas of Pakistan. While Afghanistan has often had hundreds of Western journalists reporting back to their organisations, Pakistan has had only a few resident Western journalists and is largely dealt with by correspondents outside the country or on brief visits to Islamabad.

During the course of this research I discussed the issue with Jon Lee Anderson who reports on Pakistan and Afghanistan for the *New Yorker* in a series of conversations starting in late 2010 and carrying on into 2011. We agreed that the evidence showed that Pakistan was the story much more so than Afghanistan. Anderson made some interesting and critical observations about reporting from Pakistan[17].

Serious under-reporting of Pakistan

"There has been lot of coverage but almost no in-depth reporting. Why? For one thing, it's very difficult to report from Pakistan – especially from the tribal areas. And fear is a deterrent, too – with good reason. The murder of Daniel Pearl [in early 2002] was the world's first snuff movie, in a sense, and it was of a journalist. Carlotta Gall, of *The New York Times*, was beaten up badly by ISI agents at the Serena Hotel in Quetta where she was staying. This was in 2006. Very few, if any, journalists have been to Quetta since. It's very dangerous to report in Pakistan; you simply don't know who is who."

The Western media, Anderson suggests, has become too dependent on official sources in Islamabad. "There's been very, very little independent US reporting in Pakistan beyond the kind of thing they are told by the US Embassy and GOP officials. The same is true with most of the British reporting. There are many good journalists in Afghanistan but there are probably only half a dozen serious Western journalists in Pakistan at any one time – if that – when it is 'Terror Central'. The Afghan Taliban is based there, and now there's the Pakistan Taliban as well, not to mention al-Qaeda, the Kashmiri terrorist groups like LeT, and others. Journalists are at great risk, but there should be journalists there."

Anderson pointed out that US government sources had been very reluctant to talk about Pakistan and what was going on there while US officials stationed in Pakistan usually only spoke off-the-record or unattributably. These officials played down rifts with the government of Pakistan and have pointed journalists towards Afghanistan as the story. As a result, journalists had had very little idea of what was actually going on there with the US involvement, much of which had been covert.

"Certainly during the Bush years, when all the US policy eggs in Pakistan were in the Musharraf basket, so to speak, reporters were discouraged from digging too deeply into his deficiencies or the regime's weaknesses. There was an implicit appeal not to do so on the basis that he was indispensable to the US in securing Pakistan against al-Qaeda and the Taliban," Anderson observed.

Dangers in reporting Pakistan
"Because of the dangers, the hermetic nature of politics in Pakistan, and the high stakes for the players involved, there's something of the same problem for reporters as there was in 'Green Zone-era' Iraq. Journalists talk to officials who have little idea about what's happening in the streets. The US officials may know what's going on with US and the government of Pakistan but don't know what the person on the streets of Islamabad thinks – not to mention in North Waziristan or Quetta. Little of what we see reported in our newspapers or on our television screens comes from talking to the man on the street.

"In terms of public awareness in the West – I think there is more knowledge of Afghanistan and Iran and the problems there because there has been a lot of reporting from those places and in some depth. But we are not getting that quality of reporting from Pakistan nor are we, for similar reasons, from politically-important countries like Saudi Arabia."

All the important politics and action was taking place in Pakistan and, in effect, Afghanistan was just one place where the fighting over these political decisions took place. That many US, UK and other Western national troops were losing their lives in Afghanistan gave it a much higher priority for the Western media.

Of course, there has been a wealth of reporting on the Pakistan's floods (which began in July 2010 and killed at least 1,600 people) and consequent humanitarian disaster at the time though the media quickly passed on to new stories in other countries. Of Pakistan's role in the "war on terror" there has been coverage but much of it in the realm of editorial commentary; but again Anderson emphasises that it is not sustained by regular in-depth reporting. Pakistan is the more important story and it's been that way for some time, he said.

"Pakistan is so very important. It doesn't exist in isolation. While we have been watching Afghanistan, Pakistan is a haven for terrorists. Moreover, a new Taliban formed there as the West fought next door in Afghanistan to eliminate the Taliban there. Afghanistan is a battleground on which all of this plays out on. Pakistan is one way or another controlling the jihadi side. Do we know, though, whom is Pakistan supporting, or rather who in Pakistan is supporting whom? Is Pakistan playing off one side against the other to provide a buffer from India and China?

"The ISI is a major issue. It's an open secret that they – or a sector of them – manipulate some of the jihadis behind the scenes and that they probably control the Haqqani network. What does that tell you?

"Treacherous political environment"
"Because of this treacherous political environment, no one in our governments wants to talk about Pakistan on-the-record. When you are in Afghanistan the Americans and Brits talk all the time, constantly, but off the record, about the problem of Pakistan. Then publicly they make statements about how much Pakistan is helping in the war on terror, how it is an valuable ally in the war against extremism. This is for public consumption. The US-GOP relationship is a mutually deceitful relationship."

He continues: "I think it's fair to say that, for all the reasons I've given, the US elite media in the West has collectively failed to report Pakistan effectively. I think that sometimes reporters are too close to, and too often take their cue from the US government. That's one of the reasons why they have been concentrating on looking at Afghanistan and not as much on Pakistan. I think that we will look back and say the US and to some extent the other Western media, failed to report the Pakistan story."

Jon Lee Anderson had a prescient comment in December 2010: "There is always the element of luck. If Osama bin Laden or Ayman al-Zawahiri [often viewed as Osama bin Laden's No. 2 in al-Qaeda] were killed it would help break the spell of invincibility their continued survival has cast. Their survival gives a mystical quality to al-Qaeda and attracts new recruits." And so it has proved. bin Laden's assassination has focused media attention on Pakistan with the realisation that seismic events within this troubled nation had been overlooked and seriously underreported.

With the help of the WikiLeaks documents we can see how scant and insubstantial Western reporting in Pakistan was during the last few years. As more and more of the WikiLeaks documents become available journalists and academics will have some empirical evidence to analyse coverage of many other countries.

The drift towards human interest reporting
For my own part I see this as part of the drift away by media organisations from in-depth reporting to human interest stories. The increasing commercial pressures on the Western media leave it ill-equipped to provide the in-depth reporting that is necessary for their citizens to make informed decisions about their own government's policies. Where the media fail propaganda flourishes.

Notes
[1] Could there be no better example of the diversion of funds to gossip than the *News of World*'s phone hacking scandal in what would be frivolous if it wasn't so sinister use of resources within a newspaper
[2] Interview with Jon Lee Anderson and subsequent email comments 15 January 2011
[3] http://en.wikipedia.org/wiki/WikiLeaks
[4] http://213.251.145.96/cablegate.html
[5] May 2011. As WikiLeaks has itself been subject to leaks of the material it is hard to be precise about the exact number of documents in the public domain. This number is from cablesearch.org an independent online journalism document repository.

[6] http://www.voanews.com/english/news/White-House-Reiterates-Support-for-Pakistan-Afghanistan-104310209.html

7 http://www.reuters.com/article/idUSTRE69J5X520101020

[8] "Afghanistan war logs: the unvarnished picture", Editorial, *Guardian* 25 July 2010
http://www.guardian.co.uk/commentisfree/2010/jul/25/afghanistan-war-logs-guardian-editorial

[9] "Afghanistan war logs: the unvarnished picture", Editorial, *Guardian* 25 July 2010
http://www.guardian.co.uk/commentisfree/2010/jul/25/afghanistan-war-logs-guardian-editorial

[10] Waldman, Matt: The Sun in the Sky: the relationship between Pakistan's ISI and Afghan insurgents. LSE Discussion Paper No: 18 (series 2) June 2010

[11] Hypocrisy of Pak, US gets exposed, *Asian Age*, editorial, 18 Jun 2010
http://www.asianage.com/editorial/hypocrisy-pak-us-gets-exposed-093

[12] The WikiLeaks embassy cables at a glance. *Guardian*. Day three 1 Dec 2010. http://www.guardian.co.uk/world/2010/nov/29/wikileaks-embassy-cables-key-points

[13] SCENESETTER FOR FBI DIRECTOR MUELLER'S FEBRUARY 24 VISIT. Available online at
http://213.251.145.96/cable/2010/02/10ISLAMABAD416.html , accessed on 1 June 2011

[14] 08ISLAMABAD3010: CORRECTED COPY: THE 2008 US-PAKISTAN ECONOMIC DIALOGUE. Available online at
http://213.251.145.96/cable/2008/09/08ISLAMABAD3010.html, accessed on 1 June 2011

[15] SCENESETTER FOR FBI DIRECTOR MUELLER'S FEBRUARY 24 VISIT. Available online at
http://213.251.145.96/cable/2010/02/10ISLAMABAD416.html, accessed on 1 June 2011

[16] WikiLeaks shows America's imperious attitude to Pakistan: The WikiLeaks US embassy cables reveal just how dangerously involved the Americans are in every aspect of Pakistan's affairs, Simon Tisdall, *Guardian*, Wednesday 1 December 2010. Available online at
http://www.guardian.co.uk/commentisfree/2010/dec/01/wikileaks-us-embassy-cables-america-pakistan?INTCMP=SRCH

[17] Interview with Jon Lee Anderson and subsequent email comments 15 January 2011

Note on the author

Paul Lashmar is a journalism lecturer at Brunel University. He has been an investigative journalist for three decades and has worked in television, radio and print. On the staff of the *Observer* (1978-89), Granada TV's *World in Action* current affairs series (1989-1992) and the *Independent* (1998-2001), he covered the "war on terror" for the *Independent on Sunday* from 2001-2008. In addition, he has worked as a freelance for many major news organisations. See www.paullashmar.com.

Investigative journalism on its "deathbed" in Pakistan

Pakistan was the deadliest country for journalists in 2010. Six were murdered in the first half of 2011. And since 2004, the US has been killing al-Qaeda and Taliban commanders in the lawless tribal areas through drone strikes though this, for all kinds of reasons, has gone largely covered in the local and international media. Here Sher Baz Khan examines the enormous pressures facing investigative journalists in the country on the frontline in the "war on terror"

"Investigative reporting is on its deathbed in Pakistan," said a journalist friend of mine when I recently visited his office in Peshawar. He added another horrifying comment while offering me a cup of strong milk tea: "These days, death seems to be the ultimate censorship in this country."

His words echoed in my mind as I went through the Reporters Without Borders' latest figures. On average, one journalist was killed in Pakistan every month during the last 17 months. Six were murdered only in the first half of the current year. Pakistan was the deadliest place for journalists in 2010. It was ranked 151st among 178 countries on the press freedom index, worse than even Afghanistan, Iraq and some Arab dictatorships. The country remains the most dangerous place for the freedom of expression in 2011 as well.

Journalists and their families continue to face kidnappings, arrests, assaults, intimidations and harassments. The growing use of violence which culminated in the murder of investigative reporter, Saleem Shahzad, near Islamabad, in May 2011, has now given birth to a weird climate of fear and self-censorship. Journalists are coming under constant attacks from a number of powerful players – the notorious Pakistani intelligence agencies, the numerous armed jihadi outfits, religious and sectarian groups and political parties.

Despite mounting pressure and intimidation, Pakistani journalists are able to penetrate a number of porous areas, for instance, in matters related to the country's economy and energy sectors, in some pressing social issues such as gender disparity, in dealing with domestic violence and the low quality of education and health facilities, and when it comes to elections and political parties.

Silence over a wide range of issues
But, there are also some other issues of immense importance about which journalists are supposed to remain mum. Such examples include:

- Islam;
- the country's byzantine security apparatus and its decades-long love-love affairs with a multitude of jihadi outfits and political parties;
- Pakistan's nuclear assets;
- the country's foreign policy, which is literally drafted and implemented by the military's General Headquarters (GHQ) in Rawalpindi rather than the Parliament in Islamabad;
- and the so-called "war on terror" and the various actors and directors involved in staging this tragedy of the 21st century in the theatre of the rugged mountains of the tribal areas.

In fact, Pakistani investigative journalists have been unable to operate properly since the eruption of the latest wave of militancy in the country in 2005. The numerous human rights violations committed during the so-called "military operations" against armed militants have gone unnoticed or were not vigorously pursued due to self-censorship in a climate of constant fear and uncertainty. The state of investigative reporting in Pakistan could be gauged from the fact that a mere background explanatory story about controversial topics such as military operations and jihadi groups may be tantamount to a sudden death warrant or abduction.

Such acts of violence against journalists are tools through which the military and militants ensure secrecy. This fog of secrecy enabled al-Qaeda chief Osama bin Laden, the world's most wanted man, to live in hiding for years close to a Pakistani military academy in the scenic Abbotabad city. Similarly, Afghan Taliban's strongmen Mullah Omar, Haqqani and Gulbadine Hikmatyar , the entire chain of command of the Pakistani Taliban headed these days by Hakimullah Mehsud and the numerous, often officially banned, Kashmiri jihadi outfits, would not be able to hide and operate from inside Pakistan without constant official cover-ups and a muzzled press.

Sometimes, journalists who dare to cross the limits lose their jobs. Mostly, they find their own media organisations killing their stories. They find their editors labelling their articles as "controversial" or "dangerous" – often in a sneering jeering way. But, such outcomes are considered the lesser of two evils and are often accepted stoically by journalists.

Pakistan has for many years been in a state of a perpetual war, real and phony, limited and large scale, against its neighbours and, sometimes, against its own people. Truth and journalism were the first casualties of these numerous wars. The press is regarded as the fourth pillar of any democratic society after legislature, judiciary and the executive. These traditional pillars of the state are also visible in Pakistan, but the structure of the state practically stands on a single pillar, the strongest and the most durable of all – the Pakistan army. It seems as if the whole structure of the state is designed in a way that the rest of the pillars are just there for aesthetic considerations.

A history of intimidation

In the first year of the independence in 1947, the government of Pakistan issued some 476 pieces of advice to the media to control investigative and analytical reporting. Journalism remained dormant throughout the next few decades as Pakistan saw the rise of the military establishment in the shape of various takeovers, wars with India in 1948, 1965 and 1971, and the cessation of East Pakistan, now Bangladesh.

Mostly, the press remained tight-mouthed about gross human rights violations and repeated attacks on the Constitution and several democratic institutions between 1958 and 1971, during the time of military dictators Ayub Khan and Yahya Khan. Marked by deceit and sheer demagogy, the 11-year rule of Gen. Ziaul Haq (5 July 1977-17 August 1988) was, by all standards, the darkest era for the freedom of expression in Pakistan's history.

Journalists were hounded, publicly flogged, tortured and imprisoned through the orders of arbitrary military courts. Newspaper pages had to be approved by the army men sitting in the Ministry of Information before printing. Sometimes, news reports were taken out from the layouts of the papers minutes before they were about to be printed. During those times, the *Pakistan Times,* even started leaving the spaces of the censored stories blank the next day as a silent protest.

The outside world may have known about or even still remember Zia for training the Afghan mujahedeen (holy fighters) to defeat the then-USSR during the Cold War in Afghanistan with both weapons and financial support of the West and the Arab world. The other hallmark of Zia's era was his merciless muzzling of the press. The vocal and daring Pakistani journalist and poet, Zamir Niazi, quoted Zia in his book *The Web of Censorship*: "I could close down all the newspapers, say, for a period of five years, and nobody would be in a position to raise any voice against it. If they try to organise a meeting or a procession, I will send them to jail."

Official censorship continues

Sadly enough, official censorship did not end with the death of Zia on 17 October 1988 in a C130 aircraft crash. The government's interventions in the affairs of the media still continue albeit with somewhat more sophistication. An example of this is the awarding of the government's advertisements to media and the granting of multiple media ownership rights.

But, it does not mean that there were no direct attacks on media in the so-called post-Zia democratic era. The elected governments of Benazir Bhutto and Nawaz Sharif (1988-1999) were involved in direct and often prolonged confrontations with some of the mainstream media. Sharif had a dream to become a caliph of the nuclear power Islamic country with a blind and dumb press. He was, and still seems to be, inspired by the media system of Saudi Arabia, the kingdom of his saviours and friends, the Arab sheikhs.

But, the ghost of Zia continues to haunt the Pakistani newsrooms. When I started reporting with the daily English newspaper, *Dawn*, back in 2002 in Rawalpindi, background research for one of my assignments took me to a well-maintained archive at the office of the daily the *News* on a fine spring afternoon. I still vividly recall the man in charge of the archive. He was a very polite gentleman, but looked too weak for his age. The way this man guided me in my assignment made me suspect that he was merely a record keeper. He knew me from some of my stories, which had appeared on the "Metropolitan" pages of *Dawn*. Later, I found out that the man was, in fact, Nasir Zaidi, one of the few journalists who still carry on both body and soul the scars of the public flogging he underwent during Zia's despotic rule.

By journalistic standards, the story, which Zaidi wrote, and which caused him to appear before a summary military trial and face public flogging was not investigative. He had merely tried to draw an analogy between the Pakistan army's massacres of 135 protesting workers at Multan's Colony Textile Mills and the historic Jalanwala Bagh tragedy. The later incident took place in the Indian city of Amritsar on 13 April 1919, when Brig. Gen. Reginald Dyer ordered the British Indian Army soldiers to shoot at unarmed men, women and children killing a thousand of them and injuring more than 1,500 (the figures are disputed).

Imprisonment and torture during the time of Zia

One of our senior photographers at *Dawn*, Ishaq Chaudhry, used to tell me the stories of his own imprisonment and torture during the time of Zia as well as that of some of his other colleagues. The methods of torture by the army also included putting minced chillies in the anus of the victims, as well as dripping hot liquid wax from a candle on to the genitals of journalists while making them simultaneously withstand numerous stress positions. Psychological tools were also used to inflict mental pain on the inmates, as Chaudhry described it: "Can you imagine the pain and anguish when you are in captivity and have had no contacts whatsoever with your family…with your wife and children…for the last six months. And then, an ISI guy appears before you and tells you: 'Hey, do you know that we killed your son last week?'"

Today, Pakistan is once again officially part of the United States-led "war on terror" ever since it began in 2001. Since then, however, Pakistan has also remained one of the deadliest places on earth for journalists. Ironically, during the 11 years of Zia's iron-hand rule, only three Sindhi journalists were killed, while 26 journalists were killed in the first seven years of Gen. Pervez Musharraf's dictatorial regime.

Musharraf came into power in a military coup on 12 October 1999 after overthrowing the democratically-elected government of Prime Minister Nawaz Sharif. When Musharraf resigned on 18 August 2008, due to mounting domestic and international pressure, he left behind a commercially viable, but mostly a tame and toothless media system with the Pakistan army being in the driving seat. According to the Committee to Protect Journalists, 44 journalists, mostly local, but also some foreign, were killed in Pakistan between 1992 and 2010. The Musharraf era has its major share in these casualties.

Death of Saleem Shahzad

As I write these lines, the world media is abuzz over the death of a Pakistani journalist, Saleem Shahzad. The young journalist was allegedly killed by the Pakistani military intelligence service, the ISI, for writing his investigative story about the infiltration of al-Qaeda into the Pakistan Navy. The report was published on the website of Asia Times Online. It claimed that al-Qaeda's 313 Brigade, run by the quintessential jihadi and possible successor of Osama bin Ladin, Ilyas Kashmiri, had attacked the Mehran naval base in Karachi on 22 May 2011. The attack, he said, was a reaction to the group's failed talks with the military held to release two naval officials accused of having links with al-Qaeda. This was a very sensitive story as it highlighted the Pakistani intelligence agencies and their links with the militant outfits as well as the connections of jihadi groups inside the Pakistani military – an untouchable topic for local journalists.

Shahzad was among the rare breed of talented investigative reporters. He had cultivated good sources both within militant groups and the military and interviewed some top al-Qaeda and Taliban operatives. He may have also inspired some fellow journalists to emulate him. However, his death has sent shockwaves across the Pakistani journalist community. After Shahzad's murder, reporters covering the war in the tribal areas are the most frightened. The act indicated that if journalists are not safe in Islamabad, they could not be safe anywhere else in the country.

In fact, it was the third murder case in Islamabad after the high profile assassinations of the Governor of Pakistan's most populous Punjab province, Salman Taseer, in January 2011, by his own bodyguard and the killing of Minorities Minister, Shahbaz Bhatti, a few weeks later. Both these government officials had invited the anger of the religious parties and armed militants after publicly urging reforms in Pakistan's Islamic blasphemy law, which is being repeatedly misused, often against religious minorities. Now, editors have started to rethink how to keep both their reporters safe and the inflow of news coming. This means steering away from the sensitive issues which could anger either the militants or the military.

Another disturbing factor which has now come to the forefront is that intelligence agencies have been sexually assaulting Pakistani journalists in abduction in order to silence their voices. Umar Cheema, a political reporter for the country's leading English newspaper, the *News,* was allegedly abducted and beaten up by the ISI in September 2010 in the outskirts of Islamabad for writing anti-government columns. As he described it to the Committee to Protect Journalists (CPJ): "As I was stripped naked and being tortured on the back with my head down totally blindfolded, the ringleader directed one of his fellows to molest me." Cheema said he had been sodomised with a wooden pole.

Such acts are designed to humiliate journalists and make them live with social stigmas for the rest of their lives. Such torture activities are being repeatedly practised by Pakistan's powerful intelligence agencies with complete impunity.

Self-censorship

"You think 100 times before writing or saying anything on such issues that involve either the military or the militants no matter how credible your sources are," says Inamullah Khattak, a young reporter from *Dawn*. Khattak recently published a story on a meeting of the Pakistani and Afghan Taliban with the elders of the Shia Tori tribe from Para Chinar. The meeting was held to hammer out a solution to the years-long Sunni-Shia sectarian conflict in Kurram Agency and to allow the Haqqani Network of Afghan insurgents to cross over to Pakistan's Kurram Agency from the nearby North Waziristan, where they are coming under severe and repeated drone strikes from the US army deployed across the border in Afghanistan. The meeting was held in Islamabad less than a mile away from the ISI headquarters in a local hotel. Some members of the Pakistani Parliament, a Taliban spokesman and family members of Haqqani participated in the meeting accompanied by dozens of armed bodyguards less than a couple of miles from the US embassy in Islamabad.

Khattak felt insecure and scared for months to come after his story was published in *Dawn*. Khattak's colleagues, friends and family members warned him of the trouble he could have if he continued with such stories.

Many journalists simply avoid such controversial stories. "You get a phone call from the Taliban or the ISI even if you speak a few words on a radio station about military operations or the repercussions of Taliban's policies," Haq Nawaz Khan, the Chief Reporter of the *Pakistan Today* in Peshawar and correspondent of the *Washington Post* told me in February this year when I visited Pakistan to interview a number of leading reporters covering militancy and the "war on terror".

"You are being constantly watched"

Sometimes, Khan added, "even if you do not get threatening calls from the Taliban or the secret services, they simply call you on your cell phone whenever they want and say in a polite manner, 'Assalam-o-Alykum brother. How are you doing? You are filing good stories. We appreciate your work.' Even such calls scare you. They make you feel vulnerable. You feel as if your are being constantly watched."

Generally speaking, self-censorship in Pakistan exists at two levels – individual and institutional. In the conflict zones of Pakistan, particularly in the militancy-infested tribal areas and the Baluchistan province, where an armed liberation movement has been jump-started by the neglected and exploited Baluch nationalists, many journalists simply do not take the risk to report the facts. Baluch nationalists, students, teachers, intellectual and politicians are being killed, allegedly by the Pakistani intelligence agencies. Their bullet-riddled bodies are found in the fields, streets and canals on almost a daily basis.

The province has turned into a toxic mix of nationalist insurgency, sectarianism, Talibanisation, and trigger-happy military amidst kidnappings, illegal detentions, torture, target killings and bomb blasts. There is almost a complete media blackout on what is happening in Baluchistan. In this instance, investigative journalism in the mainstream Pakistani media is, indeed, on its deathbed. The country badly needs a media renaissance and reawakening of the soul of intelligentsia to let the people know what is happening in Baluchistan.

Unfortunately, most of the reports from Baluchistan province published in the mainstream media are unsubstantiated – based on official versions and political statements. With few exceptions, there is not even good explanatory and background reporting on important events in the province. Baluchistan is becoming yet another East Pakistan – now Bangladesh – where the Pakistani army was involved in extrajudicial killings, but the press was completely tight-lipped over it, thus keeping people in West Pakistan uninformed about the other half of the country.

Self-censorship was the hallmark of reporting in the Pakistani media about the multiple-layered recent military operations against militants in Swat valley. The military conducted its last operation in the area in 2009. It displaced over three million people. Hundreds of extrajudicial killings were allegedly committed during such operations, but the media simply reported the events through official versions. In most cases, the Pakistani media focused on the humanitarian magnitude of the crisis. A large number of reports were about the arrangements made by the United Nations and various NGOs to help the millions of internally displaced people.

More harassment of local media

Some journalists were killed while many others were harassed when the local media tried to analyse the implications of the 2009 shadowy peace deal between the Pakistani government and the Taliban in Swat. Neither the local nor the mainstream media investigated the elements behind the creation of the Taliban in Swat. No questions were asked as to who was actually funding and supplying arms to the Taliban in Swat in the presence of Pakistan army and the military and civilian intelligence services.

"It is better to be silent for the moment than to be to silenced forever," says Mubarak Ali, a senior editor at a Pashto language television channel, *Khyber News*. He was commenting on the instructions issued by the army to the media on how to broadcast the images of the execution of a former ISI officer, Col. Imam. The Pakistani Taliban had killed Col. Imam in captivity and later released the video of his execution (see http://www.longwarjournal.org/archives/2011/02/video_pakistani_tali. php).

Sometimes, the intelligence agencies know about the journalists and their assignments in advance. Instead of talking to the reporter, the intelligence agencies call the desk of the newspaper or the head of the media organisation directly and stop the report without letting the journalist know about it. And on many occasions, reporters get direct calls from the intelligence agencies to stop the story or to stop writing such reports in the future. As they say in journalism: "No story is worth your life." The Pakistani journalists, after losing many of their colleagues in the line of duty, know this lesson better than most journalists from other countries.

Columnists silenced

Apart from staff reporters and correspondents, a number of prominent columnists were unable to maintain their spaces in the newspapers after they wrote about issues deemed by the Pakistani military establishment a "matter of national security" or "sensitive issue". Even some editors lost their jobs while trying to defend their reporters.

Similarly, a media organisation's editorial policy also influences the work of a reporter. Often reporters come up with good investigative stories, but are unable to have them published or broadcast as they clash with the editorial policies of their organisations. Sometimes, a reporter has to stick to only the official sources and regularly embed with the military in order to impress his editor and get a decent salary raise and bonuses the following year. Even the sect of an editor, be it Shia or Sunni, and his or her personal inclinations may be apparent in what a reporter in the field is pushed to dig for.

Some of the so-called Pakistani veteran journalists on militancy and tribal areas have a history of regularly embedding with the militant and the military. They try to keep both sides happy by staying away from filing controversial stories. In Pakistan, good journalism is often labelled as "controversial journalism". Sometimes, reporters are labelled as Indian agents or American stooges if they try to think beyond the official framework. Most of these so-called senior journalists, who massively rely on official sources, have worked with foreign journalists as "fixers" or assistants during the Cold War in Afghanistan. They are now considered the safest among reporters, and also the most successful ones in financial terms. For a growing number of young Pakistani journalists, their embedding seniors are, in fact, their role models.

Reporters are never entirely free in pursuing stories on their own. Most of the time they do get calls from their editors and are instructed on what to follow and what to ignore. The editorial policy of a media organisation is often reflected in the manner and style of reporting and the framing of different issues through a well-devised selection of criteria of not only what to report, but how to report it and where to display it. Such editorial policies also force journalists to exercise self-censorship in order to maintain their jobs.

Access to information
Most of the reports published in the Pakistani press about militants and military operations are often based on the official versions. Such statements are often exaggerated and misleading. There are only rare chances to independently verify these claims due to severe access-related restrictions and the lurking dangers in the field.

For instance, since 2004, the US has been targeting and killing al-Qaeda and Taliban commanders in Pakistan's lawless tribal areas through drone strikes. Such attacks have been increased over the last couple of years with as many as 244 by May 2011. In these strikes, thousands of people have lost their lives. It is true that a number of high-ranking al-Qaeda and

Taliban militants were killed in these strikes, but also hundreds of civilians including women and children. Despite these alarming numbers, there are hardly any investigative stories on this subject. Most of the time, anonymous intelligence sources are quoted in the media revealing the number of dead and injured. Sometimes, Taliban's claims are splashed across the media. It is almost physically impossible for journalists to get access to the tribal areas of Pakistan, where most of these drone strikes are taking place. They have to either embed with the military or with the militants in order to be able to even see the conflict zones. At the end of the day, the people get only official statements splashed across the front and back pages of the newspapers or broadcast during the prime time.

There are hardly any explanatory stories available, which could provide us a snapshot of the social and psychological impacts of drone strikes on the families of the victims, survivors and the population in general. The tribal people sometimes witness drone strikes and military-militant clashes. Sometimes, they even lose their family members either in direct attacks from the army and the militants or as "collateral damage" of these clashes. But, they are so scared that they will not talk to the media directly. They refrain from talking to journalists even via phone. They seldom have other less direct forms of communication with the media.

Journalist eye-witnesses caught in the crossfire

The same thing happened in Swat, where journalists were securing their information from either the militants or the military. Reporters, who tried to eyewitness the scenes of fighting, were often caught in the crossfire. Innocent citizens, who lost their family members in cross firing or at the hands of the military and Taliban, were scared of revealing such incidents to media fearing further attacks from both the parties.

When the Tehrik-e-Taliban Pakistan (TTP) chief, Baituallah Mehsud, was killed in a US drone attack in August 2009, there was a controversy for more than a week. Nobody knew what had exactly happened. The Taliban first denied the reports of the death of their leader and the people were not ready to buy the military's version of the event. However, only when the Taliban released some pictures of the funeral of Mehsud to the media did the people believe that the TTP's head was no more.

Journalists are also finding it difficult to carry cameras with them to the conflict areas. As a result, media images of the ongoing conflict in the country represent only a fraction of the visual reality. Journalists have rare chances to record the real war and its impacts on the local people with the lens of a camera. Most of the media images come from the settled areas of the country, many of them showing bomb blasts, official meetings, press conferences, and military PR and propaganda. Journalists wanting to visit the conflict areas on their own while carrying a camera can find themselves in big trouble as cameras can catch the attention of the countless spies of both the military and the militants operating among the people and noticing every newcomer to the area. Even children, women and beggars spy for both the parties.

Tribal culture

Most of Pakistan's leading journalists are based in the metropolitan cities and the federal capital. Apart from Pakhtun journalists, a majority of the Pakistani journalists are unable to speak the local language, Pashto, which is spoken in the tribal areas where most of the militant groups are operating and where most of the military operations are being conducted. A top journalist from Islamabad or a news anchor from Lahore or Karachi cannot even go to the conflict zones on his or her own. They have to embed with the military or the militants.

Non-Pakhtun journalists are not aware of the local culture and the local problems. They find themselves as alien as foreigners among the Pakhtuns in general and Pakhtuns from the tribal areas in particular. Interestingly, most of these non-Pashto speaking journalists are not only reporting for the Pakistani media on the northwest Pakhtunkhwa province and the tribal areas, but they are also regularly feeding the international media over the developments taking place there. One could not expect these journalists to come up with investigative stories on the conflict in the tribal areas because of their lack of knowledge of the local culture and the local language and their somewhat habitual adherence to overwhelmingly quoting official sources.

The joint family and clan system in the settled as well as tribal Pakhtun areas is also a major hurdle in the way of investigative reporting. A journalist may invite the wrath of the whole extended family or tribe if it happens that he writes something controversial about an individual member which is not liked by either that particular individual or any member of his or her extended family or clan. It is an honour society. People commit even murders in the name of honour. A journalist could lose contacts with the whole village if he points out his fingers at a single member. If a journalist even flees the area, after inviting the anger of families and clans, the journalist's family members are then targeted. As they say it in Pashto: "I cannot catch you. So, I will kill your father."

Money matters
Without strong regional and local journalism, investigative reporting in countries such as Pakistan will always remain an unrealistic dream. The local correspondents and stringers in the conflict areas of Pakistan are the most neglected. Usually, they do not receive regular salaries from their employers. Often they pay their own internet, telephone, and fax bills while digging for stories for their employers. Most of the local journalists are asked to even look around for advertisements for the newspaper in which the reporters receive some percentage in commission. Such commissions are, in fact, their salaries. If a journalist loses a limb or dies in the line of duty, his dependants do not receive any financial compensation from the media organisations.

Mostly, the cameras journalists carry with them to the conflict areas are insured against damage, but there is no insurance for the photographers and reporters who carry these gadgets. The local correspondents have to survive on their own both physically and financially. It is almost impossible to think of such journalists, who even know the local culture and language, to come up with investigative stories, without financial and moral support from the media organisations they are working for.

Conclusion
Like the state of Pakistan, journalism is at crossroads in this country. Every effort is being made to gag the press and keep the people in the darkness. Investigative reporters are either killed or harassed to the point where they start censoring themselves in order to stay alive. Good journalism can thrive in Pakistan only if the powerful Pakistan army demarcated its boundaries by letting an accountable and media-friendly democratic government and culture flourish in this county in the coming years.

Note on the author

Sher Baz Khan is a PhD scholar and a Junior Fellow at the Visual and Communication and Expertise Research Centre (VisComX) at Jacobs University Bremen, Germany. He has worked for eight years as a staff reporter for the Pakistani English daily newspaper, *Dawn*, based in Islamabad. He is currently pursuing his doctoral thesis on "The Visual Framing of the Afghan War: A comparative case study of mainstream newspapers in Afghanistan, Iran and Pakistan" at the School of Humanities and Social Sciences (SHSS), Jacobs University Bremen, Germany.

The Best of Times, the Worst of Times for Investigative Journalism in the US

The problems with investigative journalism in the US today are not so much with the field itself as with the outside influences, especially a Congress and Supreme Court in the thrall of corporate interests, argues David Cay Johnston

For investigative reporting this is the best of times; this is the worst of times; it is the age of data-driven exposés; it is the epoch of gullible belief, at least in America.

While no society has ever had enough investigative reporting, America today has lots of it, much more than just a four or five decades ago. The problems today are not so much with the field itself as with the outside influences, especially a Congress and Supreme Court in the thrall of corporate interests and eager to hide information on taxpayer spending and government actions.

The handwringing over the state of investigative reporting today lacks historical context and thus misses many of the real issues. Go back just a few decades and real enterprising reporting was rare at the best outlets and unknown at many of the most lucrative. What posed as investigative reporting at many papers, notably the *Washington Post* under Ben Bradlee, were often just leaks from Congressional and other investigators whose contributions were subtly disclosed down in the 22nd paragraph.

Investigative reporting – journalist-initiated digging – is vital to a free society. It provides more than the disinfecting benefits of sunlight on festering societal wounds; it also inhibits those tempted by the buffet of emoluments, some legal, some crooked and most of them in-between, to public servants.

Two decades ago, investigating how one of the only two executives who worked in the Manhattan headquarters of the entertainer Merv Griffin's company had mob ties when Griffin was buying an Atlantic City casino, my *Philadelphia Inquirer* colleague George Anastasia and I went to visit a New Jersey state legislator. The lawmaker asked if we knew why he had never been prosecuted for taking favours and then pointed to Anastasia, as smart and aggressive a watchdog as ever lived. The state senator said his worst nightmare was taking a bribe because he knew Anastasia would ferret it out, he would go to prison, his life in ruins and his family estranged.

When no reporters are around kleptopoliticians run wild
This subtle, but important, check on abuse of power is far from perfect. America has no shortage of people who entered public life broke and ended up multimillionaires thanks to favours, some hidden, some not. But when no reporter is around, kleptopoliticians run wild.

Consider what happened in Bell, a tiny blue-collar suburb of Los Angeles. When I started out in California in the mid-1960s every one of the 58 county boards of supervisors and virtually all of the state's cities and school boards had multiple reporters attending every official meeting. But now even the city councils of many good-sized cities meet for weeks on end with no journalist in the room. Bell's city council had not been covered in years.

The City Council voted itself outrageous pay, including a salary of more than $800,000 for the city manager. The *Los Angeles Times* won the public service Pulitzer in 2011 for exposing this after a citizen, who was twice rebuffed, finally got through to someone in the newsroom who listened and then acted. Had the newspaper sent a part-time stringer to City Hall regularly the crimes for which Bell officials were indicted likely would not have occurred.

What vexes America today is day-to-day reporting which parrots talking points and assumes the truth of statements because multiple sources all told the same lie, as we saw with the ginned-up justifications for invading Iraq.

When daily reporting lacks tough questioning
The real problem, the crisis, in American journalism is not in diligent digging to expose systemic problems, corruption and myths, but in daily reporting which lacks basic skepticism and tough questioning.

A related problem is the much too frequent failure to check the clips first. One of the ways that our digital era destroys, as well as adds, value, is the digital clip file. There are so many stories in the files of NexisLibrary and other databases that it is easy to miss key facts. When newspapers kept morgues with actual clippings you could spread them out on a desk and see the flow of the story, its emphasis and play, clearly while quickly separating the wheat from the chaff.

On the lack of basic questioning, and failure to check clips, consider two figures in American presidential politics.

Sarah Palin's financial disclosure forms give no hint as to how she and her husband, Todd, could afford their large waterfront home in Wasilla, an Anchorage suburb. Palin was elected mayor of a town with no debt. Then she had a community centre built in an out-of-they-way place, leaving Wasilla $22 million in debt.

Working his telephone from New York, the indefatigable reporter Wayne Barrett asked the obvious questions arising from this that were never addressed in the major newspapers, magazines and wire services or on the networks.

Barrett called the Wasilla community center contractors. Assuming that they had worked on the Palin home, he asked if he could come up and look at the invoices sent to the Palins. The first few contractors confirmed their work on the Palin home, but responded along the lines of "Why would there by any invoices?"

The implication that kickbacks were involved in the no-bid work on the community centre was clear, yet not a word appeared during the campaign in any of the major news outlets. Of course it could also be that the Palins paid for all the work, just without being given proper bills.

Donald Trump's background goes uninvestigated

More recently, Donald Trump was treated as a serious contender for the 2012 Republican nomination for president. Trump was never running, only trying to build an audience for his *faux* reality show, which was slipping in the ratings. Trump developed a strong lead in the polls among registered Republicans, but his background went uninvestigated.

Had anyone checked the clips, especially those by Barrett in his pioneering Trump biography and the *Village Voice*, or mine in the *Philadelphia Inquirer* and my book *Temples of Chance* (1992), they would have learned that Trump has a long history of business ties with unsavoury characters, of not paying vendors, of borrowing vast sums of money and not paying it back (thanks to help from friends in government) and making statements for which no factual basis could be established.

Trump's self-proclaimed multi-billionaire status went unquestioned. Where was the reporting on the contradiction between Trump saying he is about "the best" in everything while he uses a three decades old Boeing 727, worth a relative pittance, instead of a modern plane such as the Boeing Business Jet or a Gulfstream as proven billionaires are known to do?

After NBC renewed Trump's show, and he immediately dropped his *faux* campaign, many journalists kept referring to his candidacy as if it were real. They also ignored new revelations by Barrett at the Daily Beast about Trump's more recent and extensive dealings with unsavory Russian emigrés and others.

But the spotlight falls on Ferraro's mob links

Contrast this lackadaisical coverage with 1984, when Congresswoman Geraldine Ferraro, Democratic vice presidential nominee, was thoroughly scrutinised by *The New York Times* and even more so by the *Philadelphia Inquirer*, which dug through government records for copies of cheques her husband wrote to mob-connected characters.

On the policy front, Congressman Paul Ryan, a Wisconsin Republican who chairs the House Budget Committee, put forth a plan in 2010 and again in 2011 that, he said, would save taxpayers roughly $5 trillion in net present value (through 2084) over 75 years by reforming Medicare, the American system of universal healthcare for the disabled and everyone age 65 and older. Laudatory print and broadcast coverage described him as a serious policy wonk. Journalists accepted his figures at face value because, he said, they were based on official government reports.

I reported in *Tax Notes*, a non-profit journal, and its free website tax.com, that the same official government reports revealed that for every tax dollar saved, older Americans would spend $5 to $8 out of their own pockets. How, I mused, should people regard a politician who withholds such crucial facts that show his plan is a sham?

One might expect that a politician who proposes to save you a dollar in taxes by making you spend vastly more would be treated by reporters as at best a fool and reasonably as a liar. But as one prominent Washington reporter told me after I sent him my columns: "There is no official source telling us that…"

When stenography poses as journalism

That is stenography posing as journalism by reporters who never took the time to learn public finance, statistics or perhaps not even basic mathematics. Reporters in the era from the late 60s through the mid 1990s often asked tough questions at press conferences. Often, though not often enough, nonsense was called out as nonsense. Not so much anymore. The softballs lobbed at Presidents George W. Bush and Barack Obama are legendary.

The few reporters who ask tough questions often find no support among their peers. When a Bloomberg reporter objected that a Treasury briefing should be on the record, not be on background, no one backed him up.

The reporter later told me that one of his peers said that in an era of staffing cuts they feared for their jobs if they made a ruckus.

On the corporate front, big companies routinely bully reporters and in many cases their news organisations listen to the bullies behind the backs of the reporters instead of with them at their side. Rare is the case where the story gets killed this way. Instead, stories often run with such muddled and muted language, the hard edges softened with textual putty, that only the savviest reader can see the point.

Having dealt with the egregious problems of day-to-day reporting not being, as all reporting should be, investigative, let's turn to investigative reporting *per se*.

Evidence that investigative journalism is not sloughing towards oblivion

More than 4,000 journalists belong to Investigative Reporters and Editors, a non-profit training organisation on whose board I sit as treasurer and whose acronym is, fittingly, IRE. While membership is down by about 700 from the peak, the membership roster shows that investigative reporting is not slouching toward oblivion.

Our annual awards competition, judged under much more diligent ethical standards than the Pulitzer and other better known awards, draws hundreds of extraordinary articles, books, broadcasts and multimedia presentations. Many of the entries are about systemic problems, from drinking water safety to contracting fraud to false arrests of most of the poor and minority residents of small towns on bogus drug charges.

Work like this is expensive. At the *Los Angeles Times*, I once spent $10,000 on a single sentence in a 5,000-word exposé of charity thrift stores run by such thrifty operators that one of them bought an airplane with store proceeds, diminishing charitable benefits. The whole project involved 30,000 miles of domestic air travel in an era when the newspaper paid for first class. Such spending was possible when American newspapers raked in monopoly profits, before the creative destruction of the internet broke down the centuries-old business of linking buyers and sellers through producing news.

Today investigative reporting thrives at some outlets because it provides value and draws readers and to a lesser extent listeners and viewers. Some history here is illuminating.

My local newspaper, the *Rochester Democrat and Chronicle*, was the flagship of the Gannett chain when its patron was alive. But after Al Neuharth got control of the chain in 1973 he focused on squeezing money, not stories, out of his papers. Asked once whether the chain name should be pronounced GAN-et or ga-NET Neuharth responded "as in profit".

When I moved to Rochester in 1993, the Gannett paper was so awful, other than reporter Gray Craig, that I took to calling the *D&C* by an awful pet name based on the medical procedure of the same initials. That nickname is no longer valid. For the last few years, despite budget cuts and a shrunken staff, it has done sterling work exposing the corruption and lucrative back scratching resulting from decades of one party (Republican) rule of the local county government. My new nickname: the *Dig & Challenge*.

Washington Post's exceptional investigative work

The *Washington Post*, which in the past two decades has done a lot of exceptional investigative work, often took (or denied) credit in the Ben Bradlee era for the fine work of the *Los Angeles Times*, with which it shared a news service. More than three decades ago, walking by the *Post* after dinner with a blind date, I bought a newspaper, where to my delight my byline was on the *Post* front page over my latest *L.A. Times* piece about American influence peddling by the apartheid regime in South Africa. The next morning her copy of the paper had the same headline over a *Post* byline with a passing mention that "the *Los Angeles Times* reported..."

The same was true for some of my *L.A. Times* colleague's groundbreaking Watergate stories, as well as work by other newspapers on other stories. To be sure, the *Post* was far from unique in stealing and denying credit. The *Post* had several superb investigative reporters in those days, including Morton Mintz, whose work still resonates decades later. But the proof that the *Post* wished he would go away was in the pay – never a merit raise for work that should have won multiple Pulitzers and a written insult from Bradlee for his aggressive style and fighting to make sure editors did not muddle the facts.

At *The New York Times* there is a historical reason that for decades investigative reporting was a minor and unusual activity. Because of its unparalleled influence, many people and powers were, and are, eager to feed the newspaper material.

One of the few *Times* Manhattan reporters who knew how to dig, John Hesse, was assigned to restaurant reviews in the hope that he would stop making trouble by digging up inconvenient facts. Undaunted, Hesse's fine dining reviews included details from health inspection reports.

Until 1994 it had little capacity and little in-house talent for enterprising investigations. *The New York Times* hardly knew how to do investigative reporting, especially on the national level, when it hired Wallace Turner in 1962. For a quarter century, Turner dug into one hidden story after another while passing his skills on to acolytes working under him in the San Francisco Bureau and stringers scattered around the Western United States.

Revealing tainted medicine from China
These days *The New York Times*, where I worked for 13 years until 2008, retains an extraordinary set of investigative reporters including Walt Bogdanich, whose 2007 revelations about tainted medicine from China prompted Beijing to execute one of its high level officials, whose reports on railroad crossing safety prompted life-saving reforms and whose exposés of medical radiation errors causing injuries lead to improved practices.

This modern investigative commitment stems from a decision in 1994 by Joe Lelyveld when he was made the top editor. For the first time in nearly a century, *The New York Times* brought an outsider in as managing editor, the No. 2 slot. Gene Roberts had been a star reporter and editor at the paper, but quit as *Times* national editor in 1972 to take over one of the worst newspapers in America, the corrupt and dysfunctional *Philadelphia Inquirer*. Roberts quickly remade the paper and over the next 18 years the newspaper won 17 Pulitzers while earning the lasting enmity of the local, judiciary for revealing vast courtroom and other government corruption.

Roberts had three years back at *The Times* before mandatory retirement and he used it to hire investigative reporters, including me, who had been passed over by *The Times* in favour of those with better social and educational credentials (read: Harvard, trust funds, etc.). Roberts budgeted for an investigative unit, knowing it is much easier to reassign journalists than kill a budget line, be it for a bureau in Kansas City (which he created as national editor) or a whole investigative unit.

In America many stories of corruption and failed policies are open knowledge and yet no one writes about them. This was my prime frustration in 12 years at the *Los Angeles Times*, where I undid the reputation of the Los Angeles Police Department by exposing its massive political spying and poor investigative work, hunted down a killer to free a man framed by a cop and exposed how the Hilton (hotels) and Keck (oil and telescope) families were draining away charitable assets. Many important stories never got into the newspaper, whose top editor, Bill Thomas, revered the writer's every word but had too little backbone, the opposite of *The New York Times*.

Corruption flourishes because of weak editors

Corruption flourishes because many publishers and editors prefer softer fare, which is financed to the hilt in some places, and fear the powerful. Consider the case of Neil Goldschmidt of Portland, Oregon who, in 1972, became the youngest mayor of a major American city. Less than three years later he began having sex with a 14-year-old girl, often picking her up from school in his official limousine, driven by a Portland police officer. Goldschmidt went on to become Jimmy Carter's Transportation Secretary and governor of Oregon before moving on to a lucrative career as a political arranger.

The girl, who had been an A student, grew up to become deeply troubled drug abuser. For decades Goldschmidt paid her to keep quiet. Still, she told friends and others about it without a word appearing in the *Oregonian* newspaper even though it had become common knowledge among Portland's political elite in both parties.

Nigel Jaquiss, a former Goldman Sachs oil trader turned investigative reporter for the alternative newspaper *Willamette Week*, nailed the story in 2004. Just hours before Jaquiss got into print, Goldschmidt gave his side of the story to the *Oregonian*, which ran a Page One story describing this not as felony rape of a child, but "an affair".

The most amazing part of the story was how local officials who knew explained looking the other way (and how the *Oregonian* promised readers a full accounting of itself, but never delivered). Sheriff Bernie Giusto told Jaquiss: "You could argue that I had an ethical responsibility to do something, but other people had better information than I had and never acted."

Commercial value in investigative journalism

Newspapers as small as the *Las Vegas Sun*, which runs as an insert in the *Las Vegas Review-Journal,* and the weekly *Concordia Sentinel* in Ferriday, Louisiana, circulation 4,500, routinely run award-winning investigative pieces because exposés draw readers and help keep the papers in business. As my local Rochester newspaper has discovered, there is commercial value in investigative reporting.

Today the *Seattle Times*, after a bruising court battle with a reported $31 million legal bill to fend off a takeover by the giant Hearst Corporation, still maintains one of the best investigative reporting teams in the world, though it is half the size of five years ago. Reporters working under investigations editor James Neff have exposed billion-dollar plus stock manipulations, shown how sealed court records produce bad public policy, exposed deadly medical testing done via deception and in a 2003 series named male junior high and high school coaches who preyed on underage girls. The schools, like the Catholic Church, just moved the paedophiles to new coaching jobs until the newspaper named them.

The legal bill just to get public records cost the newspaper hundreds of thousands of dollars, but *Seattle Times* publisher Frank Blethen (who actually owns the paper, unlike most hired hand publishers) approved the spending because it was good public service and good business.

That so many newspapers (and to a lesser extent broadcast outlets) large and small dig deeply is a remarkable change from 1967 when, as a teenager, I wrote my first investigative piece about cost overruns on the Santa Cruz, Calif., courthouse. I naively thought I was just putting in the local weekly newspaper what I had learned by asking questions and looking at public records. The reactions shocked me. I was physically thrown off the construction site. A reporter at the local daily expressed annoyance that I was making them look bad. The NBC-owned radio station in San Francisco, 75 miles away, told morning commute listeners about what I had dug up and read at length from one of my stories.

A year later I joined the *San Jose Mercury*, its youngest staff member at 19. No one there held the title of investigative reporter, but the day-to-day coverage was intense, vigorous and skeptical of those in power in government and nonprofit institutions, though not generally of those in business.

One of my desk mates back then, Pete Carey, and two other *Mercury* reporters won a Pulitzer Prize in 1986 for reports which exposed the Marcos family wealth in America, prompting massive street demonstrations with people in Manila holding up reprints of the *Mercury*. Think about that – the longtime dictator in a nation thousands of miles away brought down by the digging in a newspaper which hardly circulated more than 30 miles from its printing plant.

Today Pete Carey is still there, but the newspaper's new owners are not known for investing in real digging or putting their assets at risk by doing so. And the newspaper could not afford much digging either. I bought a copy on a trip and found it thinner than the weekly section for the San Francisco Peninsula bureau that Pete and I and five others cranked out stories for four decades earlier.

The rise of smart, non-profit outfits

The newest development in investigative journalism is the rise of non-profit outfits such as the stunningly smart and aggressive ProPublica run by Paul Steiger, former editor of the *Wall Street Journal*, and his top working editor, Stephen Engelberg. (Little known fact: Engelberg was Judy Miller's editor at *The New York Times* until 2002 and he saw to it that fact-challenged nonsense did not get into print by making sure she jumped only through factual hoops. Miller's infamous WMD stories ran after Engelberg left *The New York Times*.)

ProPublica publishes online and often partners with others, including newspapers in the capital of New York State and NPR radio. First-rate investigators such as Charles Lewis, who years ago worked for *60 Minutes*, and others also run smart non-profit investigative teams from Washington to Berkeley, California

Whether these models will survive depends in part on creating endowments large enough to sustain them. To get an idea of the scale, a well-managed endowment can reliably spend 4 percent of its corpus, inflation adjusted, forever. To create an investigative reporting team equal to the estimated total $200 million newsroom budget of *The New York Times* implies an endowment of $5 billion, five times the market capitalisation of its parent company.

A $25 million annual budget, enough to do a lot of serious worldwide work, implies a $625 million endowment. Right now, the largest news endowment is the $200 million left to National Public Radio by Joan Kroc, widow of the man who made McDonalds a household name worldwide.

The big problem is that an investigative endowment would be at risk from any and every litigant, as some other nonprofit publishers have discovered to their horror. To create viable, permanent non-profit journalism that digs into wrongdoing and systemic problems requires law which shields the endowment and gives journalism equal footing under the law with the duty of managers to maintain the endowment. Unfortunately, American law is going in the other direction.

The real challenges facing investigative reporters today
The challenges facing investigative reporters these days come as much from the outside as within. And it is less the spread of soulless corporate ownership that threatens this work than the power of federal judges who bow before the corporate form, ignoring the distrust the Framers had in corporations in the era when the Constitution was written.

Everywhere in America corporate values are triumphant, though the overreaching of some politicians in 2011 in seeking to eliminate public worker unions and take away universal healthcare for the elderly is at last provoking some serious backlash. But transient political reaction is no match for statues and cases built into the framework of law, especially the *stare decisis* doctrine, which holds that even bad decisions should generally be left in the law once society has adjusted to them.

Enterprising digging into hidden facts is much more celebrated as an ideal than practised at many news organisations, some of which have built reputations on *faux* investigations while others avoid any real challenges to the established order. And make no mistake, real investigative reporting is at heart a challenge to abuse of power and sometimes to the existing order.

On the legislative and executive front, America is increasingly replacing civil servants with contractors, often large corporations like Lockheed, the biggest defence contractor. So while a newspaper historically could get the salaries of public officials and their expense reports to track their behaviour, as well as memos and studies to measure official conduct, many of these records are now secret. These contract employees typically cost twice what civil servants do, analysis of official data by Professor Paul Light, of New York University, showed.

Government by outsourcing means a lot more than higher costs. State-level American courts have ruled that the right of voting machine companies to the secrecy of their so-called software spaghetti code trumps the public interest in assuring that votes are counted accurately.

Many of the courts in America are also in the thrall of corporate power, especially Justice Antonin Scalia, who says he uses the "plain meaning" of words and interprets the Constitution as its 18th century framers would. That Justice Scalia sometimes relies on the third, fourth and even fifth definition of words has escaped press notice. And little attention has been paid to his making up history, even though Justice Stephen Breyer has politely pointed this out in some dissenting comments.

Investigative reporting, real enterprising digging driven by reporters and editors, has always been relatively rare, a few stunning jewels in a sea of stenography and glitzmongering offering a patina of substance over journalistic dross.

The real challenge to this vital work comes not from the greed and spinelessness of corporate publishers and broadcasters whose bonuses depend on the bottom line, but on a legal system that is as eager to put the handcuffs on journalists' enterprise as it has been to thwart Adam Smith's invisible hand of the competitive market.

Note on the author
David Cay Johnston, a Reuters columnist, received a Pulitzer Prize in 2001 for his investigations of the American tax system in *The New York*

Times. His work shut down so many hundreds of billions of dollars worth of tax dodges that he became known as the *de facto* chief tax enforcement officer of the United States and his work has been called the equal of Lincoln Steffens, Ida Tarbell, and Upton Sinclair. Johnston is also a best-selling author, teaches the law of the ancient world at Syracuse University's law and business schools and chairs a small lodging management company run by two of his eight children.

How to Stay Clean in the Investigative Game?

An interview with Steven Engelberg

Well there are a couple of ways. First of all you do what we have done, which is to diversify your funding. So we are now supported, we were originally supported almost entirely by one foundation run by a pair of wealthy former bankers, today they represent only 60 per cent of the funding. Our goal is to bring that down much further. So we are getting money from foundations, we are getting money from a multitude of people. We are beginning to explore small donations, we have started taking advertising on our site. Admittedly, there is only a very small amount of money so far coming in from that. I think the first step is to diversify.

The second step is to do what we have done, which is that we have an ironclad rule that no forthcoming stories are discussed with members of our board, which includes funders. Funders simply don't know what we are doing. And in the three years so far, we have never had the tiniest problem with that, up to and including when we were forced by breaking news to write a story about a board member who had come into the news and who had been criticised for something that he had done.

We wrote the story and told him about it after it appeared. And so I think it is do-able, and I don't think that one should posit that in the world of for-profit journalism we have this very pure no pressure thing, and that in the world of non-profit journalism, where you have the world of funder as well as potential for conflict. The truth of the matter is that if you are today in a news organisation which is facing these kinds of crushing economic pressures, any advertiser has the potential to influence your coverage, and you are well aware of who they are because there are so few of them. So I think on both sides – for-profit and the non-profit side – we have to be ever vigilant about this problem because we are all in a financial tight spot.

Note on Steven Engelberg

Stephen Engelberg has been managing editor of ProPublica since its inception in 2008. He worked previously as managing editor of the *Oregonian* in Portland where he supervised investigative projects and news coverage. Before that, Engelberg worked for 18 years at *The New York Times* as an editor and reporter, founding the paper's investigative unit and serving as a reporter in Washington, D.C., and Warsaw. Engelberg shared in two George Polk Awards for reporting: the first, in 1989, for articles on nuclear proliferation; the second, in 1994, for articles on US immigration. During his years at the *Oregonian*, the newspaper won the Pulitzer for breaking news and was finalist for its investigative work on methamphetamines and charities intended to help the disabled. He is the co-author of *Germs: Biological Weapons and America's Secret War* (2001).

How to Make a *Panorama* in Ten (not so) Easy Steps

Paul Kenyon reveals some of the secrets behind *Panorama*'s successes in investigative journalism – for more than fifty years at the BBC

Investigations are often said to be the most difficult form of television. They can take months, and sometimes years, to complete, with no guarantee there will be any programme to transmit at the end of it. They are often the terrain of the obsessive and bloody-minded; journalists who will keep on hunting for the story even after everyone else has agreed it doesn't exist. But, when successful, the rewards are great. They can lead to prison sentences for those exposed, freedom for the wrongfully convicted, and can even precipitate changes in the laws of the land.

Panorama has been making such programmes for more than fifty years. I agreed to explain some of the secrets behind the process for this book though, of course, there is no ready formula, no roadmap to success –

every programme is different and uniquely challenging. This is my own personal take on it, not that of the BBC. I have used examples from several *Panorama* programmes, and in particular I have tried to assist the narrative by following through the development of an award winning *Panorama* special entitled "Chocolate: The Bitter Truth". In it, we travelled to West Africa to expose the use of trafficked child labour in the manufacture of some of our most well-known brands of chocolate.

1. How did you find the story?

In my experience, few stories originate from tip-offs or leaked documents. Instead, they come from trying to morph oneself into a criminal mindset, or that of an unbridled fat cat, or a clawing politician trying to convert a little power into a lot of money. How would they behave? What would they do? So, for instance, when Spain's Costa-del-crime stopped harbouring British fugitives, they would have to think of somewhere else to hide. Put yourself inside their head...you might prefer to flee somewhere that has no extradition treaty with the UK. Iran maybe? Yes, but not necessarily a jolly place to unwind with a tin of Tennents and a stash of hooky cigarettes. Yemen? Again, the fun aspect isn't really there. Then, there's the Turkish Republic of Northern Cyprus; Full-English for less than a fiver, holidaying Brits in every bar, and hillsides of tacky pink villas with Sky dishes and giveaway names such as "The Hiding Place". You don't need a tip off for that, you just know it's the new "Fugitive's Paradise". And that's exactly what we called the programme.

Now, put yourself inside the head of someone running a leading chocolate company. They have to source their chocolate from a narrow belt of forest around the equator, because that's the only place cocoa grows (the bulk of it in Ghana and Ivory Coast). The cocoa-growing communities are poor. Alternative incomes are almost non-existent. The skills required are low. Many of the workers are illiterate and are not going to complain. So, why pay them a fair wage, and why provide decent working conditions? It's not like they are going to resign. This is the only gig in town.

I am not, of course, saying the chocolate bosses set out with an intention to exploit, I am just saying the conditions were ideal for them to tumble down that particular path if they failed to monitor assiduously what was happening to their operation on the ground. And, given the inaccessible terrain of the cocoa plantations, and the fact these workers live on the other side of the planet, monitoring the situation was never going to be easy. It would require vast amounts of investment, planning and infrastructure. All of which would slash away at profits.

So, if the monitoring wasn't necessarily there, we could hazard a guess that some of the less scrupulous individuals on the ground might be exploiting workers to squeeze as much as they could out of a cocoa plantation.

2. Sources

Jetting off to West Africa just because you had "got inside the head of a chocolate executive" would not work as a proposition. Instead, a next step might be to find an insider, someone who works in the industry at a high level and might want to spill the beans.

Motive is an issue here. It might be that the individual has seen enough; that they have tried to change things from the inside and failed, that they are now prepared to risk all to get the truth out. We might say they come with "Angel wings", not asking for money, but motivated, instead, by a strong moral desire. We do, of course, protect their identity. There may be only one member of the *Panorama* team who knows who they are. We avoid naming them in emails. In particularly sensitive situations, even telephone calls may be discouraged in favour of face-to-face meetings.

Other insiders may come to us because they are seduced by the cloak-and-dagger aspect of being a mole, leaking secret information about their own business to a journalist who is going to splash it all over the airwaves. I have met a number of those over the years, people who want to rush the minefield not to save lives, but to experience the crackle of fear. One I knew well, before my time at *Panorama*, used to be content with a curry and several bottles of wine at a rural retreat, before furtively clicking open his briefcase and slipping me folders I should never have seen. The next morning he would invariably telephone and say: "I couldn't sleep last night, had Kenyonsomnia again, convince me I've done the right thing," which wasn't difficult.

The chocolate story, like many others, had an insider – someone with angel wings.

3. Evidence gathering

We would not stop with information from the insider. Before spending money on flights, we would want to develop a network of experts; academics, pressure groups, even other journalists – anyone with first-hand experience of the issue. For the chocolate story there were dozens of interested organisations, including Anti-Slavery International, which was investigating the same story and already had researchers on the ground in key places. Then, there's the fixer. We can't go anywhere without a fixer. They are translator, map-reader, driver, tour-guide, journalist and peace-keeper. They sometimes risk their lives for us.

In Libya at the start of the uprising in Benghazi in February 2011, we hired a young man who had been in the thick of the action when hundreds of youths tried to overrun the military barracks. They were all unarmed, but Gaddafi's men fired round after round at them, and then unleashed the anti-aircraft guns. Hundreds were killed. Our fixer, Ali, saw his friend shot dead beside him. Days later Ali washed up at our hotel, among a group of young revolutionary volunteers there to help the journalists. He had never been a fixer before, but his connections in Benghazi were unrivalled. He even managed to track down a defecting soldier who had evidence that one of Gaddafi's own sons had ordered troops to fire on unarmed civilians. Within days of meeting him, he was with us on the front, and negotiating with the rebels to take us further than anyone else.

Some have been less helpful. When I sat on the pavement during a hot day in Athens, our fixer threatened to call the police because, he said, it was illegal. He wasn't with us for long.

Fixing the chocolate story on the ground for us was a Ghanaian journalist with several years experience. The role can be an uncomfortable one. We needed him to follow up leads about child labour in the cocoa industry, but the Ghanaian authorities deny child labour exists. For him to be involved with us would, in their eyes, make him disloyal to the country – a traitor. The same is true in many places; the interests of a visiting journalist are rarely consistent with those of the state, and the fixer must tread gingerly between the two. After all, when we are on the plane home toasting a successful trip, he has to live with whatever the fallout from our story.

In Ghana, when our fixer went to check out a particular cocoa farm (a plantation we already knew was using child labour) he was arrested by the local police on suspicion of child trafficking himself. They stripped him to his boxer shorts and locked him in a cell for two days. Only his connections with the region's Chief of Police succeeded in getting him out. But, by this time, we already had enough evidence and we had arrived in West Africa.

4. Secret filming

Twenty years ago, secret cameras had lenses the size of snooker balls, and came with a web of wiring and heavy duty batteries which made them, well, not that easy to use secretly. Now, they can be fitted into watches, glasses, belt buckles, and there's no point looking for them because they may as well be invisible to the naked eye.

However, there's a serious point here. As they became increasingly user-friendly, there was a tendency, for a time, to use secret cameras in the pursuit of relatively low-level targets. It was short-cut television. Splash a bit of grainy secret filming in there and it might give the veneer of an important investigation. But it shouldn't really require a secret camera to uncover a dodgy plumber. Surely there is sufficient evidence out there, in the form of witnesses, paperwork, shoddy workmanship, to carry out the investigation in the traditional way. Secret filming is a powerful tool. To overuse it on the wrong material blunts the blade.

We have used it effectively to show convicted murderers leaving their bail hostel without being monitored; corruption in horse racing; drug smugglers on the run in Northern Cyprus; patients with learning disabilities being abused by their carers – all of them stories for which secret filming was justified and which could not have been told as effectively without it.

In West Africa, we could not just indulge in a fishing trip; bowling up to random plantations and hoping we would find child labour. The BBC has strict rules about when secret filming can be used. There has to be a *prima facie* case, which is why we go through all the processes above.

The problem with the cocoa plantations was that, as soon as we – a group of white people – stepped from the vehicle, all the workers mysteriously vanished from the forest. They would sometimes leave a single adult behind who would tell us they had all moved across the valley, only a couple of miles walk through the rainforest in forty degree heat and total humidity. It was always a false lead.

When we finally located a ten-year-old boy called Fatau working in a plantation with a machete, we had a problem. A local village elder claimed it was his son, and that he only worked in the school holidays. That would make it pretty much a non-story; children are allowed to do certain types of work, so long as it doesn't take the place of school, and that they are living with their family. Fatau seemed to fulfil both those criteria and was sitting their nodding along with his "father". We were just about ready to leave when one of our team realised he wasn't talking to the rest of the children. There was a reason. It turned out he did not know the language. He wasn't from the region at all – he had been trafficked from his home in Burkina Faso, and the man who claimed to be his father was one of the traffickers.

5. Voyage of discovery
In the end, we need to make a television programme, and simply patching together some secret filming and a few interviews simply isn't going to do it.

But think of stages 1-4. There are several significant moments in there, during the actual research and preparation of the story which, if filmed, might make it into the programme. It means the audience can follow events as they unfold, in real time, side-by-side with the reporter. It allows an element of jeopardy to emerge. We might even allow viewers to experience some of the inevitable dead ends we had to endure. In other words we are exposing the actual process of the investigation, drawing the curtain back to reveal some of the cogs and wheels grinding away in the background.

For example, you might want to film debriefings with the fixer, or the reporter in the rainforest trying to nail a key piece of evidence on the satellite phone, or a clandestine meeting with an informant – their face always hidden, of course...and, inevitably, the reporter travelling from one place to the next, through narrow mountain roads or across scorched and empty deserts, or even just struggling through a busy Egyptian souk. It's all part of the drama.

6. Production devices

I don't want to call them stunts; that would imply they were attention-seeking and without any purpose. A strong production device will add to the story, whilst giving a break from the main narrative.

I once covered a story about people who faked their own deaths so they could fraudulently claim a fortune in life insurance. We discovered one of the most popular places for Americans to "die" unexpectedly was Haiti. But instead of just tracking down the people whose friends and family thought they were dead (we did find one of those) and outing them on television, we decided to go to Haiti and fake my own death. It enabled us to secretly film the whole process from being measured up for a coffin, to attending my own funeral in a dusty church on the outskirts of Port au Prince.

In the chocolate film, a colleague had a fantastic idea: we should buy our own sacks of child labour cocoa – beans we were certain had been harvested against the international conventions – and then sell them on to a dealer in West Africa. The idea was to see if they would eventually enter the supply chain. They did. Our beans ended up in the hands of one of the biggest names in chocolate. It proved a point: that sometimes no questions were asked about the provenance of cocoa beans.

Not only that. We brought some of the child labour beans back to the UK, and had them made into our own brand of chocolate. Across the wrapper, we emblazoned the words "made by child labour". Then we took it on to the streets of London to see if people would eat it. They wouldn't. Which was good: it allowed us to point out that much of the chocolate they do eat comes from similar sources, it's just that not many chocolate companies would be prepared to stick it on the wrapper.

7. Pieces to camera

Americans call them "stand ups", but it's all the same: the reporter staring into the barrel of the camera and delivering some jaw-dropping revelation that there was simply no other way of telling. At least, that's what I am saying. The allegation is that reporters only do "PTCs", as they are called, to get "air time", to "up the profile", to "get their mug on the box", none of which, of course, is true.

There are some occasions when they are, simply, unavoidable. I try to use them as a reaction to something happening in real time. So, if a reporter was attending his own funeral, for instance, it would be odd not to have something to say in the form of a PTC. If a reporter was confronting someone and was unfortunately punched in the face, the audience might feel cheated if he simply slunk away to seek medical treatment without turning to camera first and delivering a quick PTC. The scene might lose some of its impact if he tried to write his reaction into the script several weeks later.

In more authored pieces, "reaction PTCs" can be central. Not all of them have to work. If I did twenty for an hour-long film, I would expect only a fraction of those to survive through to the final cut. If you are doing them contemporaneously, you never know what twists and turns the story is going to take, and many of them are likely to be overtaken by events. Sometimes, I might do a "travelling PTC" in a vehicle just to say where we are, and where we are heading. Just a couple of words will do. It might be useful in the edit to break up a sequence or to give a sense of momentum in the investigation.

There are also occasions when PTCs can be used simply to show the reporter's there, in the middle of the rain forest, in the cut and thrust of the investigation, and not back in West London waiting for the team to return with the rushes.

In investigations, I would rarely put any of the big allegations in a PTC, not whilst out on location. I would leave that right until the end of the process, when the words have been checked by a lawyer and we have a clearer idea of exactly what the programme is saying.

8. Interviewees
Interviewees carry a significant weight within the programme. If they are dry as old leaves, it doesn't matter how you light them or how dramatic the backdrop, or even how wizard the reporter, you still have a programme full of dry old leaves. Merely being the most well-informed person on a particular subject does not necessarily make someone an ideal interviewee. Other qualities are key too. They must have the ability to simplify a complicated subject into digestible spoonfuls, and to do so with panache and flair, whilst retaining their authority. And they must have something new to say. Such characters are rare beasts.

Go and meet them first. Don't say you're considering them as an interviewee, just tell them you are still in the research stage. That allows you to turn to someone else if they are a disaster. Or you could just save yourself some time, and go to America.

In the chocolate film, we needed an international cocoa trader to help us contrast the dollar-a-day existence of those who actually harvest the beans, with that of the fat cat investors who make a fortune out of trading them the moment they leave Africa's shores. Now, if you proposed that, even in the most innocuous of terms, to a British cocoa trader, they would quickly sense they might be cast as the baddy in all of this. The ones we did contact were prepared to talk about market conditions, the history of cocoa trading, the reason prices were so volatile. But that was all. Understandably, any talk about trafficked labour on the ground would not suit them at all. They did not believe it existed.

America was different. In a smart New York office, we sat before a bank of computer screens and watched as traders bought and sold hundreds of tonnes of cocoa with the click of a button. Sometimes they would buy an entire ship-full. All eyes would be fixed on the tiny digital figures in the corner of the screen, the world price of cocoa as it skipped ever higher. They'd wait, guzzling Diet Coke and giant pizzas, and then, when they thought the price could not rise any further, they would click the mouse again, and sell the lot. Sometimes, they would make a million dollars in a day, adding no value to the product, just speculating on a commodity harvested by people living a desperate hand-to-mouth existence on the other side of the world.

Now, it's a scene any UK cocoa trader would probably not want us to see, but when I hesitantly asked our American trader if he would mind awfully us filming whilst he made his deals, he could not have been more obliging. When I asked him to describe what he was doing, on camera, he replied: "This is legalised gambling, this is our casino right here." Gold dust. In the interview itself, he provided us with this extraordinarily honest exchange:

Me: "Do you care about the quality of the bean?"
Him: "No, we do not care about the quality of the bean at all."
Me: "Do you care about how it was harvested?"

Him: "No, we don't care how it was harvested."

Me: "Do you care about whether or not child labour was involved in the production process?"

Him; "Personally I do, but from a business point of view, no, we don't care how it was harvested, we just care what the price is going to be for our bet we're going to have that day."

It's one of the stand-out moments of the film, a breathtakingly honest series of answers, and something we would have been unlikely to achieve in the UK.

9. The resolution

We cannot just lay out our findings and then let the credits roll. The audience requires some sort of resolution: What's happened since we stopped filming? Are the police investigating? Has anyone gone to jail? How have the victims faired, is anyone helping them? In the cocoa fields of West Africa, we had located a ten-year-old boy, trafficked to work on a plantation, but how could we resolve his story? We could not just leave him there, but neither could we remove him ourselves. If we tried there could easily be violence from the traffickers, and if the police got involved, they could accuse of us of kidnap. Not only that, if we did manage to free him, what then, where would we take him? But an idea was starting to take shape.

We knew his mother lived somewhere in the neighbouring country of Burkina Faso, so we contacted a radio station and persuaded them to put out an appeal for the boy's parents to come forward, a process we filmed. Amazingly, in a remote rural village, where a single radio served the entire community, the message was heard by the boy's mother. She travelled to the capital to meet us. Stage one had been a success.

The next step was to contact the Ghanaian police to tell them what we had discovered. They agreed to rescue the boy, but said the plantation was a long way off, so we'd have to pay for the petrol. We agreed. The plan was coming together.

The idea was to reunite the child with his mother, and to film the emotional scene as a resolution to our film. We planned to do so at the police headquarters in Accra. However, the chief of police insisted we must interview him, in his office, before mother and son could be reunited. Again, we agreed. There he was, an extremely senior police officer, surrounded by his juniors and assorted officials, and each time he responded to one of my questions, they would all burst into polite applause. It was an unconventional interview. Then we came to my question about just how successful the BBC investigation had been: "You know," he said, smiling and nodding at his admirers, "this was a very successful operation by the Ghanaian police, from our early inquiries right through to the rescue, my men did it all." And with that, he beckoned us into an adjacent room where he had invited all the Ghanaian media to interview him about his "historic" success, and where it was he, in the middle of an almighty press scrum, who reunited the boy with his mother, as we wrestled with the rest of the television crews to get a shot.

10. Doorsteps

What about the perpetrators? Ideally, there should be some kind of resolution for them too. Viewers like to see them challenged, but it's not always easy to persuade them in front of a camera for a sit-down interview. This is where the "doorstep" comes in, when the reporter gets the chance to throw questions at an unwilling, and an often fleeing, interviewee.

Roger Cook is still unrivalled in the field, blending theatre and journalistic inquiry in a fashion no-one has quite been able to match. I still recall him chasing an errant doctor down the street shouting: "You gave your patients Hell, didn't you Dr Heaven!"

The real purpose of a doorstep, though, isn't for entertainment. It's to give the alleged offender a right to reply, a chance to answer the questions raised in the programme. By this time, the audience is right behind the reporter, they want to hear the perpetrator's defence, they want to see his reaction to the list of charges, and they don't want to end up with a shot of a reporter shouting questions through a letter box. For this reason, a great deal of time goes into preparing for doorsteps.

Even then, I have been knocked out by a dodgy septuagenarian businessman wielding a briefcase; had dogs set on me whilst trying to ask questions of a Brit conman living in Spain, and been chased in my car by a criminal gang who tried to ram me off the road.

If I can assume no criminal elements will ever read this book, I'll let you into a secret. The most difficult doorstep I ever had to deal with was in rural Norfolk. Our target was a man we had been investigating for months, a gang master who, we knew through research, was a hefty 6 and a half foot tall, and could be fairly judged as "pretty handy". We waited for him for hours, accompanied by a similarly "handy" minder, just in case there was any trouble. He arrived. We rushed over, breathless and just a little excited that we'd finally caught up with him. I threw the first question, perfectly-crafted and deliciously unanswerable. He stood his ground, and calmly responded: "Those are my newly laid flower beds, why did you have to run over them, look what you've done to the roses."

Note on the author

Paul Kenyon is one of the UK's leading investigative journalists, and has been a reporter at *Panorama* for more than a decade. In 2011, he was the first journalist to report from both sides of the Libyan conflict, exposing a massacre of unarmed civilians ordered by one of Gaddafi's own sons. In 2010, the Royal Television Society gave him the "Specialist Journalist of the Year" award after he followed the world's most dangerous migration route out of Africa and into Europe. He also wrote a book about the experience entitled *I am Justice*. Before *Panorama*, he had his own investigative series on BBC1 called *Kenyon Confronts*.

The Flower of Investigative Journalism Begins to Blossom in China

Though it may be hasty to declare that investigative journalism is "alive" across the whole of China, it is possible to say it is beginning to emerge in many significant ways, according to Homson Shaw

To an outsider it might appear that censorship is overwhelmingly strong in China and there are few spaces in which investigative journalism might flourish. Though it may be hasty to declare that investigative journalism is "alive" across the whole of China, it is possible to say that it is beginning to emerge in many significant ways.

For instance, one of the most popular programmes is *Topics in Focus* on China Central television. Launched 17 years ago, the programme aims to "focus on hot current events, offer in-depth background analyses" and significantly features examples of investigative journalism. The production team invites members of the public to send in information and tip-offs – and they are constantly rewarded with a rich harvest of exposés of serious violations of civil rights and state laws. Indeed, being the watchdog for the public good has now become a central mission for the media.

Going undercover to expose the exam cheats

The Higher Education Entrance Examination is the most important test in China. It determines the fate of millions of Chinese high school students in a matter of two days, in which five or six examinations are given on major subjects such as mathematics, Chinese language and literature, English, the sciences and other subjects. Any student caught cheating will have all the results of their exams cancelled. The Chinese refer to the exam regulations as "high voltage power lines", meaning you die instantly if you dare touch them.

Culminating 12 years of learning from primary to high school, the examination is generally viewed by the majority of Chinese students as the only gateway to a decent education and a promising career. However, developing the technology to help cheaters during the examinations has grown into a lucrative industry in some parts of China.

In January 2011, a group of journalists arrived in Siping, a city in Jilin Province in northern China. They found in communities surrounding university campuses scores of little advertisements saying that they could help any student pass the exams and would provide necessary facilities that would outwit the metal detectors at the entrance of the exam venue and the roaming supervisors in exam rooms. The journalists disguised themselves as undergraduate students seeking assistance in their post graduate entrance exams. The dealer, after some brief questions, told the reporters they could provide a bean-size earphone which the student could utilise.

Of course, the device was very expensive! Some dealers even offered to collect the money only after the earphone's effects were proven in the examinations! As part of the service, the dealer also trained the buyer in the most effective use of the earphone. At 8.30 am on 15 January the first test began. About an hour after the examination began, noises in the earphone suddenly diminished and a clear voice began to announce the answers to the exam topics. At the end, the voice added: "By now you have received enough information to pass. Randomly try a few other questions to avoid appearing to have cheated."[1]

All this was exposed on *Topics in Focus*. Those who were involved in the cheating were duly punished. More importantly, the investigation helped improve the supervisory regulations for higher education entrance exams, both at the undergraduate and the graduate levels.

Local level investigations

At a local level, many broadcast programmes and newspapers are involved in important investigations. And many of these exposés, which often involve the work of freelances, are publicised on the internet.

Yunxiao Min, an investigative reporter of *Fortune China*, recently wrote an investigative article revealing the hidden interest chain in the private coal mining industry of Hengshan County in western China's Shaanxi Province. As a result of the investigation Yuanzhong Fan, 38, could finally return from his life as a fugitive. He had been forced to flee his home village last October after he and his fellow villagers tried to stop the illegal operations of a private coal mining company, DFH. It turned out that 48 villagers were held in custody by the local police and nine who ran away were declared wanted fugitives.

Six months earlier, on 23 April, five of the villagers in custody were charged with "mass disturbance of social order" and "gambling". Surprisingly, all five were released on bail five days later. Why such an abrupt turnabout? Rumour has it that some villagers petitioned higher authorities in Beijing and their case shocked senior officials who ordered the investigations that resulted in the removal of the Party Secretary Zhang and Lü, the Head of the County Public Security Bureau.

All this followed eight years of strife between the DFH Coal Mine and the local residents. Many local officials were said to be deeply involved. Baicha, in which Fan lived, is a remote mountain village with a resource-rich coal mine close to the residential areas. The operations of the DFH Coal Mine caused caused serious damage to properties. As a result, DFH had to offer compensations to the local residents following an agreement negotiated between the two sides. However, the mining operations beyond the designated areas caused still further damage to properties. A 70-year-old villager, Bai, and his wife visited the DFH office and demanded both an explanation and a solution, but they ended up being held in custody for more than 20 days at the local police station. Bai died soon after his release. Bai's two sons protested to DFH but they were treated in the same way. Significantly, official investigations into the company in 2006 and 2007 had resulted in the county's Mining Administration Bureau ordering a halt of their mining operation for "rectification" – yet this never happened.

Other villagers were infuriated by the activities of DFH but their complaints were similarly rejected by the company. Finally, DFH sued two of the villagers at the local court which ruled that after the "rectification" DFH had stopped their illegal operations and, therefore, should be protected by the law. The court ruled that the seven villagers pay 8 million RMB to DFH. Soon afterwards they appealed to the Municipal Intermediate Court, which affirmed the original judgement but reduced the compensation from 8 million to 1.3 million.

Following on from these two court judgements, the Yulin Municipal Coal Mining Design and Construction Co. Ltd conducted a technical evaluation and concluded that two of the five DFH mining operations had gone beyond the designated areas. DFH agreed to pay 2.9 million RMB for the moving of 120 households. But this payout was rejected by the villagers who claimed it inadequate compared to the damage caused to their homes. With an average of 24000 RMB per household, this was is barely sufficient to cover the cost of the façade, let alone the whole house. The negotiations broke down and two villagers were arrested for "refusal to abide by the court judgement".

A further evaluation by China University of Mining and Technology revealed that the area of designated mining zones for DFH should be 222084 m^2, but their illegal mining operations covered 623406 m^2, three times the designated area. The illegal operations caused serious damage to the villagers' houses and made them virtually uninhabitable. By the end of 2009, the County Party Secretary, Zhang, called a civil complaints and appeals meeting at which the villagers received 21.2 million RMB in compensation. However, the company and its top management escaped punishment and their production continued.

In January 2010, the water pipeline under Tingcai Fan's house was broken by DFH mining operations. A massive row erupted. That same night five of the Fan's family members were attacked by a "chopper team" of 10, who cut off three of Tingcai's fingers in their attack. In March 2010, 12 masked "chopper team" gangsters armed with hacking knives and steel clubs stormed into a local inn and attacked Baicha villagers. The villager chief Yonghong Wang's legs and hands were disabled. It was said that the county police took no action even after the inn's video footage of the attack had been turned in to the police station. All this quickly provoked nationwide protests on the internet that resulted in the arrest of the "chopper men" in the two attacks,

Yet still the conflict between DFH and the villagers continued. A local villager told a reporter that some small coal mines had turned into "underworld gangs", saying that "there are obvious collaborations between the mining bosses and the local officials. That's why the officials are always helping them". Some villagers revealed that many officials had shares in the local mines, 80 per cent of which were "hidden shares", held under the names of others. In the end, a major investigation into the whole controversy was launched by the top management of Hengshan County, now led by a newly appointed Party Secretary. As many as 1,000 investigating staff, organised in 18 teams, were sent to investigate small size coal mines, their illegal activities and their conflicts with local residents.

Meanwhile, investigations were also conducted by the government in an attempt to root out the links between the coal mines and corrupt officials.[2] As a result many illegal miners and officials who abused their administrative power were prosecuted. Such prosecutions are hardly sufficient to restore public confidence in the mining authorities and local officials. But the exposure of illegal industrial operations has, at least, brought them to public attention and serves as an important first step towards a final solution of the problem.

The flowers of millions of investigation bloom

These are just two examples of millions of other investigative reports. If we type in the words "investigative reports" in Chinese on the search engine baidu.com, there will be 91,300,000 results. That indicates how much the public are concerned about the topics under investigation. In addition to the *Topics in Focus*, all the 30 provincial television operations in China now have investigative programmes of their own. Though still constrained by top management and by the central government, investigative programmes are winning more and more acclaim from the public and, therefore, becoming increasingly worthy of their title "watchdogs."

It has to be pointed out that from a professional perspective the performance of investigative journalists is far from perfect, but they are undeniably improving their skills. The authorities, particularly at higher levels, are increasingly using investigative journalism as a powerful anti-corruption weapon. The economic rewards of airing high quality investigative reports improve audience ratings which, in turn, generate more advertising revenues. Moreover, public concern about major social and economic issues will ensure the popularity and continued development of investigative journalism in China.

Notes
[1] See http://baike.baidu.com/view/43125.htm, accessed on 1 May 2011
[2] See http://minyunxiao110.blog.sohu.com/173996213.html, accessed on 2 May 2011

Note on the author
Homson Shaw (Shao, Hongsong) is Associate Dean International of Zhejiang University of Media and Communications and an executive member of the Council of Directors of Hangzhou Translators' Association. Awarded his first degree in English literature by Liaoning Normal University, he became a teacher of English at Yingkou Teachers' College in 1986. In 2004, he began to teach bilingual broadcasting at ZUMC School of International Cultures and Communications and started his studies of mass communication. Shaw is a translator of Edward Herman and Noam Chomsky's *Manufacturing Consent*, which is scheduled to be published by Peking University Press in the autumn of 2011. He also has a number of articles published in the journals of colleges and universities in China.

New Media and Investigative Journalists in China

Hugo de Burgh examines the genre of investigative journalism in China where it is seen essentially as helping to promote good government, the welfare of the people and institution-building. So, he concludes, investigative journalism in China is more supervisory than adversarial

Investigative journalists were dubbed "kings without crowns" when, almost 10 years ago, I introduced fellow students of the media to the idea that there is energetic analysis and exposure in the Chinese media[1]. Since then the media environment has changed utterly. What has happened to investigative journalism in China?

My Father is Li Gang – New Media trumps Investigative Journalism

If you go on Youtube today and type in "My Father is Li Gang" you will find a rap song and many pictures, to say nothing of gigabytes of comment. They all refer to the story of a student who was driving on the campus of his university when he knocked down two girls. The driver tried to get away, but the car was surrounded by angry students who called the police. When they came, he is supposed to have cried out: "You can't touch me, My father is Li Gang!"

Li Gang was one of the city's senior police commanders. Once upon a time, under Mao and before the internet, the son's boast would have saved him. Not any more. Today people protest and the central government logs the protests as legitimate manifestations of grievance; people sue, and sometimes they win; people publicise through the internet what the media are too constrained to broadcast or publish, and the authorities are obliged to accept the popular verdict.

Not only has the phrase "My father is Li Gang" become a rap song, it has become a popular figure of speech; thanks to the internet, the whole nation was enraged. The local authorities did try to prevent discussion of the case in the offline media, but this only redoubled the rage of the netizens seeing that there are people who think that, because of their parents' power, neither the law of the land nor the moral law applies to them.

Before the Communist Party came to power the concept of the rule of law was gaining ground in the 1930s and 1940s. Then, 62 years ago, the Party swept it all away. Now it is gaining ground again. The second most popular CCTV programme is *Law Today*.

As we can see from three cases, initiated by netizens and then taken up by investigative journalists, the media are changing the law, or pushing for it to be implemented. With the *Xiamen paraxylene Plant* case netizens mobilised public opinion against a proposed development and stopped it. A principle was established that people affected by such proposals must be consulted and their permission sought. Familiar around the world is the *Chongqing Nailhouse* case, in which a family of victims of urban development held out over three years for greater compensation for the loss of their home. A picture of their house, sticking up like a nail in a cleared building site, was posted on the web and moved millions of netizens before becoming an icon all over the world. The nailhouse dwellers eventually won the compensation they wanted.

In the story of the *Shanxi Brick Kilns*, netizens exposed the collusion of civil servants and police with employers to exploit and enslave child workers in brickmaking. Their activism forced the authorities to deal with the issue.

In all these cases netizens started the hare while the offline media, using their professional skills to check and deepen the stories, became the megaphones of the bloggers and tweeters. To a growing extent it seems that the internet now sets the media agenda; how this works is the subject of various student dissertations in progress.

Meanwhile investigative journalism in the offline media does what it does best – devote time and resources to stories that have widespread relevance. Here is an iconic example from *News Probe*, China's equivalent of Channel4's *Dispatches*. It's called "Death in Custody".

Offline investigations

A young reporter stands outside a grim looking police station in a provincial town. The top of his head is on a level with the sill of the first floor windows. He is saying:

> When Mr Liu's body was found under this window it was clear that he had landed on his head; death was apparently instantaneous. But when Mr Liu entered the police station two hours earlier he was a 28-year-old professional athlete, fit and healthy. We are told that, irritated with his discussions at the police station, he ran across the room and jumped out of this window. I ask you: would a man regarding himself as wronged by a third party, who had gone to the police station innocently to request help, jump out of a window? Would a fit young man land on his head? Viewer – let me show you the evidence. You decide!

The reporter is Yang Chun and he has for several years fronted the weekly 30-minute national investigative series. It employs all the techniques we associate with the genre: careful desk and field research, checking of evidence and finding of new testimony, secret filming and door-stepping. Its prestige gives it access to authority astray where *Panorama* would find its way blocked. There is no question but that it is part of the establishment; it was brought into existence by the Head of the Propaganda Department in the 1990s. Investigative programmes have been lauded to the skies by Chinese Prime Ministers, all of whom have visited the sets of the main shows.

That does not mean that journalists do not come up against obstacles to reporting, criticism and sometimes punishment, but the situation is not dissimilar from what is sometimes referred to as the Golden Age of Chinese journalism the 1930s, when the media had moments of being championed by the political establishment, followed by moments of persecution. Then, there was competition in political ideas, there were courageous and critical editors and there was investigative journalism.

Today, the range of investigative work is covered in at least 12 books in Chinese and two recent studies in English on the subject, by my former students Wang[2] and Tong[3]. As they both agree, investigation has its limitations; investigative journalists, also on leading newspapers such as *Weekend South* and *Southern City News*, are wise if they work *with* officials instead of against them all; of course, in a country where earning a living can be a rough struggle, there are plenty of local interests which are infuriated by journalists, so the dangers can be great. Nevertheless, as elsewhere, they help to establish norms of behaviour for officials and businesses; promote clean and efficient administration and champion the put-upon. They are calling on the government to uphold high standards and to consider themselves accountable to the public, and this is particularly noticeable with environment stories, which may earn more support from officials than other stories, because of the general alarm about the environment[4].

President Hú Jīntāo wants China to be a harmonious society, a concept straight out of Confucianism, and one of the means to achieve this is investigative journalism. At every Party Congress and Parliament since the 1980s the leaders of the country have stressed, in different ways, the scrutinising role of the media. The expression used is Yúlùn Jiāndū or "Supervision by Public Opinion". It legitimates critical media while connecting Chinese tradition with Anglophone ideas of the role of the journalist in society.

Investigative journalism is seen as one of several techniques for supervision, investigation, and holding to account. There are the courts, the Party's Discipline and Inspection Commission, the petitioning system, the Peoples' Congresses and a growing number of non-government organisations, particularly in the environment field. Investigative journalists join them as a component of the system, rather than, as in Anglo-America, face them as a privileged outsider.

In sum, the programme, *Death in Custody*, shows us the journalist as invigilator; it also shows one of the methods by which accountability and transparency are being introduced into the operations of the state.

How do we understand this idea of Investigative Journalism?

For a good long time observers of China have seen Chinese institutions as deformed or underdeveloped. We have assumed that Anglophone democracy is the highest stage of development and, nowadays, as the necessary consequence of marketisation and the internet. It is true that Prime Minister Wēn Jiābǎo has talked a good deal about extending democracy, just as President Hú Jǐntāo has talked about the importance of the media and freedom of speech. But nobody imagines they have it in mind to copy Westminster. So how do we find ways to explain that China appears not to be fulfilling our expectations?

Economists have preceded the political scientists in acknowledging the influence of *culture*, even though it is a scene fraught with difficulty and easy to ridicule. Dwight Perkins[5] and others have wanted to know why China is so much more successful than other countries with better natural resources, equally cheap labour and fewer difficult challenges to trouble their leaders. Why has China leapt ahead over the past 30 years?

They have concluded that China's success today may be in some ways because China has modernised from Western lessons, but the fact that China has done so in the manner that it has is a function of Chinese culture, now released from the ideological straightjacket of Maoist ideology.

There are some distinctive rules of Chinese culture which drive today's achievements: collectivism, obligation, pragmatism and authority: they are the subconscious rules that underpin the Chinese miracle and which may explain other Chinese characteristics. What in shorthand is called "Confucianism" is the literary expression of these rules.

They express themselves in various ways. For example, Zhejiang television has a dating programme, boy meets girl, which takes the modern form but gives it local content. And what is the local content?

That there are three people in the dating, with two doing all the talking and one keeping silent. This is because the third person is the girl's mother – and she is not the one who is keeping silent! The decision is usually made by the mother. The sense that one is part of a unit before one is an individual is strong.

As to obligation, an example is provided by the 2005 student demonstrations against Japan, fierce and all over China. Some American scholars then interviewed the editor of the *Global Times* and asked him why the newspaper had played down or even not reported some demonstrations[6]. He responded saying this would give a bad impression of China, would encourage copycat demonstrations and, although reporting the demonstrations would get a bigger readership, doing so would be bad for the country. In other words, responsibility to the unit and to the people who compose it trumps other considerations.

When pragmatism rules

Then there is pragmatism. When Dèng Xiǎopíng famously rejected ideology with the declaration that he did not care whether a cat be black or white as long as it killed mice, he also – even more symbolically – changed the name of the party's theoretical journal from *Red Flag* to *Seek Facts*. He was merely returning to Chinese tradition.

Communism brought to China the idea of an ultimate utopia, or afterlife, to be striven for: a belief in belief, in absolute truths and in missionary work. But these – like Marx – come out of the monotheist tradition. Confucius, by contrast, was not interested in exploring heaven or hell, there was too much to cope with on earth. So, you have a culture in which the educated classes shelve religion and even the simpler souls are rather insouciant about their gods.

Staunch Christians and Muslims can feel scandalised by Chinese worship. Such as the temples where joss is being burnt simultaneously to Guān Yǔ (a general who died in 220AD), Jesus Christ, Buddha, the Yellow Emperor (2697BC) and Chairman Mao (died 1976). For good measure we can add the restaurateurs' most popular god, Cáishén (Money Master).

Rejecting monotheist absolutes, many Chinese really simply cannot understand Anglo-Americans' moral swaggering and apparent determination to spread around Western notions of "truth". So, of course, they assume that moral poses, whether subversion of unsatisfactory Arab countries or exporting revolution elsewhere, are merely a cover for selfish interests. They are not usually beguiled by the idea that we are at the highest stage of development and our interference will help them catch up.

Chinese approaches to UK media and institutions

The China Media Centre at the University of Westminster has many Chinese visitors who come to take courses about the UK media or UK institutions. They do not necessarily see themselves as gratefully learning best practice. When our visitors come over they come because they want to learn how we think, to improve their communicate skills; learn about "the West" and to sift among the knowledge they acquire for what might be adapted to their own work and, perhaps more valuable, that which helps them understand the thinking of Anglo-America; understand Anglophone ideas because they are so influential in the world. They are not convinced by the ideology but attentive to it because it is that of the current dominant power. Thus, they exhibit Chinese pragmatism.

Many of the factors which led to the implosion of former communist states in Europe are present today in China, yet as the foremost scholar of the Chinese polity, Shambaugh, writes, by loosening its grip, the party has strengthened its position[7]. Consultation is becoming more real than feigned; there are elections in many parts of the polity; the CCP is improving communication; local officials are made to be responsive not just repressive and, as we have heard, public opinion is taken into account.

These changes bolster the authority and legitimacy of the CCP, in a society permeated by respect for hierarchy, expertise, age, achievement and rank. No wonder that when they are interviewed Chinese journalists are likely to explain themselves as teachers and moral arbiters. Overseeing them is the Central Propaganda Department. It is the institution which enforces conformity: so another return to the imperial past. Editors must accept the authority of the department – for example, in 2006 all editors obeyed the injunction to promote the *Eight Honours and Eight Shames*, moral precepts introduced by Hú Jìntāo.

Editors also obey when instructed to curtail what the department considers negative – for example, xenophobia directed at the USA and Japan. Editors are punished if they make mistakes.

In sum, there are four rules of Chinese society: collectivism, obligation, pragmatism and authority. They contrast with what might be argued to be the rules of Anglophone societies: the rule of law; individualism; conscience and a belief in truth. Thinking about the cultural substructure of Chinese society helps us to interpret what's going on, even in the age of transnational cyber communities, when it can appear that all boundaries are fluid; it also makes us see modern Chinese society and polity as organic rather than as some temporary scaffolding bought second hand from Lenin.

The future of censorship

In chat over dinner last year, the head of a provincial propaganda department spoke of his main worry being the opinion makers of the internet: Will they attack his province with allegations he cannot counter? Will they find the scandals before he can? He makes sure that he flies to Hainan, where Tianya[8] originates, and Beijing, where Xinlang[9] is composed, to make friends with the scribblers in the hope that he can head off criticism when it is pointed at his province. It's life or death stuff for his career; several officials in recent months, exposed as flawed, have suffered dire consequences.

It's not a pleasant thought that all around you are people with cameras in their mobile phones which can see the expensive watch you are wearing – it costs twice an annual salary – or even post a video of you and your best friend on YouTube. Because the internet is so frightening to bad officials – *naked officials* as they are called – it will force them to clean up. Digital networks are having immense impact and making it possible for netizens to coordinate, but they do not of themselves make for political action. As long as there is widespread agreement on what China's political system should be like – and the world-famous dissidents may be out on a limb – complaints will not lead to revolution.

Unlike the Old Man Who Moves the Mountain, the modern censor has no hope of ultimate success but, like Sisyphus, is condemned to rolling a great rock up a hill only to see the editors and the bloggers roll it back down again. The several thousand staffers attempting to guide and cleanse the internet will continue their Sisyphean task.

The Central Propaganda Department will continue to issue imperial instructions and it will continue to exist in creative tension with the media policy-makers and editors who regarded their sacred duty as scrutinising government. Both sides will do their duty. Often the behaviour of the authorities – as in the latest case of the treatment of the internationally celebrated artist Ài Wèiwèi (detained for several months by the Chinese authorities in 2011) – will be malevolent and stupid.

While the long-term trend may well be for more transparency and an ever widening sphere of discussion, investigative journalists and free thinkers will continue to get caught between factions. As we write (in June 2011) there appears to be a crackdown going on, in response to the Arab Spring, although it is unclear who is taking the initiatives and what is the strategy, if there is one. Opinion formers are being brought into line; to survive professionally they have to be adept at self censorship.

Conclusion
The leaders have talked of the "life and death" struggle against corruption, and the need for accountability and transparency so that it has therefore, in effect, licensed several different institutions to keep in check the power holders, including investigative journalism. The state has encouraged this and the party acts as final arbiter.

Of course, there is resistance and, as in any country, the targets of investigation and criticism try to block it. Some will not be satisfied without much bigger changes. Maybe they are right; yet, though Chinese maybe as grumpy as anyone about their lot, few have it in mind to change the system; few journalists seem convinced that the Party should hand over the setting of the moral and political agenda to their own media class.

Just as China appears to have eschewed our kind of electoral democracy in favour of what is referred to as "consultative democracy"[10], so investigative journalism is less adversarial than supervisory. It is very conscious of its purposes and effects. When, in 2010, two leading commissioners of British investigative journalism discussed their work in a forum at China Central Television, they were asked to summarise their beliefs about investigative journalism at the end and did so in concrete, practical terms, detailing the importance of evidence and techniques of research and revelation[11]. The editor of *News Probe*, however, argued in his talk that investigative journalism made for good government, the welfare of the people and institution-building in China. The different emphases remind us of the very different conceptions of professionalism in two very different societies.

Notes

[1] See De Burgh, H. (2003) Kings without Crowns? The Re-emergence of Investigative Journalism in China, *Media Culture and Society*, Vol, 25, No. 6 pp 801-820

[2] See Wang Haiyan (2010) *Investigative Journalism and Political Power in China*, Oxford: Reuters Institute (working paper)

[3] See Tong Jingrong (2011) *Investigative Journalism in China*, London: Continuum

[4] See De Burgh, H. and Zeng, R. (2011) de Burgh, Hugo and Zeng Rong *China's Environment and China's Environment Journalists*, London: Intellect

[5] See Perkins, Dwight H (2000) *Law, Family Ties and the East Asian Way of Business*, Huntington, S. P. and Harrison, L. E. (eds) *Culture Matters*, NY: Basic Books

[6] See Shirk, Susan L. (2011) *Changing Media, Changing China*, Oxford: OUP p. 230

[7] See Shambaugh, David (2009) *China's Communist Party*, Berkeley: University of California Press

[8] Tianya is one of the most popular internet fora in China and known especially for "human flesh search", or digging out intimate details of prominent people

[9] Xinlang is the largest Chinese infotainment web portal, believed to have around 100 million registered users

[10] See Yu Keping (2011) Democracy in China: Challenge or Oppportunity? Wu Jingzhuang et al (eds) *China in 2030 (Zhongguo Weilai Sanshinian)*, Peking: Central Compilation and Translation Bureau pp 100-111 and Brown, Kerry (2011) *Ballot Box China*, London: Zed Books

[11] China Central Television forum on Investigative Journalism addressed by Steve Hewlett, Kevin Sutcliffe, Zhang Jie and Hugo de Burgh, April 2009

Note on the author

Hugo de Burgh holds the Chair of the Study of Journalism at the University of Westminster and is Director of the China Media Centre. He holds a Professorship at Tsinghua University under the Chinese Ministry of Education's 985 programme. His books include *The Chinese Journalist* (2003), *Making Journalists* (2005) and *Investigative Journalism* (2008, second edition). He has also published an introduction to how China works, *China Friend or Foe?* (2006). He will shortly publish a book on Chinese environment journalism.

Drugs, Destabilisation and UN policy in Guinea-Bissau: The Role of Investigative Journalism

Daniel Ruiz examines the way in which investigative journalism focusing on drug trafficking in West Africa has helped inspire national and international efforts to combat the crime

Introduction

Organised crime is one of the main drivers behind violent conflict in our age of globalisation: from the trafficking of weapons, people, drugs or natural resources, to the laundering of money, to the extortion of the populations. They provoke direct violence (assassination, torture), structural violence (exploitation, racketeering) and cultural violence (promotion of inequalities, injustice and impunity). In this chapter I will analyse the situation of Guinea-Bissau in 2006-8, when it was captured by drug trafficking cartels, under the incredulous eyes of the international community. It was only after the denunciation of the situation by leading international magazines that the international community started to react decisively.

Guinea-Bissau

Guinea-Bissau is a small country (36000km^2) located in the West African Coast, between Senegal and Guinea-Conakry. It has a low altitude (its highest point has 300m) and most of its surface is covered by tropical jungle and mangroves in the coastal areas. It includes 88 islands (the Bijagos Archipelago, declared Reserve of the Biosphere by UNESCO) and is cut by numerous fjords and rivers. The majority of its 1.5 million inhabitants is animist, unlike the surrounding countries whose dominant religion is Islam.

It was colonised from the fifteenth century by the Portuguese, whose rights were confirmed by the Berlin Conference in 1885. It is the only country in sub-Saharan Africa that obtained independence through armed struggle (in 1974), organised by the PAIGC (the African Party for the Independence of Guinea and Cabo Verde) and its charismatic leader Amilcar Cabral (assassinated just some months before its achievement). The Marxist-oriented government established after independence by Luis Cabral was overthrown by General Nino Vieira in 1980. Guinea-Bissau and Cabo Verde were then separated into different states

During the 1990s, as in many other developing countries at the time, a market economy and an incipient multi-party political system were imposed on Guinea-Bissau by the IMF. Nino Vieira managed to hold power through cronyism and corruption, but was finally overthrown in 1999 after a short civil war initiated by a dispute with the head of the armed forces, General Ansumane Mané, over the smuggling of weapons into the Senegalese region of Casamance. A United Nations peacebuilding field mission, UNOGBIS[1], was established in 1999 to monitor the peace settlement.

One putsch and two assassinations of the chief of the armed forces later, Nino Vieira returned from exile on a military helicopter from Conakry into the main square of Bissau, and won in two months the 2005 presidential elections against all odds. As the President Lansana Conté had already been related to South American drug cartels, rumours ran that Nino's campaign had been financed by traffickers. President Vieira was ultimately assassinated during the night of 1 March 2009, in retaliation for the bombing of the chief of the armed forces, General Tagme Na Waie, some hours earlier. They were long-standing political rivals (and allegedly also rivals in the trafficking business).

According to the UNDP Human Development Index, Guinea-Bissau is the fifth poorest country in the world. Infant mortality is 20 per cent, life expectancy is 47 years, 65 per cent of the population lives below the poverty line (2$). Malaria, AIDs and tuberculosis are prevalent. The median age is 20 years old. Illiteracy rate is 60 per cent. The only official source of foreign currency is the export of cashew to India, and the reduced fishing rights paid by the European Union. The GDP in 2007 was 1.3 billion US$ PPP (purchasing power parity), or 800 US$ per capita.

There is almost no electricity production, nor asphalted roads. During the colonial war the Portuguese built some 27 landing strips, some of which have now been recovered by the traffickers to land the planes carrying cocaine from South America, in particular in the isolated Bijagos Islands. It has modest reserves of bauxite, phosphates, diamonds and oil, still untapped. In 2003 it was the third beneficiary of Official Development Aid in the world. The external debt amounts to 1 billion US$.

The political system is semi-presidential. The armed forces count some 4,000 military with an additional 4,000 irregular militias. The recruitment is done on a crony and tribal basis, with 80 per cent of the soldiers belonging to the Balanta ethnic group. It has an inverted pyramid structure, with 80 per cent of officers and 20 per cent of privates. The judicial system is corrupt and subordinate to the political and economic establishment while 50 per cent of the members of parliament in 2007 were illiterate[2].

Drug trafficking in West Africa?

According to the United Nations Office on Drugs and Crime (UNODC), trafficking of cocaine through West Africa started in 2004 in response to the reduction of demand in the US and the increase in Europe. More than 46 tons of cocaine were seized in West Africa between 2005 and 2008, against less than one ton per year previously. Based on the analysis of the seizures, 27 per cent of all cocaine arriving to Europe (or 40 tons) transited through West Africa in 2007, with a value of 1.8 billion US$, which leaves 450 million US$ of profit, representing more resources than most of the governments in the region. Guinea-Bissau's government budget is equivalent to the value of 2.5 tons of cocaine, which may transit through the country in one or two months.

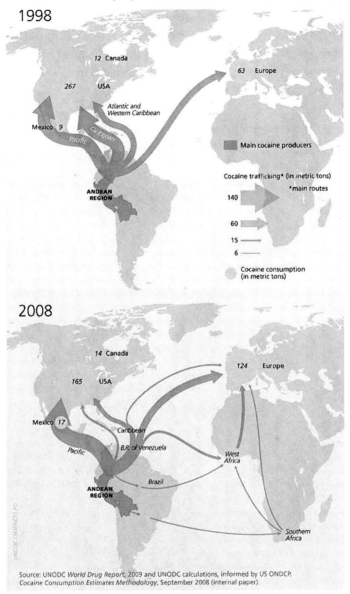

Source: UNODC *World Drug Report*, 2009 and UNODC calculations, informed by US ONDCP, *Cocaine Consumption Estimates Methodology*, September 2008 (internal paper).

Drug trafficking suspects, even when detained, are seldom sentenced and even when they are, there is no prison in Bissau, as the only one in the country was destroyed during the 1999 civil war. The drugs are transported between South America and West Africa mainly by sea and air along the 10th parallel[3]. This has been the most common route for most commodities since the fifteenth century, including African slaves.

The trafficking suffers the "balloon-effect": when it is squeezed in one part, it swells in another area, so that the final flow is not affected. This way, the preferred transportation means has shifted between sea and air, and has used different West African countries, depending on its geography and the connections with the elites.

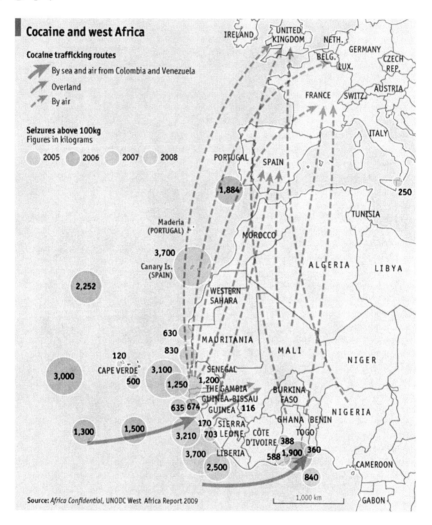

Cocaine and west Africa

Cocaine trafficking routes
- By sea and air from Colombia and Venezuela
- Overland
- By air

Seizures above 100kg
Figures in kilograms

2005 2006 2007 2008

Source: *Africa Confidential*, UNODC West Africa Report 2009

Nigeria, Guinea-Conakry and Cabo Verde had been involved in limited trafficking of drugs (heroin from South East Asia, local hashish, cocaine) in the 90s and early 2000s. Morocco has traditionally been involved in contraband with Spain, particularly of hashish. Due to pressure by the European Union from 2004, South American traffickers opted to shift one of their bases from Cabo Verde to Guinea-Bissau[4].

The South American trafficking networks include Brazilians, Mexicans and Venezuelans but are mainly controlled by Colombians, including members of the FARC (Revolutionary Armed Forces of Colombia)[5].

In Europe, the prevalence of use of cocaine is 1.2 per cent of the population. The main consumers are the UK (23 per cent), Spain (21 per cent) and Italy (19 per cent)[6].

There are two main flows from West Africa to Europe. One is transported by human *mules*, and derives from the payments in kind to the African facilitators. This part can represent up to one third of the total[7]. The other part is wholesale and is transported by more sophisticated means (e.g: hidden in containers, inside other cargo such as logs or fish.). All the countries in West Africa are involved in the transportation of the wholesale, which involves the most diverse facilitators, from government officials, to military, police, criminals, traders, fishing companies, air companies, or insurgent and terrorist groups[8].

In 2006, the International Community was reluctant to acknowledge the new developments in Guinea-Bissau, and particularly the fact that authorities at the highest level might be involved. The quarterly reports of the Secretary General to the Security Council reflected this, and only marginally mentioned the issue of drug trafficking, although some important seizures and arrests had taken place already. In September 2006, the judicial police seized 674 kg of cocaine in Bissau which disappeared after some days from the vaults of the Ministry of Finance where it had been kept, allegedly taken away by "men in uniform".

Scoop

This event attracted to Bissau a photographer specialising in drug trafficking and UNODC goodwill ambassador. On 3 April 2007 and in his presence, the judicial police seized another 635kg of cocaine and four traffickers, two of whom were officers of the army. As the judicial police did not have the budget, the photographer was asked to pay for the fuel of the vehicles. Four days later the prosecutor ordered the burning of the seizure in his presence. It was the first time that a cocaine seizure was destroyed in the country. Local journalists and human rights activists who had insinuated the possible complicity of state officials in the trafficking were harassed and forced to flee the country. The reports to the Security

Council continued to give only minimal mention of the trafficking (a maximum of 7 per cent of the paragraphs).

This spectacular operation attracted the presence of leading international magazine reporters to Bissau. On 7 June 2007, the *Economist* published the article "Guinea-Bissau, a Pusher's Paradise: The Drugs Trade in the Continent's First Narco-State is Booming". Guinea-Bissau was presented as the main point of transit of cocaine from Latin America to Europe. It denounced the complicity of high government officials, the repression against local journalists, and predicted that settlings of scores among traffickers would soon start.

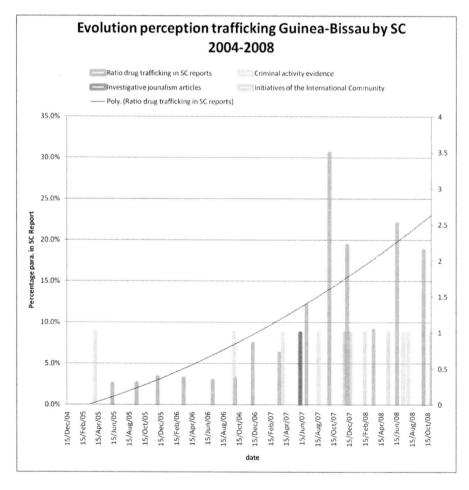

On 11 June 2007, *Time* magazine published the article "Cocaine Country", describing Guinea-Bissau as being a "narco-state" and claiming as well

that it was one of the main points of transit of cocaine to Europe through fake export companies. The reporter described how she negotiated the price for a kilo of cocaine in the centre of Bissau in the open and by day. The article denounced the complicity of high government officials, the threats against judges and journalists, and the possible connections with terrorist networks.

The reporters did not have much difficulty in conducting their investigations, as the trafficking was still done openly and with impunity. Numerous articles followed worldwide up until the present time, describing Guinea-Bissau as a cocaine trafficking hub.

Outcome

The graph represents the relation between the criminal evidence (seizures, arrests, threats), the investigative journalism articles, the percentage of paragraphs mentioning drug trafficking in the reports to the Security Council, and the reactions of the international community (statements, meetings, deployments and so on).

Although there were earlier rumours of trafficking, the first arrest of South American traffickers took place in April 2005 in the Bijagos. In June 2005, the reports to the security council included for the first time comments on drug trafficking (less than 3 per cent of the paragraphs). Despite the seizure of 674 kg of cocaine and two Colombian traffickers in Bissau on 26 September 2006, the comments only increased to 7 per cent. After the articles in the *Economist* and *Time* magazine in June 2007, the comments dramatically increased to 30 per cent and remained one of the main subjects until today (most recent: 20 per cent).

After the admission by the Security Council of the seriousness of the situation of drug trafficking in Guinea Bissau and its impact on its stability, the International Community decided to implement a series of strong interventions:

- on 27 November 2007, the Executive Director of UNODC visited Bissau;
- on 12 December 2007, the Executive Director of UNODC pleaded in the Security Council for support in the fight against trafficking in Guinea-Bissau;

- on 19 December 2007, the governments of Guinea-Bissau and Portugal organised in Lisbon an international conference on drug trafficking in Guinea-Bissau;
- on 12 February 2008, the European Union deployed a Common Foreign and Security Policy Mission in Guinea-Bissau led by a Spanish general to contribute to the reform of the security sector;
- on 15 May 2008, UNODC deployed a Special Advisor for Drug Trafficking in Bissau;
- on 29 September 2008, the report to the Security Council proposed an international inquiry to prosecute the high officials involved in drug trafficking;
- on 28 October 2008, ECOWAS and UNODC organised a conference on drug trafficking in West Africa.

Many other interventions followed with the aim of controlling drug trafficking in Guinea-Bissau and the whole region. The subject of drug trafficking has also been an omnipresent issue related to Western Africa in the international media.

Conclusions

The decline of the state after the Cold War without the establishment of new international mechanisms of governance has permitted private entities, including criminal groups, to develop transnational business networks that can put at stake the security of states and the welfare of nations. In the case of Guinea-Bissau, what was ignored was not as serious as the genocidal acts of Srebrenica, Rwanda or Eastern Democratic Republic of Congo, but it was serious enough to destabilise West Africa.

The events described show how civil society, and in particular investigative journalism, can contribute to compensate the weakness of official mechanisms by highlighting largely covert activities, and encouraging the bureaucracy (national and international) to take action. The articles were certainly successful in putting the situation of drug trafficking in Guinea-Bissau into the headlines. Investigative journalism should continue promoting transparency to encourage societies and governments to act in favour of humans and the planet, and not of obscure and illegitimate interests. Technology is making new tools available that can promote transparency and facilitate investigation as is WikiLeaks.

Reporters sans Frontières, in its November 2007 report on Guinea-Bissau, recommended the international media to continue to report on drug trafficking in order to maintain the pressure on the traffickers and their bases.

In its last research[9], UNODC announced the seizures of cocaine in Europe had halved from 2006 (121 Tm) to 2009 (53 Tm). While this does not necessarily mean that the trafficking has decreased, it means at least that the narcos have been disturbed by the disclosure of their activities and the subsequent law enforcement measures.

However, the assassination of the President of the Republic and the Head of the Armed Forces in March 2009 (allegedly due to feuds around drug trafficking), followed by the assassination of the ex-Minister of Defence and the Presidential Security Advisor (both also allegedly heavily involved in trafficking) some weeks later, and the mutiny of the ex-chief of the Navy (labelled a drug kingpin by the US government[10]) in April 2010, indicate that Guinea-Bissau is still far from having resolved its governance problems.

Dates	Paragraphs mentioning trafficking in SC reports	Criminal activities	Initiatives International Community	Articles
4-Jun-04	0/34			
15-Dec-04	0/41			
16-Mar-05	0/34			
5-Apr-05		Judicial Police raided a fake fish processing facility in the Bijagos Islands, seizing 18 kilograms of cocaine and a large cache of arms, and arresting seven foreign traffickers (three Spanish, two Venezuelan, and two Colombian)		
10-Jun-05	2.5%			

12-Sep-05	2.6%			
2-Dec-05	3.3%			
14-Mar-06	3.2%			
6-Jul-06	2.9%			
26-Sep-06		Seizure of 674 kg cocaine (disappeared)		
29-Sep-06	3.2%			
6-Dec-06	7.4%			
20-Mar-07	6.3%			
3-Apr-07		Seizure 675 kg cocaine in presence UNODC Goodwill Ambassador (destroyed)		
7-Jun-07				*Economist*
11-Jun-07				*Time*
3-Jul-07	12.1%			
18-Aug-07		Arrest of two Colombians after seizing weapons and a large sum of money in a raid on a suspected location in the Bairro Militar of Bissau (also seized documents relating the two Colombians to the highest levels of Guinea Bissau's institutional and political powers)		
28-Sep-07	30.6%			
27-Nov-07			Visit Executive Director UNODC to Bissau	
1-Dec-07			Publication by UNODC of a special report on drug trafficking in Guinea-Bissau	
6-Dec-07	19.4%			
12-Dec-07			Speech Executive Director UNODC at the Security Council	

19-Dec-07			International Conference on drug trafficking in Guinea-Bissau in Lisbon	
12-Feb-08			Establishment of a EU mission for SSR in Guinea-Bissau.	
17-Mar-08	9.1%			
15-May-08			Deployment in Bissau of a Special Advisor of UNODC on drug trafficking	
17-Jun-08	22.0%			
12-Jul-08		Seizure of 2 planes with 500 kg of cocaine (disappeared)		
31-Jul-08		Minister of Justice threatened by traffickers		
29-Sep-08	18.8%		Proposal by SC of sanctions against high officials involved in drug trafficking	
28-Oct-08			Conference ECOWAS/UNODC in Praia	

Notes

[1] UN Security Council, Resolution 1233 (1999), 6 April 1999, that establishes UNOGBIS.
[2] Discussion with the speaker of Parliament in March 2007
[3] Designated by law enforcement organisations Highway 10
[4] Mazzitelli, Antonio (March 2011) *The New Transatlantic Bonanza: Cocaine on Highway 10*, WHEMSAC
[5] ibid
[6] UNODC (April 2011) *The Transatlantic Cocaine Marke*, Research Paper
[7] ibid
[8] UNODC (October 2007) *Cocaine Trafficking in West Africa.*
[9] UNODC (April 2011) *The Transatlantic Cocaine Market*, Research Paper
[10] US Department of the Treasury (8 April 2010) *Treasury Designates Two Narcotics Traffickers in Guinea-Bissau Treasury Targets Emerging West African Narcotics Transit Route*

Further reading

al Jazeera (2009) Africa's Cocaine Coast, February 2009. Available online at http://www.youtube.com/watch?v=CrnV22bF2k8, accessed on 1 May 2011

BBC (2008) Guinea-Bissau drugs plane seized, 20 July

Casimiro, Fernando (2008) *As Nações Unidas Falharam Na Guiné-Bissau*, 13 December. Available online at www.didinho.org, accessed on 1 May 2011

Casimiro, Fernando (2009) *O Narcotráfico Na Guiné-Bissau, Com Realismo*, 24 April. Available online at www.didinho.org, accessed on 1 May 2011

Channel 4 (2007) *Cocaine Country*. September. Available online at http://video.google.com/videoplay?docid=-5576811608218107470, accessed on 1 May 2011

Comité Interministerial para a Reestruturação e Modernização do Sector da Defesa e Segurança (2006) *Reestruturação e Modernização do Sector da Defesa e Segurança, Documento de Estratégias*, Bissau, October

Economist (2007) Pushers' Paradise: The Drugs Trade in the Continent's First Narco-State is Booming, 7 June

El País (2009) El "narco" se instala en Guinea-Bissau, 22 March

Green, Matthew (2008) West Africa: Unbroken Line, *Financial Times*, November

Guardian (2008) West Africa: UN expert cites crime, terrorism hideout, 14 January

International Crisis Group (2008) *Guinée-Bissau: Besoin d'Etat*, 2 July

Le Monde Diplomatique (2009) Guinée-Bissau: questions sur l'assassinat d'un président, 12 March

Mazzitelli, Antonio (2011) *The New Transatlantic Bonanza: Cocaine on Highway 10*, WHEMSAC, March

Reporters sans Frontières (2007) *Cocaïne et coup d'Etat, fantômes d'une nation bâillonnée*, November

Security Council Report (2011) *Emerging Security Threats In West Africa*, May

UN Security Council (2004) *Report of the Secretary-General on Developments in Guinea-Bissau and on the Activities of the United Nations Peacebuilding Support Office in That Country*, 4 June 2004 to 29 September 2008. Available online at www.un.org/docs/sc, accessed on 1 May 2011

UN Security Council, Resolution 1233 (1999), 6 April establishing UNOGBIS

UNDP (2006) *Human Development Report Guinea-Bissau*

UNODC (2011) *The Transatlantic Cocaine Market Research Paper*, April

UNODC (2007) *Cocaine Trafficking In West Africa. The threat to stability and development (with special reference to Guinea-Bissau)*, December

UNODC (2008) Guinea-Bissau: New hub for cocaine trafficking, *Perspectives*, No. 5, May

UNODC (2008) *A ONUDC Adverte sobre o Tráfico de Droga como um Ameaça à Segurança na África Ocidental*, 28 October

UNODC (2007) *Cocaine Trafficking in West Africa*, October

UNODC (2007) *Drug Trafficking as a Security Threat in West Africa*, November

US Department of the Treasury (2010*) Treasury Designates Two Narcotics Traffickers in Guinea-Bissau Treasury Targets Emerging West African Narcotics Transit Route*, 8 April

Wallensteen, Peter (2001) *The Growing Peace Research Agenda*, Kroc Institute Occasional Paper, Vol, 21, No. 4, December

Walt, Vivienne (2007) *The Way-Station for Europe's Cocaine, Time*, 11 June

Note on the author

Daniel Ruiz is a Researcher at the Universities of Madrid, Trieste, Gorizia and Bradford. He is currently a senior political affairs officer in MONUSCO (UN mission in Congo). The focus of his present research is on the links between transnational organised crime and violent conflict.

Section 3. Alive and Well Locally?

Where the Freedom of Information Act is like Manna from Heaven

John Mair

So it seems that investigative journalism is just alive and well in the UK and internationally – but mainly on television. British newspapers nationally have, with one or two noble exceptions, moved to a new agenda which precludes investigation. Local newspapers are in an even more perilous economic state with little hope of light at the end of their tunnel.

The Freedom of Information Act has come as manna from heaven for many of them. They can mount an investigative splash through the simple device of a carefully targeted FoI request. But is investigative journalism dead in local papers and on local TV?

Neil Fowler is the Guardian Fellow at Nuffield College Oxford and has previously edited two morning and two evening regional newspapers in the UK. Here, he argues that local newspapers are continuing to dig deep and expose scandals, corruption and wrong-doings in the regions. So don't believe the sceptics.

Guy Lynn now works for BBC London. He has previously reported for BBC Look North with some excellent investigative pieces on stories such as dodgy, discriminating estate agents. But he had to deliver those extra pieces in addition to his daily rota job and its demands. Lynn has won three Royal Television Society Awards in the last five years. He praises the BBC locally but not without a caveat or two:

> I believe investigative journalism is alive and well, particularly at the BBC. Yet it faces occasional threats to its survival. Original journalism is regularly recited like a mantra as something audiences truly appreciate as distinguishing the BBC from its competitors. Yet, sadly, investment in investigative journalism can sometimes fall by the wayside when faced with the number crunching. Reporters can and should help the situation. The extra personal investment, the realization that we are doing a job others would kill to have, can result in huge rewards not just for us personally but for the audience we serve.

Proof that Investigative Journalism is Alive and Kicking in the Regions

Local newspapers are continuing to dig dip and expose scandals, corruption and wrong-doings in the regions. So don't believe the sceptics, argues Neil Fowler

A surprising revival happened in May 2011. Driven by the Society of Editors, new life was breathed in to the UK Regional Press Awards. Two years before, in 2009, the event had been like a wake, and a miserable wake at that. In 2010, the National Union of Journalists had arranged its own event, but it not been able to match the glamour or excitement of previous years when under the stewardship of *Press Gazette* it had been a genuine industry highlight[1].

In 2011, some 350 journalists from reporter through to editor, with a few managing directors thrown in for good measure, attended a remarkably upbeat lunch at a London hotel to celebrate the best of the local newspaper industry. But was the optimistic atmosphere merely a cheerful pre-death rattle of a sector mortally wounded in the maelstrom created by the effects of the growth of the internet? Or was it an indication that there was still resilience of some kind still propping up the industry's somewhat shaky foundations?

Interestingly, the winners of most of the 23 categories showed that if regional and local newspapers were dying, some of them, at least, were going down with a fight. The overall winner of Newspaper of the Year was the *Irish News* – a Belfast-based daily selling 45,000 – a figure more than it was selling 20 years ago. The judges praised it for being muscular, independent and serious – with strong campaigning and investigative arms. One of its reporters, Allison Morris, was named Daily Reporter of the Year; her work was said to be "serious reporting at its best" by the judges and interviews with some secretive dissident republicans was the "culmination of several months' painstaking work".

Both winners in the two Weekly Newspaper of the Year categories (for newspapers selling either fewer than 20,000 or more than 20,000), the *Derry News* and the *Essex Chronicle*, were praised for their willingness to "cause a stir" and "to dig and probe". And the Scoop of the Year award went to Jeanette Oldham, of Birmingham's *Sunday Mercury*, for her three-month inquiry into how tens of millions of pounds of government cash to help asylum seekers had gone missing. It was "an exemplary piece of investigative reporting about matters of major public interest – a scandalous waste of public money, corruption and government incompetence", said the judges.

So investigative journalism is alive and kicking in the West Midlands, at least, but examination of many of the other categories in the awards shows that it is not a geographical anomaly. The Young Journalist of the Year, Dan Warburton from NCJ Media in the north-east of England, was praised for face-to-face interviews with regional gangsters showing "bravery, cunning, legal knowledge, tenacity and great writing skill".

Two reporters in the Business and Financial Journalist category, Jon Griffin of the *Birmingham Mail* and Simon Bain of the *Herald*, Glasgow, were commended for being "brilliantly informed" and uncovering "technical matters of genuine public interest". The Weekly Reporter of the Year was Paul Francis, the long-standing political editor of the *Kent Messenger*, and named as the "scourge of Kent County Council". His stories, the judges said, were "a marvelous example of dogged determination". And the Campaign of the Year was won by the *Norwich*

Evening News which uncovered, long before BBC's *Panorama*, tales of mistreatment of elderly patients in Norfolk; and forced a complacent NHS management in to changing its ways.

Breaking new ground in data journalism

It was not just in print that investigations were seen to be taking pace. The *Manchester Evening News* won the award for Digital Innovation of the Year when it broke genuine new ground in live data journalism. It used information provided by Greater Manchester Police, on the day it tweeted every crime and associated event, to not only develop a live snapshot of what was happening in its patch but also to conduct some innovative social research at the same time.

These were the winners but there were many others on the shortlists, too, who added to the evidence of a still lively sector. The *Derby Telegraph* tracked down a known on-the-run paedophile to Switzerland before going out there and confronting him. The *Western Mail* exposed the publicly funded Welsh television shows that had zero viewers.

Catherine Lea, of the *Hull Daily Mail*, trawled through mounds of planning documents and dug out reports from long-defunct organisations to find hidden business and development schemes of huge significance to the Humberside region. Michael Ribbert, of the *Bristol Evening Post*, had to spend a great deal of time examining the small print of the government's Defence Spending Review and to make many phone calls to find out exactly what would happen to military facilities in his patch. And it wasn't just the big dailies that were producing good examples. The *Luton and Dunstable Express* traced and exposed a woman accused of murder in Pakistan living on benefits in a Bedfordshire backstreet.

Belfast investigative reporting puts WikiLeaks under the spotlight

Shortly after the awards, in early June 2011, the *Belfast Telegraph* showed that the regional press wasn't afraid of becoming involved with WikiLeaks. Working with its sister publication in the Irish republic, the *Irish Independent*, it worked its way through US embassy cables supplied by the whistleblower to detail the extent of American involvement over the years in Northern Ireland affairs.

On its first day it devoted 13 pages to what it had found, discovering talks in 2004 that took place between the loyalist Democratic Unionist Party and nationalist Sinn Fein, when the DUP was still maintaining that it would not negotiate with republicans. Two *Belfast Telegraph* journalists, along with three *Irish Independent* journalists, spent many weeks analysing almost 7,000 pages in 1,900 dispatches. They uncovered previously unknown details of the peace process, as well as unflattering assessments of many local politicians. They also came across records of private talks between Irish President Mary McAleese's husband and loyalist paramilitaries that were passed on to the White House.

So, on the face of it, investigative journalism is very much alive in the UK regional and local press. But before it is possible to determine the how deep-set that wellbeing is, it is important to ascertain what is really meant by investigative journalism and if the practice was ever that commonplace over the years in the sector.

Steve Weinberg in 1996 defined investigative journalism as "reporting, through one's own initiative and work product, matters of importance to readers, viewers or listeners"[2]. That covers many aspects of reporting that will be found in most newspapers and magazines. However, most items, even trivial news briefs, can be said to be of importance and relevance to at least one person. How much can be said to come from "one's own initiative" is, of course, arguable, in the debate provoked by Nick Davies's *Flat Earth News*.

In the 2005 book, *Key Concepts in Journalism*, Mark Hanna was not so sure about it[3]. He said that the term investigative journalist smacked of pretension but that it did help to define the skills and methods "which sustain a journalist through a complex lengthy assignment". Hanna said that investigative journalism had appeared as a distinct area of interest in the UK in the 1960s, evolving from the wider subjects of campaigning journalism and press exposure. He said that the perception in media and academic circles was that investigative journalism had declined since its "1970s heydays". He didn't supply any evidence to say where that perception came from – but if the genre only began in the 1960s and has been in decline since the 1970s, its primacy was somewhat short-lived.

Hanna does not differentiate between national and regional newspapers over this alleged decline, but he is scathing about the local sector: "Cost-cutting, to facilitate massive profits, in the regional press means many reporters who aspire to investigations, can rarely free themselves from mundane tasks." That assumes, of course, that aspiring reporters were ever in history allowed to free themselves in such a way. They weren't. They were always generally working on the mundane task of writing stories that their readers might find interesting.

Investigative journalism – up until the mid-1980s

So what investigative journalism has there been in the regional press and how widespread has it ever been? Until the mid-1980s most regional newspapers were relatively unadventurous organisations. They were generally small in pagination, despite the growth of classified advertising since the early 1960s, they made relatively little money, they invested little in technology because they believed existing arrangements with the print unions made such risks of little value, and they didn't have legions of reporters working incognito on "investigations".

What they were good at was reporting local councils, police and the courts, asking difficult questions to those involved in the local community and, of course, finding good human interest that enterprising freelances would then sell on to the nationals. That was, and still remains, the basic *raison-d'être* for the regional and local press. There never was, therefore, any golden age of regional investigative journalism as such, so there can be no claims for the practice to have died. But regional newspapers would uncover the occasional nugget that might be termed "investigative journalism".

A good example of this was in 1977 when the Preston-based *Lancashire Evening Post* investigated allegations of serious wrong-doing by the then Chief Constable of Lancashire, Stanley Parr. The investigation was led by the *Post's* current editor Barry Askew who included in his team Bob Satchwell, now executive director of the Society of Editors, who was his assistant editor at the time. Satchwell said: "We heard that a detective sergeant had complained during an annual inspection of the force. It all went very quiet, but we were being briefed by senior figures describing (the DS) as mentally ill and dismissing the rumours."[4]

However, the team then heard that an outside force had been brought in to carry out an investigation in to a whole range of serious complaints and it strived to get a copy of the report that many were trying to keep secret. Eventually a copy was obtained and published. Parr was sacked and his career ended in disgrace with 26 breaches of discipline including showing favours, improper use of police vehicles and falsification of records.

When regional reporters scooped national awards

Askew and Satchwell, as well as the *Post's* chief reporter David Graham, were named Journalists of the Year in the 1977 British Press Awards, an honour rarely given to anyone from outside Fleet Street. This was perhaps the best instance of the 1960s and 1970s in the regions, but there would have been other titles producing stories of a similar nature.

In 1993, the *Derby Evening Telegraph*, under the editorship of Mike Lowe, succeeded in having the chairman of Derbyshire County Council's finance committee, Sean Stafford, prosecuted for fraudulently claiming £13,500 in loss-of-income expenses from the authority. He was jailed for 18 months. The newspaper had used regulations in the 1982 Local Government Finance Act that allows scrutiny of all council invoices, expense forms and payments at specific times of the year.

This was a tactic that had been adopted enthusiastically by the *Telegraph's* then-deputy editor Keith Perch in a previous role as a freelance in the Hull area in the late 1980s, where he had used the Act to ask questions of the then chief constable of Humberside police's expense claims. This relatively straightforward method of keeping local authority characters under scrutiny was subsequently picked up by other regional and local publications.

Many regional dailies through the 1980s and 1990s would have published similar stories. Probing local councillors, acting as conduits for concerned readers, questioning planning applications – all were staples of their diets. Not ground breaking on a national scale but very important locally. Larger weeklies, such as the *Kent Messenger*, would also break similar stories, smaller weeklies with their smaller and less experienced staffs generally didn't to the same degree – but they never had, although they would have done so from time to time.

Campaigning on issues that touch the national conscience

What regional and local newspapers were exceptional at, and remain so today, was campaigning, mainly on local issues, but sometimes on subjects that touched the national conscience. The best of this latter was the *Northern Echo* which, arguably, undertook and succeeded in possibly the finest campaign ever undertaken by any British newspaper, when it battled in 1965 for a posthumous pardon for Timothy Evans, who had been hanged in 1950 for the murder of his baby daughter in the horrific story of 10 Rillington Place.

Harold Evans (no relation), later to become editor of both *The Sunday Times* and *The Times*, raised the issue, raised it again and continued to raise it until the government and courts agreed to review the case and (Timothy) Evans was eventually pardoned[5]. This wasn't investigative journalism (although Evans did originate investigations on the *Echo*, such as an exposé on the cause of noxious fumes on Teesside), as Evans pointed out all the evidence was there to show that (Timothy) Evans was innocent and that John Christie, executed in 1953, was the culprit. But it was campaigning journalism at its best and a story that set the gold standard in the industry.

Since then the regional and local press have continued to campaign on matters both large and small, local and sometimes not-so-local. The *Western Morning News* in Devon and Cornwall and the weekly *Cumberland News* in Cumbria, for example, both campaigned separately but most effectively for better deals for farmers in the foot and mouth outbreak in 2001[6].

Jon Austin, a reporter on the Southend and Basildon *Evening Echo*, has won numerous awards for the investigations he has given time to undertake since the mid 2000s. Examples include digging in to controversial land dealing by groups of travellers in south Essex as well as the safety of furniture on sale in local shops. In 2011 he is still a staffer on the *Echo* and still coming up with exclusives.

And on a smaller scale, the weekly *Tamworth Herald's* five-year campaign from 2002 to 2007 to honour forgotten war hero Able Seaman Colin Grazier, who played a key role in cracking the Enigma code, was also significant. Staff at the paper became aware of Grazier, who drowned with two other men after recovering two weather books from a German U-boat during the Second World War, following a chance remark in an unrelated interview that a Tamworth man had "won the war". It was known that Grazier had been awarded a posthumous Military Cross, but the exact reasons were kept secret. After careful and prolonged checking the role of Grazier was confirmed. The weather books, which were an integral part of the Germans' Enigma system, led to code-breakers at Bletchley Park cracking the cipher, paving the way for an earlier end to the war.

The *Herald's* ensuing campaign, under deputy editor Phil Shanahan, led to streets (and beers) being named after the men, and a sculpture being erected in Tamworth city centre. Grazier, the local man, and his two comrades, were finally given the public recognition they deserved. This investigation by the *Herald* may not have had the importance of bringing down a chief constable, but is a good example of what the local and regional press can achieve. It was a story to which the national media would be unlikely to devote time and resource, but, as its presence in its own display at the Bletchley Park museum indicates, was a story that needed bringing to the public's attention.

Don Hale's long campaign to clear man accused of murder

Occasionally, the weekly press has been able to take up a case that catches the national imagination. Such was the case with the small *Matlock Mercury* which in 1994 under its editor Don Hale (and with just a staff of three) began a long-running campaign, as well as some of his own investigations, on behalf of Stephen Downing who had been jailed for life for the 1973 murder of Wendy Sewell in Bakewell. Downing had always professed his innocence and was therefore ineligible for parole. The campaign was to last for seven years until Downing was released in 2001 and the conviction quashed the following year.

It was the kind of case that seemed so secure when it happened that a national newspaper would be unlikely to take it up. But the *Mercury* did, Downing was found to be innocent – and Hale was named Journalist of the Year, another accolade normally given only to those working for nationals, by *What the Papers Say*.

The regional and local press have also been very good at covering major stories on their own patches to a high level of detail. The *Evening Star*, Ipswich, won awards for its in-depth coverage of the 2006 murders of five prostitutes on its patch, the subsequent jailing of Steven Wright and its launch of the charity, Somebody's Daughter, to support vulnerable young people in the Ipswich area.

These examples may be slightly in the past, but the pages of the Hold The Front Page[7], the website that covers the regional press, as well as media magazine *Press Gazette*, maintain a steady flow of reports on the latest campaigns undertaken by newspapers both large and small.

But what does this all mean in these days of reduced numbers of reporters who are tending to be more office based that perhaps they used to be? The evidence of the 2011 Regional Press Awards above shows that there is still scope and resource for investigations. And there are senior figures in the industry who believe that while the internet has brought about a whole new level of competition it is also enabling new ways of conducting investigations.

Optimism as web makes investigations more affordable for the locals

Neil Benson, Editorial Director for Trinity Mirror Regionals, is optimistic and believes the web has made investigations more affordable for local titles. In the past, he says, information was hard to come by, now the internet is a source to be mined pro-actively. He says it makes investigations easier with fewer dead ends and a higher strike rate.

It needs new skills, he says. The present day reporter must have a mix of old-fashioned nose for news combined with being conversant with the use of Freedom of Information (FoI) legislation, having the ability to utilise all kinds of social media and increasingly to understand and interpret data. Trinity Mirror has run seminars on how to conduct investigations using experienced journalists from its nationals' division.

Benson cited the *Liverpool Daily Post* as an early user and exploiter of such techniques. In 2007, the *Post* learned that the airline Flyglobespan's daily Merseyside to New York flight was becoming increasingly delayed. The *Post* used crowd sourcing methods to tap in to niche online forums to find out what was happening, including that the airline had lost a key safety licence and that many passengers were not being paid compensation due for delays.

Another of Trinity Mirror's publications, the *Manchester Evening News*, in early 2011 appointed an investigations reporter tasked with finding unique content for both print and web. And Benson praised its award-winning supplement that analysed Greater Manchester Police's tweeting of every crime call on one day as the perfect example of what regional news organisations should be doing to maintain their relevance and credibility. The *Birmingham Mail* used forums to investigate and analyse how many pupils gained their first choice schools, put the data on line and ran reports in print for three days gaining a 2 per cent lift in sales.

The power of the group helps, he says. Editors have been encouraged to bring FoI in to their planning schedules and, while data journalism is in its infancy, reporters are being trained to read and understand spread sheets. Daily routines have changed too, so that as well as police calls there are now regular checks on what is being searched for on newspapers' own websites, as well as monitoring hourly on what classifieds have been placed. David Higgerson, the Head of Multimedia for Trinity Mirror Regionals, blogs internally and sends out tips such as 100 FoI ideas.

All trainees in future years, Benson believes, will have to come armed with these skills, as well as total familiarity with however social media develops. Digital media is an important way of keeping journalists in touch, he says, especially with what readers are interested in, rather than the journalists themselves.

In a major group like Trinity Mirror, with its big city-based papers and often multi-title centres (Manchester, Liverpool, Birmingham, Cardiff, and Newcastle) the resource to keep investigations on the agenda is more available. In smaller titles and communities it may not be so easy but some efforts are being made.

Another scoop – tracking down a paedophile in Switzerland

The *Derby Telegraph's* scoop on tracking down a paedophile in Switzerland, shortlisted in the Regional Press Awards, was achieved through being circumspect. The paper knew where he was and arranged a contra deal with the airline to fund flights for a reporter and photographer. The newspaper got its man – and the airline got its travel feature later on, produced by the same pair of journalists.

Steve Hall, the *Telegraph's* editor, says that the paper still has the resource to carry out investigations, to deliver comprehensive backgrounders when appropriate and to launch campaigns. In the last year, in addition to the Swiss report, his newspaper carried two lengthy supplements on the teenage girl grooming ring in the city and chipped away at what he sees as the secretive nature of some of the local authorities and health-related trusts in his patch. He says this kind of work is ingrained in all that the newspaper does.

A simple example was the strange case of two new fire appliances leased by the Derbyshire Fire and Rescue service. They would have been wonderful additions to the service's fleet if they had not been too noisy for the crews to operate. Very embarrassed to waste money like this when facing stringent cuts, the service did its best to cover the trail. But the newspaper got wind of it, dug away, checked minutes and called contacts before the service admitted the problem. A small issue, perhaps, but a good illustration of what the local paper should be doing.

Hall says that they use all the tools that they can – FoI, financial book opening times at councils and social networking – and that his belief is that his newspaper is producing as much investigative work of this kind as it ever has. However, tighter resources do mean that news editing is paramount. Although there will be attrition of some ideas, he says, the paper cannot really afford for stories not to happen.

So investigations are very much alive in the regional and local press. They may not the big showstoppers that brought down chief constables in the 1970s (and in reality there were relatively few of those) but editors and their teams are adapting to changing circumstances. They are using the new tools available to question and scrutinise.

If the role of the local journalist is to inform and to give some context to what is happening through the interpretation of reports and facts and figures, many are still able to carry out that function. Smaller weeklies and many frees may not be doing that, but they never did. The evidence is that larger weeklies and many dailies are hanging on to some level of investigations. The subject matters may not be the stuff of legend, but again, in reality, many never were. They were generally the simple stories that readers wanted examining.

The big challenge to come is whether editors can retain big enough teams to carry on the harrying and the probing if the existing business model continues to unravel. The jury is out.

Notes

[1] See www.pressgazette.co.uk

[2] See Steve Weinberg, *The Reporter's Handbook: An Investigator's Guide to Documents and Techniques*, New York, St. Martin's Press, 1996

[3] See Bob Franklin and others, *Key Concepts in Journalism*, London, Sage, 2005

[4] See www.lancashiretelegraph.co.uk

[5] See Harold Evans, *My Paper Chase*, New York: Little, Brown, 2009

[6] See Barrie Williams, *Ink in the Blood*, Woodfield, 2007

[7] See www.holdthefrontpage.co.uk

Note on the author

Neil Fowler is the Guardian Research Fellow at Nuffield College, University of Oxford, where he is researching the decline and future of regional newspapers in the UK. He has spent much of his career in the UK regional press, having edited two morning and two evening daily newspapers. He has also been publisher and CEO of the *Toronto Sun* in Canada and has been editor of the UK's biggest selling consumer magazine, *Which?*

Going Undercover (with help from the make-up artist) to Expose Discrimination in Estate Agents

Little in your work as a television reporter, doing "lives" in dicey environments, rushing from one stressful situation to another, can prepare you for the adrenalin rush of going undercover, says Guy Lynn

There are a few moments in this job when you ask yourself what you have done to deserve this? This is one such moment. It is 530 am, pitch black outside and I am sat in a freezing house in Boston, Lincolnshire, having my make-up done. I'm into hour number two of not blinking and uncomfortable things being done to my hair and face.

I console myself that this is an Oscar-nominated make-up artist, with years of experience transforming Hollywood actors into aliens. Now her challenge is somehow to make me not look like me. This is not some grand, frustrated vision of mine to tread the boards but a critical part of the BBC's infamous health and safety form to ensure nothing whatsoever will blow my cover as I proceed to expose letting agents who are prepared to discriminate and break vital race relations laws.

Little in your work as a television reporter, doing "lives" in dicey environments, rushing from one stressful situation to another, can prepare for the adrenalin rush of going undercover. I have done this before but never putting myself on the frontline in such an exposed way. The strange house I am in is not mine, but a property loaned to me by John, a dedicated member of the public, worried by suspected abuse of migrant workers in his town. With his full cooperation, I am putting the house on the open market after migrants approached me in a terrible state, unable to rent a property.

Many suspected they were being discriminated against because of "where they were from" though none can prove this. Subsequent research of mine reveals a shocking fact: nearly one in two agents here are prepared to flout UK race laws (as an aside – I should state many reputable agents in the town were not). The highest echelons of the BBC have approved the secret filming on the basis of this body of evidence. Within minutes, the first letting agent will arrive to assess this property and I am slightly nervous.

Undercover investigative journalism can be tough in smaller newsrooms. Editors are under enormous pressure to distinguish, to make their 18.30 programme (where this story will air in a long version, additional to the news pieces that will run on BBC network outlets) different from what else is on offer on other networks. Time and again, high impact original journalism is seen as one way to do that. Yet by nature, those stories can be high risk, high wire and with an inbuilt licence to fail (from the first research calls to just minutes before broadcast).

Editors need to show a leap of faith to allow the time and investment to take leading reporters off air while under pressure to deliver more with fewer resources. Other writers in this volume have argued for more investment in investigative journalism. I would, of course, second that but investigative journalism also needs to survive in newsrooms where resources are tight. One can wish for the magic wand to bring in more cash but investigative reporters (especially up and coming ones) need to deliver hard-hitting investigative pieces in newsrooms where that money does not exist now and may not in the future.

Working as a one-man-band has its rewards…

The rewards of hard-hitting investigative journalism can be enormous (such as your piece on all national radio and television bulletins) but there often needs to be a substantial personal investment. With less money around, more just has to come from the reporters themselves. I am often asked about the evolution of stories I have bought to air. They have often originated from large amounts of research in my own time, working in the early stages as a one-man-band and after a long day's work doing more "standard" stories.

My full title is Environment and Rural Affairs Correspondent. At Look North I have never worked (in a dedicated fashion) as an "investigative reporter". I always find the concept strange: all reporting is by nature investigative and to divide the reporting world up into investigative reporters (as opposed to standard ones) feels a bit like boasting to be a GP who uses a stethoscope. Delivering investigative pieces has come at the same time as juggling the demands of being a correspondent for on-the-day and off-diary stories, feeding a programme with fewer staff but which is expected to deliver half an hour of quality news each day. The day before going undercover in the estate agents story, I have been broadcasting live about a train crash and the following morning I am expected a hundred miles north of Boston to report on the impact, several years on, of the foot and mouth crisis.

I have to admit to being nervous. Chirpy John and Amber, the make-up artist, have both left. It's just me now in this strange, cold house. There are so many things that can go wrong. Operating the equipment (a tiny, button hole camera sewn into my shirt) is a nightmare in itself and notoriously unstable. Then there's playing the part: a landlord showing agents around his treasured property who stoops, as if with a bad back, the whole time. This is the only way I have discovered to get the right angle from the secret camera to capture the face of the person talking.

Then there are the literally scores of conversations with editorial policy, health and safety and BBC lawyers, darting through my mind with every breath. Of course, nothing I say or do can be construed as entrapping the agents in any way. Suddenly, I realise I am not quite sure where all the rooms in the house are. How strange will it look for a landlord to usher a letting agent into a kitchen that is actually the upstairs toilet?

But then how strange is it that I am here in the first place? John, the owner of the house, has allowed me to pretend I am him and put his property on the market (after I had gathered substantive *prima facie* evidence against agents in this town). Achieving this has (despite him being entirely behind the idea of exposing the illegal practices) come about through vast amounts of time spent cultivating a relationship. I recall the pubs, the dodgy curries, the walks, the visits to his house late at night to hear John practising his piano.

The core of ever story is a relationship of a sort

Many of the stories I have done have required similar investment and it's never come during a 9-5 day. In a world of electronic media, Twitter, Facebook, Google and RSS feeds where stories often just appear on your computer screen, relationships can get overlooked. The core of many of my high impact stories has been a relationship of a sort so getting it right is critical to getting the story to air.

When I strived to expose the abuse of migrant workers in the fields, picking the broccoli and cauliflower we all buy in the supermarkets, it relied on a Portuguese agricultural worker to do the undercover filming. There was no other way to infiltrate a community (the largest Portuguese community outside London, in South Holland, Lincolnshire) without the cooperation of "Vincenzo". I remember visiting him (an hour and a half's drive away) at the end of many a day. Some Saturday nights could be spent chatting to him, helping out with bailiffs, his children and I guess I just grew to become his confidant. Of course, I would never see this as some kind of *quid pro quo*, or manipulation, but you end up spending so much time with someone (who wants to expose something illegal) that the relationship has to go both ways.

Similarly, when I went undercover to expose a fake vet at the centre of an illegal and black market trade in animal medicines – I was reliant on a dog lover from the illegal hare coursing community who knew Leonard French very well. Again, that relationship (long walks with his dogs, dinners with him and his wife while trying not to sneeze from my chronic allergy to his 15 dogs) was critical to the story airing and French being jailed for a year at Lincoln Crown Court as a direct result of the piece (it was the longest sentence for this kind of crime to date).

I try to memorise the property's geography when I hear the doorbell. The first agent is early. I show him around, reeling off details of the house's anti-flooding features on the River Haven. Before long, after discussing his agency fee and deposit, he boasts how easy it is for those in his office to discriminate on behalf of the landlord against the town's migrant workers. I ask him if this extends to religion too, say if I didn't want any Muslims to see the property? No problem, he replies. Just specify it in the application he is clutching along with "no cats and dogs" and his office will sort it out.

Scary moment as a burly estate agent probes me

There is one dicey moment when a particularly burly estate agent looks at me and asks: "Don't I know you from somewhere, where have I seen you before?" He starts investigating me (just reward perhaps to have the tables turned!). He wants to know exactly what do I do, where am I from, what is the exact nature of the business I am and the orders that I take in my job? I start to get nervous, it feels as if he is leading somewhere, perhaps has blown my cover and I'm starting to slip out of my comfort zone and I'm sure that is obvious, especially as I have heard that some of the estate agents will not in any way take kindly to being exposed in this fashion.

I remember the first time I got a whiff of what was going on. It was an aside while talking to someone, face to face, about a totally different topic. In this case, it was a vicar complaining about the lack of attention shown to migrant burials and then just slipping in he had encountered some migrant workers who were confused as to why properties advertised in the newspaper had gone so quickly when they walked into the shop the next day. He had put it down to their bad English. I subsequently discover they hadn't "gone" – the properties were just not being shown to anyone who was foreign, in clear breach of the Race Relations Act: one of the most important post-war pieces of anti-discrimination legislation enacted.

The jailing of Len French started life in a conversation with a vine pea farmer whom I had gone to visit at his farmhouse to discuss the impact of European regulations on the employment of overnight workers in pea processing. He slipped in, as an aside, the huge parking problems at a country show from a man who was wheeling up and selling animal drugs to the show's visitors. That man was jailed the next year after I went undercover to bust his black market trade in animal medicines and expose how he was breaking the law, pretending to be a vet and treating animals at great danger to both humans and animals.

The ability to empathise is the investigative journalist's best tool

The ability to empathise is the most critical tool that investigative journalists can sharpen and is also the most overlooked. High impact stories rely on getting information out of those who don't necessarily want to give it, taking you inside places they would never normally take a journalist. The key to those hidden jewels is, in my view, always with empathy and ideally face to face.

Before any conversation, however insignificant on the phone or in person, I will always plan what I want that conversation to deliver and then try to imagine the world exactly as seen from the person that I am talking to. The world will appear very different from his or her island than it does in mine. Yet the two are always linked: getting information out of someone is entirely connected to a demonstrable understanding of the world that person inhabits.

This can come in the most subtle of forms. I remember trying to gain access to film the world of illegal hare coursing and clocking the way in was a true and detailed understanding of who came first in these men's lives: the dogs (without irony, who were loved more than the wives or partners). I always made it my business to write down and memorise the names of every lurcher and recited the details at every conversation, asked how they were, tracked their dog birthdays and ensured I used the correct terminology ("lurchers" rather than "dogs").

The renowned American communications expert Leil Lowndes argues that perceived similarity between two people (in this case when trying to date) is often accompanied by an understanding of the way they talk, the kind of language they use. Subconsciously the person speaking to you believes that you are one of them. Of course, you are not, you are a journalist who is disconnected but the ability to come as a friend rather than as a foe can be invaluable in terms of getting the access you want, or the information that you need.

By the end of the day, I have shown eight agents around "my house". This project is far from over. It is one thing for letting agents to say they will discriminate, another to actually do it in practice. Soon, with the help of another BBC producer and a Polish migrant, it will be put to the test.

Both will be told when they walk into letting agencies, within twenty minutes of each other that the property is available for the British man but "gone" for Daniel, the Polish worker.

Amazing waves generated by the piece

When the piece I have used as an example in this article is broadcast, I am amazed by the waves it generates, not just in the UK, running on all BBC network outlets but across the world. TV stations in Poland and China, I am told, have broadcast segments of the piece and are talking about it. Human rights lawyers are "horrified" and UK organisations pop out press releases to condemn the practices. Above all, it appears to have made a difference. The Equality and Human Rights Commission agrees to investigate further. The National Association of Estate Agents announces an immediate investigation and a retraining programme. Some businesses subsequently change their race relations policy as a direct result. The report wins a prestigious Amnesty International media award for best coverage of the year 2010, labeled "outstanding, shocking and emblematic of a deeper malaise in UK society" by the judges.

I believe investigative journalism is alive and well, particularly at the BBC. Yet it faces occasional threats to its survival. Original journalism is regularly recited like a mantra as something audiences truly appreciate as distinguishing the BBC from its competitors. Yet, sadly, investment in investigative journalism can sometimes fall by the wayside when faced with the number crunching. Reporters can and should help that situation. The extra personal investment, the realisation that we are doing a job others would kill to have, can result in huge rewards not just for us personally but for the audiences we serve.

Note on the author

Guy Lynn is a correspondent for BBC Look North and currently investigative reporter for BBC London News. In the last five years, he has won three Royal Television Society RTS Reporter of the Year awards, an Amnesty International Media Award 2010 for reporting on human rights and two BBC Ruby TV news journalism awards. He has worked as an environment correspondent for BBC network news, reported and presented for BBC local radio, Channel One and Reuters TV. He has also written and directed documentaries including *100 Years of Terror* for Emmy award-winning Set Productions and *Ordinary People*, a six-part series that aired on TV stations/festivals around the world.

Section 4. Alive and Well: Thanks to Whistleblowers

Leaking in the public interest?

Richard Lance Keeble

Leaks (and their strange bedfellows, unattributed quotes) lie at the heart of contemporary journalistic routines in the mainstream. Politicians, the police, the intelligence services, business leaders – they and many others release confidential data to trusted journalists hungry for exclusives. So hardly a day goes by without some significant revelation of private or confidential information.

Yet there are some significant differences in the leaks and the consequent reaction of the authorities to them. Many leaks occur as one faction within the elite competes with another faction (in the Great Theatre of Excessive Power) – for influence and media presence. And the journalists relaying these leaks into the media are generally left untroubled by the police.

But when the leaking appears to threaten the elite in any significant ways – then the full force of the law is thrown at them. So the fate of whistleblowers is mixed. For instance, the *British Medical Journal* reported recently that medical whistleblowers often found themselves "the subject of retaliatory complaints and disciplinary action" (see Nick Cohen's article "Let the law save whistleblowers, not silence them", the *Observer*, 10 July 2011).

Cohen wonders why no whistleblower spilled the News International beans before "hackgate" exploded in July 2011. "If they had spoken plainly, their editors would have fired them and in all likelihood they would never have worked in the media again because no other manager would want them to do to him what they had done to his predecessors."

In the first essay in this section, Duncan Campbell, former crime correspondent of the *Guardian*, stresses how governments leak on a regular basis. "They leak to sympathetic journalists information that may damage their opponents or enhance their own reputation. Most of the time it is not called leaking – stories refer to 'a senior source...a friend of...a normally reliable source...an insider'. It is still leaking."

He goes on to **examine three cases where brave whistleblowers suffered harsh penalties for their principled leaking of highly sensitive material.** Daniel Ellsberg faced a long term in prison and death threats aplenty after his release of the *Pentagon Papers* in 1971 to *The New York Times* which is credited by many with helping to end the Vietnam War. The leak ultimately led to a Supreme Court ruling that "only a free and unrestrained press can effectively expose deception in government".

Thirty years ago, Philip Agee, then a 41-year-old former CIA officer living in Cambridge, was told that he was to be deported from Britain as a threat to the security of the state following the publication of his damaging exposé of the CIA in his book, *Inside the Company*, published in 1975.

Finally, Campbell looks at the case of **Mordecai Vanunu,** who leaked details of Israel's nuclear weapons programme to *The Sunday Times* in the mid-eighties and, as a result, was jailed for 18 years. Campbell roots his study of these whistleblowers in the interviews he has conducted with them.

Next Adrian Quinn, of the Institute of Communication Studies at the University of Leeds, studies four other celebrated cases of whistleblowing this century (involving two women and two men) and again uses interviews to discuss motivations and the consequences of brave acts. Quinn ends by considering WikiLeaks' complex and troubled relationships with the mainstream.

Over three extraordinary years WikiLeaks has published leaks on corruption in Kenya, the Church of Scientotology, a cache of 75,000 documents on the Afghan war (in collaboration with the *Guardian*, *New York Times* and *Der Spiegel*) and a further cache of 400,000 documents relating to the Iraq War – while in November 2010 five newspaper began publishing selections from more than 250,000 diplomatic cables from US embassies around the globe.

Quinn concludes: "The news values observable at WikiLeaks locate the organisation well outside the value system of the mainstream media with which WikiLeaks has recently collaborated, despite the occasional incorporating and amplifying of the dissenting voices of whistleblowers."

Whistleblowing – from the Xerox Machine to WikiLeaks via Ellsberg, Agee and Vanunu

Duncan Campbell examines investigative reporters' reliance on whistleblowers – highlighting three celebrated cases from the last forty years

So here we have this remarkable invention which, at the touch of a button, revolutionises the ways in which we can communicate. It allows the dissemination of information to countless people around the world. The operation can be carried out with complete anonymity. Suddenly, leaking and whistleblowing can be done on a grand scale –so who needs time-consuming investigative journalism? I refer, of course, to the arrival of the photocopier.

It was the photocopier which, in 1971, allowed Daniel Ellsberg, a former US marine commander and Pentagon official, to take 7,000 pages of top secret documents about the US decision-making process in Vietnam and disseminate them, first to *The New York Times*, then to the *Washington Post* and finally to a series of other newspapers across the US. In this way he established himself as one of the most significant figures in the history of whistleblowing and leaking. The photocopier was hailed at the time as a fabulous conduit for information, as, in many ways, it was. There must be many grateful journalists who have received, often anonymously, the fruits of some troublemaker's afternoon at the Xerox machine.

Now, forty years after the *Pentagon Papers*, we have a combination of the internet, WikiLeaks, Twitter and "citizen journalism", all changing the ways in which we communicate and digest information. But do they really alter the basics of reporting much more than the photocopier did?

Daniel Ellsberg is a good starting point for the debate about the future of investigative journalism, not least because he has remained engaged in the action and is prominent today in his defence both of Bradley Manning, the young US marine accused of leaking information to WikiLeaks, and of that outfit's founder, Julian Assange.

There are three cases, taken from the last four decades, which seem particularly worth exploring in light of what is happening to the exchange of information. First, there is Ellsberg, who leaked in the hope that it would bring the Vietnam war to an end; secondly, Philip Agee, the former CIA man who passed on information about the agency in the mid and late seventies; and thirdly, Mordecai Vanunu, who leaked details of Israel's nuclear weapons programme in the mid-eighties.

All three worked in cooperation with journalists and the end results were all spectacular. I have chosen those three partly because they are fascinating and significant cases but mainly because I had a chance to meet and interview all three of them more than 20 years after they made their decision to reveal secret information by which time they had been able to assess what sort of impact they had had.

Ellsberg – unbowed

Daniel Ellsberg faced, like Agee and Vanunu, a long term in prison and death threats aplenty after the release of the *Pentagon Papers* which is credited by many with helping to end the Vietnam war. Ellsberg remains unbowed. In the preface to his book, *Secrets: A Memoir of Vietnam and the Pentagon Papers*, he makes it clear he believes the risks he took were worth it. He writes of the lesson that emerged from his trial: "Telling the truth, revealing wrongly kept secrets, can have a surprisingly strong unforeseeable power to help end a wrong and save lives."

Thirty years ago, Philip Agee, then a 41-year-old former CIA officer living in Cambridge, was told that he was to be deported from Britain as a threat to the security of the state. He had already published a damaging exposé of the CIA in his book, *Inside the Company*, published in 1975, and had made clear his intent to destabilise the organisation further by revealing the identities of CIA agents. In Britain, he worked with publications such as *Time Out* – which then had a substantial news section – to name the agents, leading to many of them being sent back to Washington, their cover blown. The US government was livid and vowed vengeance.

Agee wept on the ferry that took him away from Britain after his deportation but he died in 2008 at the age of 72 and remained unrepentant. He had been motivated initially by his horror at discovering the backing given by the CIA and US government to the military dictatorships and death squads operating at that time in Chile, Argentina, Brazil, El Salvador and Guatemala. Reflecting on what he had done and the damage it has caused to him and his young family years later, Agee told me in an interview in Hamburg not long before he died that he had no regrets.

"There was a price to pay," he said. "It disrupted the education of my children and I don't think it was a happy period for them...But it made me a stronger person in many ways, and it ensured I would never lose interest or go back in the other direction politically. The more they did these dirty things, the more they made me realise what I was doing was important."

Under the US Freedom of Information Act, Agee was able to see the scope of the operation mounted against him by an unforgiving CIA who accused Agee of being a boozer and a womaniser. "They admitted to having 18,000 pages on me. I figured out there were 120 pages a day for seven or eight years...I thought it was so foolish, such a waste of money, because I don't do anything that's not public."

Agee: accused wrongly of putting lives at risk

He was also, like WikiLeaks, accused of putting lives at risk. The name most frequently invoked was that of Richard Welch, the CIA station chief in Athens who was assassinated in 1975. Although Welch was named not by Agee but in other publications, Agee has often been blamed for his death. "George Bush's father came in as CIA director in the month after the assassination and he intensified the campaign, spreading the lie that I was the cause of the assassination."

Not everyone who decides to leak or whistleblow manages to escape the harsher penalties. Mordecai Vanunu, who leaked details of the Israeli nuclear weapons programme to *The Sunday Times* in 1986, was jailed for eighteen years and spent eleven in solitary confinement but remained convinced that he had done the right thing. If he has regrets about what he did, it is about the way he chose to leak the story.

"It was a mistake to go with one newspaper but I didn't have any experience with the media," he said when we met in Jerusalem after his release in 2004; significantly WikiLeaks worked with five separate publications in five different countries when it made its major release of embassy cables in 2010. "My target was to bring information to the world, so the best way would have been a press conference or to send it to 20 newspapers so that it would not be controlled by anyone. Now things have changed and the internet has made it much easier for information to be passed on."

Vanunu: keeping his spirit free
Vanunu had had plenty of opportunities to recant and is still not allowed to leave the country as part of his ongoing punishment; bogus suggestions are made that he might still have secrets to impart although no-one seriously believes this; the decision to stop him leaving Israel seems to stem more from the authorities' irritation that he did not leave prison a broken man. "There was a lot of pressure, a lot of attempts at brainwashing," he said. "I decided from the beginning that they could have my body in prison but my spirit, mind, brain, I would keep free, under my control; that would be my way out."

There are some common threads in these three stories that remain relevant today in a climate of leaking and whistleblowing on which much investigative journalism depends: each of them was accused of putting lives at risk; each of them was subject to a smear campaign about their personal life using media sympathetic to the government; and each of them was pursued by the government concerned in a punitive and vindictive way.

There are similarities in the WikiLeaks case. In early 2011, Bradley Manning was accused of "aiding the enemy", an offence which could involve him spending the rest of his life in prison while two American politicians, at the time both would-be presidential candidates, Sarah Palin and Mike Huckabee, indicated that either Manning or Julian Assange should be killed. Palin said that whoever was responsible should be hunted down like an al-Qaida terrorist and Huckabee said the person responsible for the leaks should be executed.

Of course, one person's terrorist is another's freedom fighter and one person's whistleblower is another's traitor. Just as Hillary Clinton would congratulate a Chinese or North Korean leaker or whistleblower for telling truth to power or an Israeli politician would praise an Iranian who did what Vanunu did, so one's admiration for leakers may depend almost entirely on where you stand politically. It is also worth bearing in mind that governments themselves leak on a regular basis. They leak to sympathetic journalists information that may damage their opponents or enhance their own reputation. Most of the time it is not called leaking – stories refer to "a senior source...a friend of...a normally reliable source...an insider". It is still leaking.

How to define "investigative journalism"?

I have always been slightly wary of the term "investigative journalism", with its implicit suggestion that its practitioners were in the business of something loftier than mere earthbound reporters, composing symphonies rather than, say, pop ballads or, perish the thought, commercial jingles. Where is the line drawn? Is it "investigative journalism" to buy a database of MPs' expenses and then mine it, even if the inquiry is diligent and lengthy? Is it "investigative" to publish a sensational leak which might arrive on a reporter's desk ready to run? Is writing a non-fiction book on a serious subject "investigative" *per se*? I suppose the answer is that we all have our own notions of what passes the test, the kinds of story to which we doff our hats, which qualify as works of diligent and exemplary journalism and that make us think: "Gosh, I wish I could have done that."

Surely that kind of journalism will never die. Its only essential tools, none of them button-operated or dependent on the internet, are the same ones that have been used by writers and journalists and muckrakers since the invention of the printing press: an inquiring mind, a lack of deference and great patience. W. T. Stead made a name for himself and "investigative journalism" — although it was not called that — more than 125 years ago with his articles in the *Pall Mall Gazette* which exposed child prostitution. In 1885, by "purchasing" a 13-year-old child, he shone a light on one of the darkest places in Victorian England with his series of articles, "The Maiden Tribute of Modern Babylon". He perished on the Titanic but his form of proactive journalism lives on.

What may perhaps make that kind of journalism harder now is that people who make their living as reporters are under greater constraints than they were in the heyday of "investigative journalism" in Britain, like the seventies, say, when *The Sunday Times* "Insight" team was in its pomp and money was no object. Life has changed in television, too, since the nineties, when both the BBC and Channel 4 had genuinely investigative programmes dedicated to uncovering miscarriages of justice in *Rough Justice* and *Trial and Error*, both now abandoned as too expensive and time-consuming.

But some national newspapers and, to a lesser extent now, television documentaries, still expose injustice and wrong-doing on a regular basis along with all the waffle and the triviality. Another obstacle, again the result of financial constraints, is that it is harder for reporters to get out of the office now. The days when journalists could hang around courts covering cases and picking up tales and tip-offs from lawyers, coppers, criminals, witnesses and fellow-reporters have almost passed. No national daily can afford to have their reporters tied up in such a way and local papers have almost abandoned that beat, too. That essential human contact of trust which requires personal contact – meeting rather than tweeting – means less likelihood of stories emanating from what was once a productive arena.

The internet and the spread of rumours
What is also different today is the speed with which information — and disinformation – can travel the globe. We should not be too precious about the disinformation. Newspapers have used their authority too often in the past to spread falsehoods for them to hold up their hands in horror at all the fantasies and rumours that fly around the blogosphere now. The problem is that the internet has multiplied the opportunities for rumours and planted tales to make their way round the world unchecked. Fast

journalism, like fast food, smells tasty, is cheap and easily available but often isn't very good for your health.

Even serious newspapers now deal routinely in unsubstantiated celebrity gossip which they would have disdained a couple of decades ago, even if it is done from an "ironic" perspective; the stories don't need to be checked, a single "allegedly" in front of a piece of tittle-tattle can be substituted for the bother of making a telephone call or doing a bit of research.

But yes, "investigative journalism" is alive not dead. And it will survive as long as there are dishonest chancers in power. Which means for ever.

Note on the author
Duncan Campbell is a former *Guardian* crime specialist and Los Angeles correspondent. He was previously news editor of *Time Out* and *City Limits*. He has written a number of books, including *If It Bleeds*, a novel about crime reporting.

All Roads Lead to Assange: Wikileaks and Journalism's Duty of Care

Drawing on interviewers with some celebrated whistleblowers and the journalists who have worked with them, Adrian Quinn highlights some of the major ethical issues involved

On a Sunday evening in March 2003, the scheduled episode of BBC2's current affairs series *Correspondent* was due to be *Israel's Secret Weapon*, the story of Mordechai Vanunu, an Israeli nuclear technician who blew the whistle on his country's efforts to build a nuclear weapon[1]. Vanunu had smuggled photographs out of the bomb factory where he once worked and his story appeared in *The Sunday Times* in October 1986. Vanunu was soon kidnapped by Mossad agents operating in Rome and taken to Israel where he was tried as a traitor and imprisoned. At the time of the broadcast, Vanunu had been in jail for 18 years, 11 in solitary confinement. The *Guardian's* television writer Ali Catterall, who had seen a preview tape, called the *Correspondent* programme "courageous, timely, utterly essential viewing"[2].

Then it was spiked.

The BBC's website offered this statement: "It was unfortunately necessary to postpone the billed programme...due entirely to the overrun of an unscheduled news bulletin about the Azores summit...There is no suggestion that any political pressure affected a scheduling decision by the BBC." Some will have thought that the BBC did protest too much.

Interviewed outside the Israeli prison where Vanunu was being held, Peter Hounam, formerly of *The Sunday Times*'s "Insight" Team, said: "He's in there because he spoke to me and we published his story. I feel a sense of responsibility that we should be helping him get out."[3] Speaking on a different occasion, Hounam added a crucial, ethical caveat: "I'm absolutely convinced that if we had not published the story, Mordechai would probably have been killed."[4] On this reading of Vanunu's abduction, a newspaper story cost Vanunu his liberty, but saved his life.

This chapter looks at four significant incidents of whistleblowers from the present century, two men and two women, plus that of Julian Assange and WikiLeaks, whose theory of journalism also informs this chapter. The revelations under discussion range from spying and international security to the delivery of front line services, including nursing and policing. The emphasis in this chapter is on the testimony of the whistleblowers themselves and the testimony of the journalists who worked with them.

Margaret Haywood: The undercover nurse

WikiLeaks highlights the many disconnects in contemporary journalism. While in some respects WikiLeaks conforms to classic whistleblowing, there are features of the WikiLeaks case which depart from past experience. Julian Assange says that WikiLeaks is both "a publisher of last resort" and the publisher which provides us with "information about how the world actually works"[5]. The whistleblower is what the philosopher calls a "moral agent" and for Margaret Haywood, a nurse of 20 years and a mother, the BBC was the last resort for her to realise that moral agency.

In 2005, Margaret Haywood helped the BBC's *Panorama* make *Undercover Nurse*[6]. At a hospital in Brighton, Haywood secretly filmed elderly and dying patients experiencing suffering and neglect and in doing so she broke the confidentiality rule contained in the code for standards of conduct, performance and ethics for nurses and midwives. "As soon as I walked on that ward, I knew there were major problems," she said. "There was blood on the curtains and I could hear people crying and shouting. It was absolutely awful."

In April 2009, Haywood was found guilty of misconduct at a hearing of the Nursing and Midwifery Council and was struck off. The *Nursing Times* reported Linda Read, chair of the panel, saying: "Although the conditions on the ward were dreadful, it was not necessary to breach confidentiality to seek to improve them by the method chosen."[7] Later that year, in October, Haywood was reinstated and received a caution.

In an essay for the *Journal of Medical Ethics*, Paul Grant applied what he called four ethical lenses to the Haywood case: purpose, principle, people and power. Grant determined that Haywood's was a "morally ambiguous situation in which both the protagonist and the organisation compromised their core values"[8]. But he also noted what he called the pragmatic reality of her particular situation: "She successfully highlighted travesties that would have otherwise been ignored and she brought about significant real change at the Royal Susses County Hospital and nationally."[9] In an interview in Liverpool, Haywood told me that she was prepared for:

> ...a smack on the wrist, "don't do it again". But no one was prepared for my nursing registration being taken off me. The nurses and carers who'd been abusing and neglecting the patients were still working and here's me getting struck off for trying to do something about it.

She also spoke candidly of her collaboration with public service broadcasters:

> I made clear to the BBC that my responsibilities to the patients had to take priority and the filming was a secondary issue. They're journalists, I'm a nurse, but I knew I was key to what they wanted. As soon as I went on that hospital ward with that camera, I knew I was breaching confidentiality and I had to keep reminding myself of the reason why I was doing it: to improve standards of care. It was

stressful and I did feel like a double agent, but revelations of abuse and neglect have to take priority over confidentiality. I'm well aware of my code of conduct, but as far as I was concerned the benefits outweighed the risks. My nursing registration was a drop in the ocean compared to what was happening to the elderly patients on that ward. I never thought of myself as a whistleblower, I thought of myself as a caring nurse who was trying to raise standards for the elderly in *that* hospital, in *that* ward. It never even crossed my mind[10].

Three years before Haywood blew the whistle to the BBC, Robert Heddle, a surgeon, also used secret cameras to help ITV's *Tonight* made *Sick and Tired*[11], a film not dissimilar to *Undercover Nurse*. He was not struck off. I asked Heddle to comment on how Margaret Haywood was censured and what it says about the management culture in the National Health Service when a female nurse was dealt a stricter sanction than a male surgeon, when both had knowingly transgressed their respective professional codes. "I was outraged by that. It was bloody scandal," Heddle said. "I remembering thinking, they're persecuting her, because it looks easy." He also commented on the ethics of using surveillance technology in a hospital environment:

> It's not a very elegant way of doing it, because it's confrontational and it puts the managers with whom you have to work on the back foot. The element of trust which, ideally, should exist, doesn't exist, because they're wary of you. But the very worst thing, from the point of view if a doctor, is when patient welfare suffers. And damn it, we're supposed to be helping patients, not damaging them. If it takes the media to do it, so be it[12].

I also asked Heddle if he sees whistleblowing, in the context of health, as an extension of the duty of care and not as a breach of it. He replied: "If you can't get attention through the proper channels, then I honestly think it's the only way."

Nina Hobson: Undercover copper

In October 2003, the BBC broadcast *The Secret Policeman*, an undercover investigation by Mark Daly who for seven months trained as a police recruit in Manchester. Quite unlike *Israel's Secret Weapon*, no preview tapes were made available and on the same night as the rest of Britain, chief police officers will have viewed evidence of the institutional racism that

Sir William Macpherson had reported on in 1999. "A dog born in a barn is still a dog. A Paki born in Britain is still a fucking Paki." These and other remarks from police recruits, captured by secret cameras, were a stark confirmation of the truth. Donal MacIntyre called *The Secret Policeman* "the most significant and important undercover documentary that has ever been done in this country"[13].

Less well known than Mark Daly's investigation is *Undercover Copper*, made for Channel 4's *Dispatches*[14]. Where Mark Daly's film was confined to trainee police officers, *Undercover Copper* was made with the assistance of a veteran insider, Nina Hobson. A commended police officer, Hobson had joined the police as a teenager and later she blew the whistle on routine sexism in the police force in Leicestershire. Hobson found officers watching and discussing extreme pornography instead of patrolling, and dealing with rape victims with callous and sexist policing methods. And where Mark Daly was a reporter turned policeman, Nina Hobson had served in the police for most of her adult life before becoming an undercover reporter and whistleblower.

Knowing that it would end her career in the police, Hobson surveilled her colleagues for four months. Where Daly's film largely featured police recruits boasting of their racist policing, Hobson captured evidence of actual dereliction of duty. Officers were shown playing cards when they should have been patrolling and failing to attend an incident of man roughing up a woman in the street. When Nina Hobson appears in *Undercover Copper* the final time, she speaks into her own camera as part of her video diary. She breaks down momentarily on the words "16 years I've been with the police" and she gathers her feelings to say:

> Now it's over and I knew it would be over when I went into making this programme. The reality is a lot harder than I thought it would be. I hope everybody realises why I've made the programme and I hope that it changes things for the people who are still in the police. The people who give up so much to be good police officers and who should be supported and not totally browbeaten by the bureaucracy and the government and the system[15].

Speaking to me from Australia, Hobson made clear the risks she faced:

> From the beginning the decision was made that once we had the film we wanted to make, I would resign from the police. The very difficult thing for me was that I might be caught with my cameras without my realising they'd caught me and I'd be in even more trouble. My lawyer said to me: "If you get caught you'll go to prison, you do understand that." That's something I had to consider before going in there because, you know, I have children. The decision to run that risk was taken because I was so passionate about telling that story.

Hobson's actions, like Margaret Haywood's, can be contextualised alongside the growing body of scholarship in the area of feminist journalism studies. In her contribution to the *Handbook of Journalism Studies*, Linda Steiner summarises Liesbet van Zoonen and says that there is a virtue in a woman's ability to "challenge male journalists' detachment...that men use objectivity as a shield against the sensitivity and sympathy that journalism requires"[16]. Writing then in her own voice, Steiner concludes by imagining a feminist journalism that is rooted not in women's innate values, but in a new political sensibility and a feminist epistemology. "Feminist theorising," she writes, "suggests the value of more contextual and situated journalistic forms that get at reasons, consequences, impacts; and of collaborative, non-competitive, horizontal work structures that allow for integrating domestic responsibilities."[17]

Losing a source: David Shayler and MI5

In 1997, Mark Hollingsworth and Nick Fielding, of the *Mail on Sunday*, broke the story that the British intelligence service MI6 had plotted to kill Colonel Khadafi of Libya. It was also revealed that MI5 held files on two men who were serving in the government of then-Prime Minister Tony Blair and that MI5 had failed to act to stop the car bombing of the Israeli embassy in London in 1994. The *Mail's* source was David Shayler, who had been an officer with MI5 from 1991 to 1996. Shayler stands on its head the suggestion that whistleblowing is altogether a breach of confidence. Speaking alongside Mark Hollingsworth after his return from exile in France, but before his trial for breaking the Official Secrets Act, Shayler said: "Whistleblowing is a very noble tradition. To not blow the whistle when you know something makes you morally dubious."[18]

Like the Vanunu revelations and unlike the Haywood and Hobson ones, David Shayler's story appeared in the press. Hollingsworth says that the number of people involved in producing a television programme means that further leaks are all but certain. Camera operators, sound recordists, electricians, graphic designers – what Hollingsworth calls "an army of people" any of whom could leak details of the programme for no other reason that "they're drunk in the pub and blurt it out to impress people". This would have resulted in an injunction against the Shayler story and the arrest of the source. Hollingsworth says that other than his co-author Nick Fielding, only the editor of the *Mail on Sunday* and possibly one other executive knew of the story before publication.

There are two lines of criticism that most whistleblowers such as Shayler face. The first is that they are too swift to involve the media and should first have spoken up within their place of work. The second is that they do it for the money. Margaret Haywood is sure that had she spoken up at the Brighton hospital where she was working she would have simply been moved on. She remembers: "I knocked on the ward manager's door and said I wanted to speak to her about care standards on the ward and she spent the next 45 minutes talking to me about budgets. I knew that if made too much noise, they'd have got shut of me and carried on in their own way." Similarly, in the case of Nina Hobson, the *Guardian* reported Matt Baggott, Chief Constable of Leicester police, saying:

> I'm sure that many will share my disappointment that Nina Haywood chose not to raise these matters of concern at the time. There are number of ways colleagues can do so – if needs be anonymously. Sadly Ms Hobson appears to have chosen not to use any of the channels available. Because of this, the incidents of poor behaviour that she filmed were allowed to go unchecked for months[19].

Then there is the issue of money. The summer before his arrest, Kirsty Wark from the BBC's *Newsnight* asked Julian Assange how he supported himself financially. Assange replied:

> Since January when we started fund-raising in earnest, from the general public, we have received a million dollars from mums and dads, from people like you: journalists and human rights workers.

Not a single dollar from any institution, not a single dollar from a company, not a single dollar from a government[20].

These two, standard criticisms were also levelled at David Shayler. On the first question – that Shayler's approach to the media was premature – Hollingsworth has spoken in defence of his source, saying:

> One of the most crucial points, which was later corroborated, was that he'd raised his concerns internally. The government and MI5's case against David was that he should have brought these matters to the proper authorities before he went public. The point is: he did. That gave us a legitimacy and a public interest to publish these stories. It was quite clear that MI5 and the authorities were not prepared to investigate seriously.

The presence of money, and so-called chequebook journalism, can cloud a journalist's relationship with a source as it is often seen as providing an inducement beyond helping to establish the truth. Much was made at the time of the fact that David Shayler received payment after his revelations appeared in the *Mail on Sunday*. Under the 1989 Official Secrets Act, which Shayler had breached, there is no public interest defence. Equally, the voluntary codes of conduct for journalists and broadcasters frown on paying witnesses, unless there is a clear public interest justification for doing so. Hollingsworth says the £39,000 paid to Shayler amounts to "petty cash" and that the money was given to Shayler for a specific purpose: to allow him to "eat and pay rent" while living in exile in France. In a letter to the *Guardian*, written in response to the headline "Shayler guilty of revealing secrets"[21], Hollingsworth and Fielding said:

> The notion that David Shayler "traded state secrets for cash from the *Mail on Sunday*" is risible. Shayler's revelations about incompetence, mismanagement and abuse of power by MI5 were made to us long before documents were ever mentioned. A contract was signed and Shayler agreed to go ahead with the articles solely on that basis. He was later paid a limited amount because it was accepted he would have to leave the country and would need financial support while living abroad. Even the judge accepts that Shayler was not motivated by financial reward[22].

On 4 November 2002, David Shayler was found guilty at the Old Bailey of breaching the Official Secrets Act. The same day, Paul Burrell, butler to the late Princess Diana, sold his story to the *Daily Mirror* for £300,000, considerably more than was paid to Shayler. While certainly of interest to the public, little of what Burrell had to say corresponds to any objective sense of the public interest when lined-up next to the revelations about derelict police, neglectful hospitals, nuclear bombs and general unaccountability as discussed here.

In a letter to the *Guardian*, Hollingsworth and Fielding speak of their source and of the documents he provided. Julian Assange says that at WikiLeaks: "We verify documents, we don't verify sources."[23] This position represents a break with past practice in investigative journalism. However explosive was the evidence that Mordechai Vanunu captured at the Dimona bomb factory in Israel (57 photographs) that evidence was only made credible in combination with the verbal testimony of the source. Similarly, the *Mail on Sunday* was at first concerned with establishing the authenticity of its source and later its reporters asked to see documents. Mark Hollingsworth also reports being sceptical when David Shayler first came forward: "He could have been a plant. This could have been a disinformation campaign, or an entrapment operation. He could have been a tabloid reporter. He could have been Ali G. for all I knew."

Julian Assange and WikiLeaks

WikiLeaks, however, disaggregates this relationship between the source and the revelations they offer. Speaking to the Graduate School of Journalism in Berkeley, California, Assange drew a further distinction between whistleblowers and "people who are leaking secrets for no reason at all"[24]. When interviewed by Chris Anderson of TED (Technology Entertainment and Design) Assange added that, in fact, WikiLeaks very seldom knows the source of the material it publishes. "And if we find out at some stage we destroy that information as soon as possible," he said[25].

It is useful to recall something of the etymology of the term whistleblower. In sport, blowing a whistle draws attention to a foul, at which point all eyes and all cameras turn to the person in whose lips the whistle rests. WikiLeaks' method of an electronic "drop box", where whistleblowers can anonymously share what they know is significant, though for the moment it is uncertain whether leaked information can routinely stand in for the verbal testimony of the insider.

Hollingsworth's testimony on the Shayler case which he broke, is also important in anticipating the current concerns over super injunctions. In these, in addition to not being able to report a story, the news media also cannot report that a judge has granted an injunction in the first place. In 2001, Hollingsworth said:

> The accusation against us that was that journalists cannot be and should not be arbiters of what is sensitive and damaging to national security. My point is: in a lot of investigative work, whether it's about big business, the police, the environment or nuclear, the other side will say "If you do this story, lots of people will lose their jobs." But at the end of the day, journalists have to make that judgement. And it can only be done through experience really. If we decided to submit stories to the authorities, regardless of the subject, there would be no investigative journalism. It would be dead. They would kill the story, or do spoilers, or try to shut everything down and you would lose the story. You would be hit with injunctions constantly and there would be chaos. Nothing would be exposed. Everything would be done in internal inquiries. We *can* be the arbiters, we *can* be the judges and of what's sensitive and not sensitive. If we didn't take on that role, there would be no stories of an investigative kind.

Conclusion: Locating WikiLeaks

In some very important respects, Julian Assange falls through the cracks of past practice of journalists handling whistleblowers. Though Editor in Chief of WikiLeaks, Assange's involvement with the mainstream media saw him lose the autonomy that goes with a true editorship. *Guardian* editor Alan Rusbridger seems to acknowledge this in his introduction to David Leigh and Luke Harding's book *WikiLeaks: Inside Julian Assange's War on Secrecy.* Rusbridger writes of "Assange's status as a sometimes confusing mix of source, intermediary and publisher"[26].

Nick Davies is the *Guardian* reporter who first approached Julian Assange and persuaded him to work with the *Guardian* to convert the raw data received by WikiLeaks into what Davies calls "meaningful stories". Davies, whose own book *Flat Earth News*, blows the whistle on falsehood, distortion and propaganda in his own profession, says that his involvement with WikiLeaks led to the most impactful journalism of his career. 'From the White House down to the lowliest, littlest house, people were responding to it.'[27]

Assange, however, does not appear to have benefited from the protection afforded to many of the whistleblowers discussed here. In his interview with Mark D'Arcy for BBC's *Booktalk*, and elsewhere, David Leigh has reported intimate details of the restaurant meal he bought Assange and of the night Assange spent in his house[28]. Where Mark Hollingsworth has here been quoted on the importance of protecting whistleblowers, and of appreciating the pressure they bring on themselves, David Leigh seems to delight in breaking Assange's confidence. Leigh justifies his behaviour by asserting that Assange is neither editor, nor source. Leigh de-humanises and de-professionalises Assange, calling him an "opportunist" and "computer hacker", adding that, as a journalist, Assange is "a reckless amateur" and "for all his personality quirks, a function of the technology"[29].

In his teaching, David Leigh has likened the work of the investigative journalist to that of the policeman. Indeed, one observes in Leigh the contempt for his source that a jaded detective might have for his informant, his rat. In *Understanding News*, John Hartley discusses news values and their role in "mapping the outsiders". He says "the often rough handling of dissent and alternative views of social structures is not the result of personal animosity on the part of individual broadcasters and journalists towards those views"[30].

If not personal, or exclusively so, how does one explain Leigh's disdain for Assange? Helpful here is the critical thinking on the media's attitude to dissent and its role in the bounding of debate. Speaking in Canada in 2007, Noam Chomsky said that journalists at the most critical end are "the guardians of orthodoxy. They set up the limit: you can do this far, no further. If you go a millimetre further than that, the reaction is hysteria, vituperation and slander. And that's the media that consider themselves critical. I think that's true universally: England, France, everywhere"[31]. The news values observable at WikiLeaks locate the organisation well outside the value system of the mainstream media with which it has recently collaborated, despite the occasional incorporating and amplifying of the dissenting voices of whistleblowers.

240

Both Margaret Haywood and Nina Hobson spoke in detail of the moral and practical support they received from their respective broadcasters. In fact, Haywood reports that the advice offered by the barrister provided to her by the BBC was: "Don't do it, don't do it." By contrast, in an interview with the Russian-based, English language news channel RT, Assange claimed that the *Guardian* abused the material that WikiLeaks provided through "over-redaction". He also claimed that of the three mainstream titles with which he collaborated in 2010 (the *Guardian* in the UK, *Der Spiegel* in Germany, and *The New York Times* in the United States) the *Guardian* was the "worst offender" but that *The New York Times* also broke an agreement made with Assange in November 2010 that the only acceptable redactions were those needed to protect lives - not profits or reputations[32].

Assange has complained that *The New York Times* redacted a 62-page cable down to two paragraphs. In some respects, Assange seems to have anticipated this. Speaking at Berkeley the spring before his collaboration with the mainstream media, Assange said "leaking is an anarchist act. To be a mainstream publication [like *The New York Times*] you can't be lionising sources doing anarchist acts all the time"[33].

In closing, Julian Assange says: "Wikileaks is an activist organisation. The end goal is justice. The method is transparency. Part of the method is journalism. When our sources give us material, our promise is that we'll protect them, but we'll also try to get maximum impact from that material."[34] The long term impact of the material brought into the public domain by WikiLeaks in an open question and that question has met with both dismissal and hyperbole.

On his website, Phillip Knightley, formerly of *The Sunday Times* "Insight" team, wrote: "It is becoming clearer day by day that the WikiLeaks saga has changed journalism and citizen's relationship with government forever. This is not about some temporary embarrassment to governments and their leaders but a sea change in the way we are ruled and the information we are entitled to expect about how decisions about our future are made."[35] The *Guardian* journalists seem less certain and wonder if WikiLeaks might come to be seen as "a brief comet that had streaked across the sky in 2010"[36]. As this book goes to press, the question of the true impact of WikiLeaks has not been answered, but neither has it gone away.

Notes

[1] *Correspondent* was *Israel's Secret Weapon*, BBC2, 16 March 2003
[2] *The Guardian*, 15 March 2003
[3] BBC2, 16 March 2003
[4] *Nuclear Secrets: Vanunu and the Bomb*, BBC, 5 February 2007
[5] 30 April 2010
[6] BBC1, 20 July 2004
[7] Nursing Times.net, 17 April 2009
[8] Ethical lessons from the "undercover nurse": Implications for practice and leadership, *Journal of Medical Ethics*, 2010, Vol. 36, No. 8 pp 469-472
[9] ibid
[10] Interview, 14 April 2009
[11] *Tonight*, ITV1, 8 February 2002
[12] Interview, 14 April 2009
[13] *The 50 Greatest Documentaries*, Channel 4, 9 October 2005
[14] *Dispatches*, Channel 4, 27 April 2006
[15] ibid
[16] Karin Wahl-Jorgensen and Thomas Hanitzsch (eds) *Handbook of Journalism Studies*, New York and London: Routledge 2009 p. 120
[17] ibid: p. 129
[18] A Crash Course in Investigative Reporting, Sheffield, 17 June 2001
[19] David Smith, Undercover PC exposed sex bias, *Guardian*. 23 April 2006 p. 15. Available online at http://www.guardian.co.uk/uk/2006/apr/23/ukcrime.gender, accessed on 1 May 2011
[20] *Newsnight*, BBC2, 27 July 2010
[21] 4 November 2002
[22] 9 November 2002
[23] *Newsnight*, BBC2, 27 July 2010
[24] 18 April 2010
[25] 16 July 2010
[26] *Wikileaks: Inside Julian Assange's War on Secrecy*, by David Leigh and Luke Harding, London: Guardian Books, 2011 p. 7
[27] Omroepcongres, 30 September 2010
[28] BBC Parliament, 12 March 2011
[29] TechCrunchTV, 12 February 2011
[30] 1982: 83
[31] 20 Years of the Propaganda Model, 17 May 2007
[32] 2 May 2010

[33] 18 April 2010. See
http://fora.tv/2010/04/18/Logan_Symposium_The_New_Initiatives#
WikiLeaks_How_Safe_Are_Confidential_Sources, accessed on 1 May
2011
[34] ibid
[35] Phillipknightley.com, 8 December 2010
[36] Leigh and Harding op cit: 241

Note on the author

Adrian Quinn is a graduate of the Centre for Journalism Studies, in Cardiff, Wales and he recently joined the Institute of Communication Studies at the University of Leeds. For the past ten years he has lectured at the University of Liverpool. He has written on the Front National in France and on academic standards for the *Times Higher Education Magazine*. His work with the Glasgow University Media Group has appeared in *Media, Culture and Society* and the *International Journal of Media and Cultural Politics* (see www.glasgowmediagroup.org). He is currently working on his first book, *The Bad News Debates*.

.

Section 5. Alive and Well and on New Platforms

Using the Web and Social Media as Tools for Investigative Reporting

Richard Lance Keeble

A typical refrain heard in newsrooms across the country is that investigative reporting needs time and above all substantial resources and so is unlikely to emerge on alternative internet sites since they are generally lacking those vital elements.

Yet, as Paul Bradshaw, award-winning blogger and Visiting Professor at City University, argues here, investigative journalism does not have to be pursued – or funded – in one particular way. "The newsroom investigative journalist was an endangered species well before the internet arrived, while over the last decade NGOs and activist organisations have taken on an increasing role in funding investigations."

He says the internet has made it possible to separate the "investigative" from the "journalism": students, bloggers, activists, and anyone else with a burning question can begin to investigate it. "They can raise questions openly with thousands of others online, submit FoI requests at the click of a button or analyse datasets and documents with free tools, regardless of whether or not they are employed as a journalist. The vast majority do not *want* to be a journalist. What they want are *answers*."

Sean McGrath, winner of the John Pilger Award for Investigative Journalism at the University of Lincoln, highlights the ambivalent attitudes to growing role of the data journalist:

> Although data journalism is being embraced by the journalism community at large, there seems to be the inherent antipathy that comes with any major shift in technique and theory. Conventionalists continue to argue that sitting in front of a computer is not "real journalism". From the opposite side, there is much talk of data journalism being "the future", as if some form of digital enlightenment will take place and those who do not have a complete command of the world of data, will be left by the wayside.

McGrath patiently takes us through a list of sites useful to the DJ – such as www.google.com/fusiontables, http://www-958.ibm.com and http://www.socrata.com. He concludes: "The information super-highway is rapidly becoming the most powerful tool in the journalistic arsenal. While it is fanciful to say that computer-aided reporting is the future of journalism, it is also naïve to simply reject its potential."

The internet has certainly made the news a far more participatory experience for consumers. As Tom Standage comments in a special report on the internet and the news industry in the *Economist* of 9-15 July 2011: "Referrals from social networks are now the fastest growing source of traffic for many news websites. Readers are being woven into the increasingly complex news ecosystem as sources, participants and distributors." And it's now not just WikiLeaks which is opening doors into the secret world of the "war on terror": Al-Jazeera has created a "transparency unit" inviting leaks from its readers into a WikiLeaks-style anonymous drop box while the *Wall Street Journal* has also started its own drop box. Whether sufficient protection is being offered the leakers remains to be seen.

Next in this section, Shane Croucher, who gained a First Class Honours on the BA Investigative Journalism and Research at the University of Lincoln, focuses on the new technique of crowdsourcing – involving consumers in the active production of news. New media and the web, according to Croucher, have opened up a previously untapped resource – the civic-minded public – presenting an opportunity to broaden the field of investigative journalism and who participates in it.

Finally, Tom Farmery, who also gained a First Class Honours on the BA Investigative Journalism and Research at the University of Lincoln, impressing the examiners in particular with his daring probe into bare-knuckle fighting, explores, controversially, the possibilities of Facebook as a tool for investigative reporting – and some of the ethical issues involved.

Has Investigative Journalism Found its Feet Online?

As the pioneers unearth, tell and distribute their stories in new ways, we are beginning to discover just what shape investigative journalism may take online, according to Paul Bradshaw

We may finally be moving past the troubled youth of the internet as a medium for investigative journalism. For more than a decade observers looked at this ungainly form stumbling its way around journalism, and said: "It will never be able to do this properly."

They had short memories, of course. Television was an equally awkward child: the first news broadcast was simply a radio bulletin on a black screen, and for decades print journalists sneered at the idea that this fleeting, image-obsessed medium could ever do justice to investigative journalism. But it did. And it did it superbly, finding a new way to engage people with the dry, with the political, and the complex.

Now the internet is growing up too, finding its feet with the likes of Clare Sambrook, Talking Points Memo, PolitiFact and VoiceOfSanDiego all winning awards, while journalists such as Paul Lewis (over the death of news vendor Ian Tomlinson on the fringes of the G20 demonstration in London in 2009), Stephen Grey (for his work on extraordinary rendition) and James Ball (WikiLeaks) explore new ways to dig up stories online that hold power to account. As these pioneers unearth, tell and distribute their stories in new ways we are beginning to discover just what shape investigative journalism may take in this new medium.

Funding investigative journalism

There is a now-familiar refrain that rumbles across the newsroom as regularly as a train: that online publishing cannot support what is needed for proper journalism – the journalism we have to call "investigative". The argument is simple. Done the way it has been done for the past 50 years in newspapers and broadcasting, investigative journalism requires a reporter's time – and, therefore, money. Online publishing – or at least, online advertising – does not currently offer a publisher the same margins that they enjoyed in the past.

But investigative journalism does not have to be pursued – or funded – in one particular way. The newsroom investigative journalist was an endangered species well before the World Wide Web arrived, while over the last decade NGOs and activist organisations have taken on an increasing role in funding investigations.

Indeed, the argument that the commercial pain of news organisations leads to cuts in investigative journalism is contradicted by research undertaken by Dutch-Flemish investigative journalism organisation VVOJ. They found that there was no relationship between the financial health of a news organisation and the amount of investigative journalism that was undertaken there[1].

It is notable that some of the biggest investigative stories in decades have come during one of the worst commercial periods for the newspaper industry: and while the MPs' expenses and WikiLeaks stories may not prove anything about the health of investigative journalism as a whole, they do serve as canonical examples of how it is changing. Because the web specifically – and digital technology more generally – offer new business models around investigative journalism. Primarily these come down to two features: a lowering of costs, and a broadening of revenue streams.

One of the costs of investigative journalism, for example, is that of organisation: the internet makes it significantly easier to collaborate and communicate with others; the need for a formal news organisation is much reduced. The way that the WikiLeaks revelations were managed both with that organisation and between publications in different countries is just one very visible example. My own project Help Me Investigate, meanwhile, proved that it was possible to conduct investigations (such as that into a £2.2m overspend on a council website) with the help of self-organising groups of individuals.

Another cost is time – and here, again, the internet offers efficiencies: a visit to the library is replaced with a visit to the library website, or a database. The FoI Act and related online services make it easier to obtain official documents. Social networks and forums make it easier to find leads, sources and experts. This is not to argue that investigative journalism can be replaced by an entirely online process, merely to point out that previously time-consuming elements of the process have now been considerably sped up.

The funding opportunities presented by the web are particularly interesting. Print and broadcast journalism relied on three streams of funding: advertising, for most; cover sales for some; and the licence fee.

Online, those organisational capabilities and reduced costs have opened up other streams: donation-funded investigations, for example, may not be new for charities and NGOs, but even those middlemen are now not always needed. The US website Spot.us, for instance, has successfully facilitated the sponsorship of numerous investigations by users. Other crowdfunding platforms offer the same possibilities to non-journalistic organisations. It is also difficult to pick apart how many subscribers to a platform such as Malaysiakini, for example, are paying for content, and how many to support a cause – its founder notes how subscriptions rise and fall in direct relation to negative actions by the government.

Meanwhile, the funding of the Bureau of Investigative Journalism, ProPublica and the Huffington Post Investigations Fund (coming from sources other than traditional advertising or cover sales) suggest that we may be seeing a partial separation of the investigative and watchdog roles of the media from those of entertainment, information and current affairs which previously subsidised it. It is not yet clear, of course, how sustainable the individual examples are – but the broader trend towards a wider diversity of funding streams and business models remains.

Online investigative journalism as a genre

Over many decades print and broadcast media have developed their own languages of investigative journalism: the spectacular scoop; the damning document; the reporter-goes-undercover; the doorstep confrontation, and so on. Does online investigative journalism have such a language? Not quite. Like online journalism as a whole, it is still finding its own voice. But this does not mean that it lacks its own voice.

For some the internet appears too fleeting for serious journalism. How can you do justice to a complex issue in 140 characters? How can you penetrate the fog of comment thread flame wars, or the "echo chambers" of users talking to themselves? For others, the internet offers something new: unlimited space for expansion beyond the 1,000 word article or 30-minute broadcast; a place where you might take some knowledge, at least, for granted, instead of having to start from a base of zero. A more cooperative and engaged medium where you can answer questions directly, where your former audience is now also your distributor, your sub-editor, your source.

The difference in perception is largely a result of people mistaking parts for the whole. The internet is not Twitter, or comment threads, or blogs. It is *a collection of linked objects and people* – in other words: all of the above, operating together, each used, ideally, to their strengths, and also, often in relationship to offline media.

Networked, multimedia, participatory

This deconstructed but linked nature is fundamental to the shape that online investigative journalism often takes. Paul Lewis's reporting, for example, for the *Guardian* allows users to see both its parts – as it takes shape – and its whole when it results in a more traditional narrative. All this before it breaks down once more into ongoing updates on subsequent court cases, demonstrations and inquests.

The "story" – a form that was created for print and then broadcast media – is broken down online, providing multiple points of entry across the network of its parts, as well as points of control, such as what medium you experience the story in.

Because, rather than being restricted by the qualities of the medium – rejecting a lead because it will not make "good television" or "doesn't have a clear angle" – online investigative journalism sometimes takes advantage of its multimedia qualities. Frontline's investigation into police shootings in the aftermath of Hurricane Katrina, for example[2], adds text reports to broadcast video, online updates and resources, providing users with the ability to explore the subject through individual cases – and even supply a tip via email. This requires a different mindset from the journalist: an ability to see how a story might play across different platforms to have maximum impact. In other words, not to take the medium for granted.

Finally, online investigative journalism is often participatory: those points of entry across the network are also potential points of interaction. Paul Lewis's investigations into Ian Tomlinson's death during the G20 protests in central London in April 2009, into undercover police infiltrating the environmental movement, and into the death of a man being deported to Angola all benefited from ongoing participation through online networks. Clare Sambrook's investigations into child detention took place on blogs and social media where its campaigning nature found a natural home. Talking Points Memo's investigation into the firing of US attorneys won a George Polk Award thanks largely to the participation of its users who looked through thousands of emails and internal Department of Justice documents. There are dozens of similar examples[3].

This is often called "crowdsourcing" – a memorable term for what is, simply, collaboration with people who don't share the same employer. The key is to remember that there has to be mutual benefit – calls to "send us your stories" will not be enough. That involvement of the former audience can be confusing, and drag us into endless debates about who gets to be called a journalist, or a publisher – even whether something gets to be called "investigative" or not. This is an egotistical waste of time. Journalists' job titles are not important: what they produce is.

What next for investigative journalism in a world of information overload?

But this identity crisis does highlight a final, important, question to be asked: in a world where users have direct access to a wealth of information themselves, what is investigative journalism for? I would argue that it comes down to the concept of "uncovering the hidden", and in exploring this it is useful to draw an analogy with the general journalistic idea of "reporting the new".

Trainee journalists sometimes see "new" in limited terms – as simply what is happening today. But what is "new" is not limited to that. It can also be what is happening tomorrow, or what happened 30 years ago. It can be something that someone has said about an "old story" days later, or an emerging anger about something that was never seen as "newsworthy" to begin with. The talent of the journalist is to be able to spot that "newness", and communicate it effectively.

Journalism typically becomes investigative when that newness involves uncovering the hidden – and that can be anything that *our audience* couldn't see before – it could be a victim's story, a buried report, 250,000 cables accessible to 2.5 million people, or even information that is publicly available but has not been connected before ("the hidden" – like "the new" is, of course, a subjective quality, dependent on the talent of a particular journalist for finding something in it – or a way of seeing it – that is newsworthy).

So what if all of the investigative journalist's material was public: documents, sources (witnesses, experts, victims, actors in the story), and information? The role of the investigative journalist would perhaps be as follows:

- to make the "hidden" (to their audience) "visible";
- to hold power to account;
- to make connections;
- to verify;
- to test hypotheses - the why and how of journalism.

This doesn't sound very different to how we see the role now. Of course, in reality, all of the investigative journalist's material will most likely not be online, so if we leave that thought experiment behind we can add other roles to acknowledge this:

- to make the invisible visible (i.e. digitising offline material, from paper documents and witness accounts to the "invisible web" of databases);
- to make the disconnected connected: publishing information in such a way that others can make further connections with other sources of data;
- to identify gaps in information – and fill them.

These are all, in fact, "making the hidden visible" in another form, whether they fill those gaps with material that is in the public domain or which only exists in a single witness's diary.

Narrative and authority

The role of a journalist in creating a narrative comes through strongly here: *hypotheses* are about narratives; making *connections* is about making narratives. Narratives are important – they help people find their place in a story – but online investigations can have multiple narratives and different users can find different entry points across those.

The other role that comes through strongly is institutional: *holding power to account* involves (but does not require) being in a position of power to do so; *verification* involves (but does not require) the stamp of institutional "due process".

My own experience with Help Me Investigate suggests that these two roles remain important bases for journalism as a profession: in crowdsourced journalism, "writing the story up" did not particularly appeal to non-journalists (the story was in their minds already) – only journalists wanted to do that. And it took an established media outlet to get official reaction.

This is not to suggest that only journalists can "have impact" – there are plenty of examples of groundswells of opinion online instigating media coverage. Indeed, impact can be seen as a combination of the clarity of a story and its distribution (not just how many hear the story, but who) and that requires not just journalists but publishers and, as distributors, users.

No excuses

So what does this mean for future investigative journalists online? Firstly, we may have to accept that many parts of investigative journalism will lose their air of mystery: from gathering information to publishing and distributing it, there are now dozens of new opportunities for the aspiring investigator: FoI tools such as WhatDoTheyKnow; free data gathering and interrogation tools such as Yahoo! Pipes and OutWit Hub, leak-hosting sites, and tools to combine and clean data such as Google Refine and SQLite. I see students now able to do work that would baffle many full time journalists.

That's no bad thing: distinguishing investigative journalism from other types of reporting was always problematic: "All journalism should be investigative" is a near-cliché because it goes to the heart of what we should be doing as journalists. Now we have the opportunity to act on that sentiment.

Journalists will be – and already are – more collaborative, learning how to work with and across networks. The internet has made it possible to separate the "investigative" from the "journalism": students, bloggers, activists, and anyone else with a burning question can begin to investigate it. They can raise questions openly with thousands of others online, submit FoI requests at the click of a button or analyse datasets and documents with free tools, regardless of whether or not they are employed as a journalist. The vast majority do not *want* to be a journalist. What they want are *answers*.

Their efforts can have value regardless of their job title. The role of investigative journalism – online, and then in print and broadcast – will increasingly be to build on their work: to make it visible; to verify it; to connect it to other information; to hold power to account over it. (If that threatens your romantic idea of the "individual genius" and makes you feel somehow less important, then you can take comfort in calling those people mere "sources" and yourself a "proper journalist". It doesn't matter what you call it as long as journalism gets done – although you may alienate potential sources by doing so in public.)

Secondly, journalists will need to judge carefully how and when to tell different parts of their story. The medium and channel of presentation is one new element of judgement - but they will also have to balance publicness against privateness at every stage, and judge how either might improve or speed up their work, and increase its impact and reach. There are no easy answers to these questions.

Finally, aspiring investigative journalists will no longer wait for a job title – or even a job – to begin investigating. At the conference that inspired this book two journalism students were asked how they saw the problems facing investigative journalism. The first felt that institutional restrictions on time or money should not be an excuse for journalists failing to investigate important questions in their own time; the second felt that people no longer needed institutional validation to investigate something: they could publish on a blog and build an audience that way.

These are hugely encouraging sentiments for anyone who worries about the state of modern journalism. Of course, some people will always look for excuses, but thanks to the access to information, documents, sources, collaborators and tools that the internet presents, we have fewer excuses to make. Not only that, journalists and aspiring journalists have the opportunity of a generation: to define the shape of investigative journalism to come.

Notes
[1] See http://www.journalism.co.uk/news/commitment-not-cash-is-key-to-investigative-journalism/s2/a51542/, accessed on 1 May 2011
[2] See http://www.pbs.org/wgbh/pages/frontline/law-disorder/, accessed on 2 May 2011
[3] One good roundup can be found at http://www.pbs.org/mediashift/2008/04/examples-of-online-investigative-journalism116.html, accessed on 3 May 2011

Note on the author
Paul Bradshaw is an online journalist and blogger and a Visiting Professor at City University's School of Journalism in London. He manages his own blog, the Online Journalism Blog (OJB), and is the co-founder of HelpMeInvestigate, an investigative journalism website funded by Channel 4 and Screen WM. He has written for journalism.co.uk, *Press Gazette*, the *Guardian*'s Data Blog, InPublishing, Nieman Reports and the Poynter Institute in the US. He is the co-author of the *Journalism Handbook* with former *Financial Times* web editor Liisa Rohumaa, and of *Magazine Editing* (third edition) with John Morrish. Other books which

Bradshaw has contributed to include *Investigative Journalism* (second edition), *Web Journalism: A New Form of Citizenship*; and *Citizen Journalism: Global Perspectives*. Bradshaw has been listed in Journalism.co.uk's list of the leading innovators in journalism and media and Poynter's most influential people in social media. In 2010, he was shortlisted for Multimedia Publisher of the Year and in 2011 ranked 9th in PeerIndex's list of the most influential UK journalists on Twitter. Bradshaw is also a graduate of Birmingham City University (then the University of Central England), where he studied media from 1995 to 1998.

Enter: the Data Journalist

Sean McGrath argues that there are essentially three steps involved in data journalism: the gathering of data, the interrogation of data and the visualisation of data. And, as he stresses, each process requires a different skill as well as different tools

In 2010, the CEO of Google, Eric Schmidt, claimed: "There were 5 exabytes of information created between the dawn of civilization through 2003, but that much information is now created every two days" (2010 Atmosphere convention).

To place this claim into perspective, let us consider the following. This page consists of approximately 2 kilobytes of data. There are 1,024 kilobytes in a megabyte of data. The complete works of Shakespeare would equate to roughly 10 megabytes. There are then 1,024 megabytes in a gigabyte. An average-sized library, filled with academic journals, would equal roughly 100 gigabytes of data. There are then 1,024 gigabytes in a terabyte. The print collections of the US Library of Congress would equal approximately 10 terabytes. 1,024 terabytes equals 1 petabyte. All the printed material in the world would equate to roughly 200 petabytes.

Finally, 1,024 petabytes is equal to 1 exabyte. Recent research suggests that we are now producing 6.8 exabytes of information every two days. Given print, film, magnetic, and optical storage media produced about 5 exabytes of new information in 2002 alone, it would seem that Schmidt might have been slightly sensationalistic with his statistic. However, his overriding point remains valid.

In the information age, both governments and big businesses are being continually pressured into releasing an increasing amount of data. While this suits the journalist, it may also suit those releasing the data – for where better to hide secrets, than in plain view? Amongst the centillions of "0"s and "1"s that make up the digital world we now inhabit, there are infinite journalistic stories waiting to be discovered. All we have to do is find them.

Enter: the data journalist
Data journalism is really an amalgamation of roles, each of which could take a lifetime to master. The perfect data journalist would be a skilled researcher, statistician, programmer and, of course, journalist. In reality, it is unlikely that an aspiring data journalist would possess complete knowledge in each of these areas but fortunately it is not necessary.

The phrase "data journalism" is still taboo. The juxtaposition of the words "data" and "journalism" in the same sentence, inevitably conjures up images of computer programmers huddled over a MacBook, frantically writing code. While this certainly is one element of data journalism, it does not tell us everything. As Martin Moore, Director of Media Standards Trust, states: "Data journalism is shorthand for being able to cope with information abundance. It is not just about numbers. Neither is it about being a mathmo or a techie. It means being able to combine three things: individual human intelligence, networked intelligence, and computing power." Let us consider each of Moore's criterion individually.

Individual human intelligence
To turn raw data into a story, we still need implement fundamental journalistic techniques. For technology to find an answer, a question must still be asked. There is currently no technology in the world that fully

understands the prerequisites of a good story. In other words, the data journalist must rely on the exact same skill set as the journalist. Instinct, experience and training are all fundamental.

Networked intelligence

In October 1997, Distributed Computing Technologies (DCT) successfully cracked a 56-bit key as part of the RSA Secret-Key Challenge. The challenge, set up by RSA Laboratories was designed to demonstrate the strengths and weakness of various encryption methods. However, what DCT revealed in the process was the strength of "grid computing".

The concept was that instead of using one "supercomputer" to carry out intensive calculations, the internet enabled the calculations to be spread out among thousands of computers. Operations that would have previously been impossible could now be divided up between anyone with a computer. This technology has expanded to perform tasks such as the Search for Extra-terrestrial Intelligence (SETI) and cures for cancers, with millions of users lending their spare computing power to carry out potentially world-altering research.

The same Peer-to-Peer (P2P) concept has also seen illegal file, music and video sharing bring their respective industries to their knees. More recently, the notion of network distribution has retreated away from the computers and focused instead on the people operating them. Crowdsourcing could be seen as the twin sister of data journalism, utilising the internet to bring a network of people together to contribute and investigate.

Computing power

If an abundance of data is the core reason behind the need for data journalism, computing power is the reason that data journalism can now be practised. In 1965, the co-founder of Intel, Gordon E. Moore, wrote a paper observing a trend and predicted its continuation into the future. The prediction, now known as Moore's Law, claimed that the transistors that can be placed on an integrated circuit double approximately every two years. Moore's Law has proven to be remarkably accurate. So much so, that the computer industry uses the law to forecast future trends.

Essentially, Moore's Law means that the technology powering a Personal Computer doubles in power every two years. Although this does necessarily equate to a doubling in computing speed, it goes some way to demonstrating the rapid and exponential increase in computing technology. In 1999, an Intel flagship commercial Central Processing Unit (CPU) was capable of performing 2,054 million instructions per second (MIPS). Their latest CPU, which is often referred to as the "brain" of a computer, is capable of performing approximately 159,000 MIPS. What was once a "supercomputer", reserved for advanced medical research or taking on the grandmasters of chess, is now simply a "computer" available on the high street for a few hundred pounds.

With a little bit of knowledge and a few choice pieces of software, the household computer can now mine, interrogate, analyse and visualise even the most complex data.

The process: Learning to work with data
If one were to break down the processes involved in data journalism, there would essentially be three steps involved. The gathering of data, the interrogation of data and the visualisation of data. Each process requires a different skill as well as different tools.

Data gathering
Of course, it is impossible to work with data, until there is data to work with. Renowned data journalist Paul Bradshaw suggests that instead of becoming overwhelmed by the amount of information available, the aspiring journalist should start with a question and then search for the data that will answer it. As previously mentioned, the sources for reliable and newsworthy data are ever increasing. The following examples are simply the tip of an iceberg. Creative thinking and experience will reveal an unlimited number of data sources.

http://www.data.gov.uk
The government's official data hub is a fantastic source of primary information, ranging from crime figures to traffic statistics. All data can be used for both private and commercial use, although should be acknowledged by including an attribution statement specified by data.gov.uk, which is "name of data provider" data © Crown copyright and database right.

http://www.data.gov
Although the US counterpart is a good site to become familiar with, the data available is much less forthcoming and, therefore, will probably need to be used in conjunction with other sources.

http://www.factual.com
An open data platform and community with a wealth of data sets covering a wide range of subjects.

http://www.socrata.com
Socrata is geared towards non-technical internet users. Although quite UScentric, Socrata is an excellent source of government, healthcare, energy, education, and environment data.

wikileaks.org
WikiLeaks needs no introduction, but is proving to be one of the most valuable sources of data available.

The Freedom of Information Act
Although sites such as data.gov.uk aim to take emphasis away from the FoI Act, freedom of information remains one of the most pertinent tools in data retrieval. Heather Brooke's *Your Right to Know* (Pluto Press, 2004) is an essential read in order to maximise the effectiveness of information requests. http://www.whatdotheyknow.com is also a useful tool. Not only does it give useful advice, but also it acts as a gathering point for previous requests.

Delving Deeper: Hacks meet hackers
For those who are not content with using the tools freely available for data gathering, there is another option. At the very apex of the data-driven revolution are those who are combining a level of programming knowledge with journalism.

Screen scrapers are bespoke pieces of code that are able to trawl the internet looking for data relevant to the programmer's specification. For example, if you wanted to crawl every local police authority's website in the UK, looking for press releases relevant to police corruption, scraping would make this feasible. Not only could it be done, but it could done several times a day for a year, or for five years. Scraping turns the World

Wide Web into the tool and the only restraint is the creative foresight of the journalist.

Again, the word "programming" often summons feelings of anxiety for the uninitiated and in all fairness, even basic programming is not something that can be learnt in a weekend. However, many journalists reading this will be fluent in shorthand and if interested, should view learning basic programming as on par in terms of complexity. Python, Ruby, PHP and SQL are all languages that one could use as a basis for writing a scraper.

For those who feel that learning a programming language is simply too daunting a mountain to climb, there is a simpler option which can yield equally impressive results. There is a growing community of programmers who are working in conjunction with journalists, each of them able to bring something different to the table. If you have a good idea for a scraper, you are almost certain to be able to partner with someone able to write your scraper for you. Scraperwiki.com and hackhackers.com are both excellent sites to meet communities where such collaborative work is possible.

Interrogation of data

Once the data is collected, it will need to be organised, filtered and cleaned up. While data is readily available, it is an unfortunate fact that it is usually not presented in a way that makes it easy to work with. As Paul Bradshaw advises: "Look out for different names for the same thing, spelling and punctuation errors, poorly formatted fields (e.g. dates that are formatted as text), incorrectly entered data and information that is missing entirely."

There is no one-size fits all, automated approach to data interrogation. Many of the inbuilt functions of Microsoft Excel such as "search and replace" and macro recording will help. There are also tools such as Freebase Gridworks and Google Refine that can help clean up your data.

Visualise the fruits of your labour

Visualisation is at the heart of all data-driven journalism. The aim of the journalist is to take data, which is vast and incomprehensible and turn it into a story which is simple to understand. It is important to recognise at this stage that data journalism is not attempting to reinvent the wheel.

Anyone has encounter a pie chart has encountered data visualisation. The same can be said for anyone who has watched a weather report on the news or watched the half-time statistics during a televised football game.

There are, however, a growing number of tools that are specifically designed to aid you in your quest to understand your newfound data. Each tool carries different copyright restrictions and if the visualisation is to be published, this should be considered.

http://www-958.ibm.com
This rather un-catchy web address is the home of IBM's Manyeyes, a free data visualisation suite. While some of visualisations are rather basic, it offers a variety of original visualisations. It is worth noting that in order to see the visualisation, the user must agree to allow their visualisation to be published on the site. This means that it may not be suitable for all types of journalistic work.

www.google.com/fusiontables
Google's Fusion Tables is still in a Beta phase but shows signs of promise. Not only are you able to integrate with Google Documents, but you can map your data directly on to satellite imagery of earth.

Conclusion: The era of the network
Although data journalism is being embraced by the journalism community at large, there seems to be the inherent antipathy that comes with any major shift in technique and theory. Conventionalists continue to argue that sitting in front of a computer is not "real journalism". From the opposite side, there is much talk of data journalism being "the future", as if some form of digital enlightenment will take place and those who do not have a complete command of the world of data, will be left by the wayside.

As is often the case with opposing views, neither is entirely correct. One thing that can be said with certainty, though, is that we are resolutely in the era of the network. Google is searched in excess of 300 million times per day while there are 35 hours of footage uploaded to YouTube every minute and 110 million tweets per day.

There is still an argument to be had for finding a balance between conventional journalistic technique and this new breed of data journalism.

However, the information super-highway is rapidly becoming the most powerful tool in the journalistic arsenal. While it is fanciful to say that computer-aided reporting is the future of journalism, it is also naïve to simply reject its potential.

Note on the author

Sean McGrath has recently graduated from the University of Lincoln with a First Class BA (Hons) in Investigative Journalism and Research. He was also the winner of the John Pilger Award for Investigative Journalism. As well as having worked as a researcher for the BBC, he is an active blogger and has a background in social media technology, web design and search engine optimisation. As for being a data journalist…he will, he says, always remain a student.

The Wisdom of Crowds? How Crowdsourcing Feeds into Investigative Journalism

New media and the web have opened up a previously untapped resource – the civic-minded public – presenting an opportunity to broaden the field of investigative journalism and who participates in it, argues Shane Croucher

Most investigative journalism of the past was conducted by professional journalists as individuals or in small groups, such as *The Sunday Times's* "Insight" team, shrouded in secrecy and hidden away from prying eyes. It was all a bit MI5. Some investigative journalism still happens like this because the investigation may necessitate secrecy owing to its sensitive nature.

However, new media and the web have opened up a previously untapped resource – the civic-minded public. This presents an opportunity to broaden the field of investigative journalism and who participates in it. Investigative journalism is not dead, it is growing and no longer the preserve of trained journalists.

Anyone with a computer and a thirst for holding power to account can join in. Temporary and permanent online communities focused on investigative journalism are being built. This is the crowdsourcing phenomenon and it is something we should celebrate. Crowdsourcing is a useful means of getting as many hands on deck as possible. Lots of websites and online tools are dedicated to crowdsourcing information, content and expertise from willing contributors.

Where the crowds are forming

Helpmeinvestigate.com is an excellent resource for collaborative investigative reporting. It describes itself as "a platform for you to organise and pursue questions of public interest you think should be investigated". Site users can submit questions, an example being: "How much is my local council spending on advertising?" and other users join in to find out. Once the information is collated, it is there to be used by anyone who needs it or simply wants to view it. The site is actively promoting holding authorities to account and can spawn significant news stories.

An example is when one of its investigations uncovered a £2.2 million overspend by Birmingham City Council on its website[1]. In February 2011, Help Me Investigate announced it would go open source, allowing anyone to use its coding to adapt and develop for their own crowdsourcing investigative platforms. Paul Bradshaw, who founded the website in 2009, wrote in a blog post[2]:

> Going open source addresses a number of legal weaknesses and geographical limitations that the project has encountered, as well as providing an opportunity to improve the technology that we simply don't have in our current form. We've had dozens of requests to join the site from people in South America, Australia, the US, Middle East and South Africa that we couldn't comply with for legal reasons. There have also been those who wanted private investigations, or completely public ones. Now there is a way that those people can use and change the technology accordingly. It also allows us to focus our efforts on what I believe is the most important feature of the site: its community and resources.

Whatdotheyknow.com, part of the My Society project that encourages digital transparency and democracy, invites users to openly submit freedom of information requests to those bodies up and down the country subject to the Freedom of Information Act.

Reams and reams of data are being uploaded to the website, free for everyone to view, whereas it may have previously been hidden away from public view in someone's email archives. Its open nature can also holds the bureaucrats handling the requests up to scrutiny, in theory lowering the chances of an individual being fobbed off or ignored.

Whatdotheyknow is doing what many authorities should, but are not. They are making information held by public bodies available online for all to see. Social networking sites such as Facebook and Twitter can be a great way of finding willing volunteers to assist in investigations. Update your status saying you need people to help with an investigation you are working on and you might be surprised at the response.

An article on Mashable[3] highlighted how Wendy Norris, an American investigative journalist, used Twitter and Facebook to recruit local people in her community to work on an investigation with her. She put out the message: "Heading to the grocery or drug store this week? Join a fun, stealth crowdsourcing project. No disguise needed. Direct message me if you are in Colorado."

What Norris was trying to do was find out if rumours that condoms sold in shops in Colorado were locked away behind the till and could only be purchased by asking staff to unlock the cabinet. This, it was rumoured, was making it difficult for teenagers to get hold of condoms, because it was too embarrassing.

From Twitter, Norris recruited seventeen volunteers, who went to 64 shops in the area and disproved the rumours. Condoms were widely available from the shelves and very rarely locked away. Norris gave Mashable seven tips for using social media to crowdsource (ibid):

1. Employ a sense of fun with the request.
2. Make the task discrete and easily accomplished.
3. Explain the purpose as a larger public service.
4. Set a reasonable time frame for task completion.
5. Allow volunteers to overlap tasks as built-in fact checking.

6. Provide immediate feedback to questions/responses and encourage retweets for additional recruitment.
7. Build public interest in, and anticipation for, the story.

Crowdsourcing does not just lend itself to finding volunteers to physically take part in activities. It can also be used to find people with certain expertise to help analyse documents, data and information. A great example of using crowdsourcing to trawl through data is the *Guardian*'s coverage of the MPs' expenses scandal[4]. Once all of the details of MPs' expenses, dating back from the past few years, were published by Parliament, the *Guardian* uploaded all of the data on to their website. They built a tool whereby readers could look through all of the documents, MP by MP, and highlight if something looked like it should be investigated further.

This will have saved *Guardian* journalists a lot of time trawling through the information. They could jump straight to the areas flagged up by users as worthy of a second look. The tool was also "gamified", to an extent, as users could work to "complete" sections of the data. The newspaper used the public anger to engage its readers in democracy by giving them a simple investigative platform from which to scrutinise their elected representatives.

Issues in crowdsourcing

There are, of course, problems that can arise in crowdsourcing. One is verification. Journalists are at risk from being fed sophisticated propaganda, or being hoaxed. How do you know that the information you are receiving is *bona fide*, or that the person you are talking to is who they say they are? These are particularly an issue with social networking sites, where anonymity and fake profiles run rife.

An answer may be found in traditional journalistic methods: simple fact-checking. Do not just take what is being said or offered at face value, ask for proof. Ask for a phone number so you can contact someone directly. Ask for supporting evidence.

At a day of workshops laid on by the Media Standards Trust and the BBC College of Journalism in March 2011, the *Guardian*'s Special Projects Editor Paul Lewis spoke of how he used Twitter to find someone who was on a particular flight where an alleged assault by a private security firm on an asylum seeker had taken place. Someone came forward on the site to say they were on the flight. Lewis then simply asked them to scan him a copy of their boarding pass to verify that this person was indeed on that flight.

Another issue that may arise is longevity, or keeping people motivated, in a crowdsourcing project. People can get bored and quickly lose interest. Some may argue that crowdsourcing can only work over a short period of time. Kevin Marsh, of the BBC College of Journalism, wrote about a crowdsourcing project by the French newspaper *Le Journal de Montreuil*[6].

Using Google Maps during a petrol drivers strike, the newspaper got its readers to update which petrol stations in the area had received deliveries and which petrol stations had not, to save readers wasted journeys in search of fuel. Initially, it worked well. However, after about four days, problems began to arise. Marsh writes:

> After the first few days, the rush of info slowed – so the map never became complete. Worse than that, as the blue flags sprung up over the map, car owners started to panic. For most of the region, there are only three or four petrol stations within 10km. Once the nearest one was flagged, people got in their cars, with tanks 7/8 full, and headed off to the next nearest without a flag. Just in case. Of course, the absence of a flag didn't mean the presence of petrol, just that no-one had flagged it. So when the slightly panicking driver turned up at an unflagged station to find it had no petrol...slight turned into total turned into queues, forecourt fistfights etc, etc. Wise crowd? After four days, deliveries restarted. Again, at first the newly replenished stations were flagged...until there was enough petrol in the system for no-one to care enough about the map to email the paper – though not enough to ensure there was petrol everywhere.

One way to keep people interested is to "gamify" a crowdsourcing project, as highlighted in the *Guardian's* coverage of the MPs' expenses scandal. Set specific tasks that need to be completed, which when finished will lead to a further level of tasks. Reward users with levels of prestige within a community, perhaps even more responsibility, like comment moderation powers. Perhaps, even, incentives like vouchers for shopping.

Verification and longevity are just two of many issues surrounding crowdsourcing in journalism. As crowdsourcing develops, so will issues, both practical and ethical. These challenges must be met with discussion and learning by doing, refining and reflecting along the way.

Following the crowd

These are merely a few examples of crowdsourcing in investigative journalism on the web and the issues arising around it. There are countless more. This open arms approach to investigative journalism will not always be appropriate. There will still be sensitive investigations that need to be kept hidden from the public until publication.

Back in the day this was pretty much the only type of investigative journalism going on. Now, the web has made access to data and information simple. Communities of investigators are being built, motivated by working in the public interest not for money, and this is spreading. Increasingly, people are lining up to hold power to account. The expenses scandal was a catalyst to a wider yearning for more openness and transparency in our political society, and this is feeding into the development of investigative journalism, and crowdsourcing in particular.

Not only can the internet provide excellent – and free – crowdsourcing opportunities for investigative journalism, but there are also many free-to-use tools. As citizen journalism grows and more and more hyperlocal start-ups appear across the country, these tools facilitate investigative journalism from anyone who is interested.

Notes

[1] See Dale, P. (2009) Cost of new Birmingham City Council website spirals to £2.8m. Available online at http://www.birminghampost.net/news/politics-news/2009/08/04/cost-of-new-birmingham-city-council-website-spirals-to-2-8m-65233-24, accessed on 30 May 2011

[2] See Bradshaw, P. (2011) *Help Me Investigate is changing*. Available online at http://helpmeinvestigate.com/help-me-investigate-is-changing, accessed on 30 May 2011

[3] See Lavrusik, V. (2010) How investigative journalism is prospering in the age of social media. Available online at http://mashable.com/2010/11/24/investigative-journalism-social-web/, accessed on 30 May 2011

[4] See *Guardian*. (2009). Investigate the MPs' expenses 2. Available online at http://mps-expenses2.guardian.co.uk/, accessed on 30 May 2011

[5] See Marsh, K. (2010) The attention deficit of crowds. Available online at http://www.bbc.co.uk/journalism/blog/2010/11/the-attention-deficit-of-crowd.shtml, accessed on 30 May 2011

Note on the author

Shane Croucher has just graduated with a First Class Honours from the innovative BA Investigative Journalism and Research at the University of Lincoln.

Facebook: the Investigative Network

How ethical is it for reporters to assume false identities in their operations on the web? Tom Farmery discusses this and some of the many possibilities and pitfalls of using Facebook as a tool for investigative journalism

Launched in 2004, the social networking site Facebook now boasts more than 600 million members worldwide. It can sometimes reveal surprising bits of information. For instance, in July 2009, soon after he was announced as MI6's new chief, Sir John Sawers was shown by the *Mail on Sunday* on Facebook while on a family holiday. This was a result of his wife, Shelley, posting pictures of her and her family quite innocently on Facebook.

But what does this mean to journalists, and can Facebook become a reliable research tool in investigative journalism? Well, let us first of all take the Facebook wall for example. The wall, effectively, is a reflection of a conversation in the real, physical world. It is an infinite log of what someone has said, but also, whom they have said it to. The only difference between a conversation using the wall and a chat with someone down the local is that more people overhear a Facebook conversation than they do in a pub.

As a user of the social networking site I am baffled on a daily basis by what other people post on their wall, whether it is a thoughtless comment about someone else or an album of shameful photographs from the night before. It could be argued that these same people are only reflecting their own life in their wall posts and what is wrong with that? Well, nothing but what it does mean for investigative journalists is that no longer do you have to get amongst people to find out what they are saying. Instead, if you have access to the particular user or group then you can, from a safe distance, pinpoint exactly what is being said.

Working journalists know that as much as access is key, it can, when covering sensitive, dangerous topics, also be difficult to acquire. What makes this worse when using Facebook is that the site's privacy settings have improved making it more difficult to track users. Simply searching for an individual's name will not necessarily return a single result. Therefore, it is important to consider more advanced ways of searching.

Tailoring your search

Because of its nature Facebook allows you to search in many different ways. You are able to tailor your search to whatever it is you want to discover. So, for example, if you wanted to uncover a story about racism in the ranks of the armed forces you would search for both "British soldiers" "racist" in quotation marks. Facebook's search engine will then make a connection with any information that relates in any way to your initial request. From those two search terms I was able to highlight seven groups that were either anti-Islam or pro-British soldiers.

Depending on what search is used can determine what is found. In many cases it is appropriate to use keyword or political searches for broad research – confirming that something is out there and worth following up. However, when more information is uncovered about a certain subject or person it is wise to then consider email or geographical based check.

Yet this requires the journalist to have more personal information to start off with. For example the subject's email address or location. Let's take

BBC Football Focus presenter Dan Walker. When you type his name into Facebook the search is returned with up to a hundred profiles but not one of them is Dan's.

However, when you search using his email address only one result is appears, and significantly it is his account. It is important to remember that in order to track somebody this way you must have more information than simply the person's name. But then it is expected that through various other means finding something such as an email address is not particularly difficult. Literally no Facebook profile is off limits and, with the right information at hand, any registered user can be found.

The problem in reporting quotes from Facebook

Sometimes just conducting an advanced search can retrieve the information needed for a story. However, reporting quotes from Facebook is problematic – how do you know that person said exactly what is being shown on a computer screen – without verification there is no story.

Verification on the internet can be tough to obtain and it is paramount that there is every confidence in what you have found if you are planning on publishing in tomorrow's paper. Yet if an email search was used it would be right to assume that the person who registered with that address is the same person you are looking for. This is also assuming that no one else has access to that specific email account.

The problem is, though, that more and more people are taking advantage of Facebook's improved privacy settings. This becomes a problem when you are trying to find information that you know may be there but have not got access to.

It is at this stage where the journalist may consider going virtually undercover in an attempt to clarify what has been said. In order to act covertly using Facebook, you must create a false profile. It is crucial that the implications of what you are doing are fully recognised. The same preparation must be made as if you were going undercover in the real world. The same rules apply: unless you have *prima facie* evidence that the person you are trying to uncover on Facebook then it is not advisable to take this route, and you must only do so as a last resort and with overriding public interest.

Going undercover – via Facebook

Due to the nature of this type of undercover operation it is far safer than going undercover in person. This is because at no point, at this stage, do you need to meet the person in the flesh which can be helpful on many levels. Firstly, the nervousness of going undercover is lost and more importantly the pressure of blowing your cover is removed. However, in no way must this method be undervalued or overused. The ethical issues still remain the same and it is important to remain focused and organised at all stages of the operation.

Infiltrating a group on Facebook requires a stubborn resistance and impeccable patience. The conventions of undercover journalism should always be remembered and applied. First of all the people you are looking to get amongst, virtually, must believe that you are one of them.

Forming a back-story for yourself is very important. If you were researching racism in the UK today, for instance, listing that you are a member of the British National Party and that you are in support of the English Defence League is just not good enough.

Some of the best undercover operations have only worked because of a tight, but believable back story – think of Donal MacIntyre's extraordinary Chelsea Headhunters investigation when he even had a tattoo made on his left arm to "prove" his identity as a Chelsea fanatic.

Phillip Knightley, famous for the work he did on the *Sunday Times* "Insight" team, supports the idea of going virtually undercover, but does offer these words of caution: "They [the journalist] should have exhausted every normal way of getting the information. They should not act as an *agent provocateur*. And the result should pass the public interest test."

Knightley does, however, believe that this method of gathering stories may have a short life expectancy: "I think people are going to wake up, I think you have a little window to use it now, but you have a limited time before people start taking precautions. I just have the feeling that it's not going to be too long before people wake up but people like you who'll be writing about it will find it much harder. Use it while you can."

Building trust online

Now, it is slightly different when using Facebook. Consideration must be given to how you plan on building trust online? This is how I do it: create one or several profiles, but then have them interact with each other so it makes them look genuine, yet also gives the person or group you are attempting to join, a flavour of who you are. In some cases because of the informality of Facebook, the same people you are investigating may eventually invite you to join their online group. As surprising as this may sound it does happen, especially if your back story is solid enough to gain someone's acceptance.

The fascinating element of this type of undercover work is that you can find out as much as you want about people before going any further. In July 2010, Northumbria Police were involved in a major operation in Rothbury, Northumberland after Raoul Moat shot three people only days after his release from prison – leaving tragically one person dead.

During the police's operation two men, Karl Ness and Qhuram Awan, were arrested suspected of helping Moat hide and also providing him with food. Days before Ness was arrested his Facebook page, below "Philosophy" and "Quotations" read: "all police informers must fuckin rot,,,, the horrible little kuntz". Not really damning evidence, but it was no real surprise when Ness was found guilty of murder, attempted murder, conspiracy and robbery at Newcastle Crown Court and sentenced to life imprisonment.

There are limitations to what can be dug up on Facebook. The person you are trying to get information on may not be online, and that, trust me, can be incredibly frustrating. The other downside, and I have touched on it briefly, is that if you do not gain direct access then you have no story. Incriminating evidence may be there but if it cannot be confirmed then it cannot be published.

Personal information is becoming the new currency of the internet and social networking sites such as Facebook can be an extremely useful research tool for investigative journalists. Yet it must be remembered that the consequences of going undercover this way are still very real and simply because you are hidden behind a computer screen does not mean you are any less likely to have your cover blown.

Note on the author

Tom Farmery is a recent graduate of the University of Lincoln's innovative BA (Hons) Investigative Journalism and Research programme with a First Class Honours degree and will begin the Investigative Journalism MA at City University, London, in September 2011. Tom tweets at @tom_farmery

Section 6. Alive and Well in the Academe

Aiming Higher? Investigative Journalism in Universities

Richard Lance Keeble

Can you teach journalism? Or is it best learned "on the job"? What use has learning about, say, ideology, Herman and Chomsky's propaganda model, the history of the radical press in early nineteenth century Britain or Gramsci's theory of hegemony for a hack concerned to bash out a story about a local car accident to a deadline just five minutes away? Is there a specific genre, even, of investigative journalism? Are there not some distinct research techniques – such as subterfuge, the assumption of false identities "in the public interest" – which can be associated with investigative reporting. *Should* not all journalism be "investigative"? The questions go on and on.

In this section a number of top academics stress: yes – investigative journalism can be taught! Firstly, Rosie Waterhouse, director of the Master's in Investigative Journalism, City University, London, outlines some of the reasons for the extraordinary success of its graduates – many of them holding top jobs in the industry.

Eamonn O'Neill, Lecturer in Journalism and Course Director of the MSc in Investigative Journalism at the University of Strathclyde, examines the roots of the term "investigative journalism" while reflecting critically on the steps he has taken to introduce its study at Master's level at his university. He concludes:

> Successful degree courses in the USA (both UG and PG) have existed for a number of years but this has not been the case in the UK. Therefore, it is no wonder that opinions differ about what the best process to launch a career in this category might involve, since they tend to reflect the individual's subjective experience. Undoubtedly, it would be unwise for any university, anywhere, to oversell its courses in this area, since to do so would be to ignore the constant difficulties of mounting investigations and the importance of professional experience in undertaking them. The importance of having a professional track-record in this field on the teaching staff seems to be an obvious ingredient for the course developing positively...

Finally in this section, Connie St Louis is a Senior Lecturer and the Director of the MA in Science Journalism at City University, London. She is chair of the Association of British Science Writers (ABSW) and an award-winning broadcaster, science journalist and writer. Here she argues that too few journalists are holding scientists properly to account. PR directors now set the agenda and foist their priorities on time-pressed science reporters.

Can you Teach Investigative Journalism? Methods and Sources, Old and New

Rosie Waterhouse is director of the Master's course in investigative journalism at City University, London. Here she outlines some of the reasons for the extraordinary success of its graduates – many of them holding top jobs in the industry

Can you teach investigative journalism? The short answer is yes. I teach it at City University in London. It's a Master's course, now in its fourth year. The students are among the brightest and the best young journalists starting out today. Is the course successful? If you judge by their results and the jobs they have gone into – yes, very.

I have students working on the nationals, regionals, for ITN, BBC regional TV, for *Panorama*, *Dispatches*, independent television production companies, for good trade magazines, for newspapers in Egypt, India and Cambodia, for think tanks and charities. One of them is working at Sane, the charity and helpline for the families of people suffering from schizophrenia, founded by Marjorie Wallace, a veteran of the legendary *Sunday Times* "Insight" team in its Harry Evans hey day. And five of them have gone on to be researchers at the Bureau of Investigative Journalism, also based at City University.

In January, one student from last year, Billy Kenber, won the Hugh Cudlipp Prize for Student Journalist of the Year.2011. This was for his MA dissertation project on the forced deportation and mistreatment of failed asylum seekers which was published across pages one, two and three of the *Independent*. He also secured a graduate traineeship at *The Times*. Matthew Holehouse, a Telegraph graduate trainee, was shortlisted for the Young Journalist of the Year in the Regional Press Awards for articles published in the *Glasgow Herald*.

Two former students were appointed to specially created new jobs as data reporters, one at the *Telegraph*, another at the *Guardian*, who is working specifically on investigations.

Learning on the job?

When I tell some of the old school that I teach investigative journalism, many are sceptical, dismissive. "I was never *taught* investigative journalism," they say. "I learnt it through hard graft, working on the job, over many years."

I never went to university at all. Few, if any universities had journalism courses when I left school in 1977, just with A levels, good at English and very, very nosey. So I became an "indentured" trainee reporter on the *Chester Chronicle*. I found I absolutely loved it. I gradually moved south, via Chester News Service and the *Manchester Evening News*, on to *The Sunday Times* "Insight" team, the *Independent* and *Independent on Sunday*, BBC *Newsnight*, the *Mail on Sunday*, and back to *The Sunday Times*.

My last full-time job in newspapers was at the *Daily Telegraph*. In all these places I was encouraged to indulge what I think was an instinct for digging, "finding things out", as one of my heroes, Peter Wilby, puts it.

So I am old school as well. After I started teaching in the Journalism Department at City eight years ago, I decided to develop short courses in investigative journalism for third year undergraduates. I wanted to turn out more young journalists who would be diggers. Find things out. Research. Get to the truth.

Then, I was encouraged by the former head of the Journalism Department, Adrian Monck, to develop a Master's course, specialising in investigative journalism. I have to say, apart from some fantastic highlights as a working journalist, this has become my dream job. It's my train set. It's a small course – my new head of department, George Brock, calls it "boutique" – for 17 or 18 journalism students with aptitude for in-depth research, strong ideas and serious attitude. They range in age and interests from new graduates to more mature students from various specialisms including journalism, marketing, law and the police.

Wanting to change the world

They don't know it at the interview stage, but they have to say something that persuades me and the colleague I interview with, Melanie McFadyean, that they want to change the world, or at least make a difference. And also, preferably, have fun. So you could say the course is elitist in terms of pursuing what I consider "pure", high-minded, some would say worthy, journalism. To me it's elite. I am proud to say it teaches "public interest only" investigative journalism. As I tell the students, we do not do sex or celebs.

Some people say all journalism should be investigative. In an ideal world, up to a point, yes. But it isn't. And in terms of what makes an investigative journalist different I would say there has to be a certain instinct, a nose for something not quite right, for injustice, unfairness, for corruption and dodgy deals, a sharp eye and respect for accuracy and evidence, perception, persistence, a genuine desire to get to the truth, not just a good story and a big by-line. But above all I try to teach that investigative journalism is about people. You have to be interested in and care about people.

In branding terms, it's a multi-media course with advanced research skills. The course is modelled on the skills and qualities I learnt from working with some of the best in the business, and reading some of the classics by great diggers such as Phillip Knightley (also a wonderful story teller) and David Leigh. And, of course, Harry Evans and Woodward and Bernstein were inspirational. Inspiration also came from watching some of the brilliant television reporters such as John Ware and Jane Corbyn, of *Panorama*. One of my favourite descriptions of an investigative journalist is from John Ware who came to City to give a talk: a news reporter, he said, is like a sprinter. An investigative journalist is the long distance runner.

So my course teaches the old methods of good old fashioned reporting, finding things out, being a news and current affairs junkie, reading the papers, picking up the telephone, going to meetings, talking to people, cultivating sources and contacts, using public records, pouring over documents, working nights and weekends.

Data journalism – the latest trend

Now, of course, we have email and the internet is a fantastic research tool. The latest trend is data journalism, originally called Computer Assisted Reporting, or as I explain it, getting stories from data, using spread sheets and computer software. As I freely admit to my students. I don't do it. In my role as a lecturer I don't have to. But I know what it can do. I saw data journalism emerging as the latest tool in digging at the Centre for Investigative Journalism summer school in 2005. The next year I put myself through what was to me a gruelling three days of workshops on CAR, being taught by two of the top trainers from the US.

It did not come easily. I was always the one putting my hand up to say I had not quite grasped the latest lesson, could we go a bit slower please. I almost cried with frustration. In the end I gave up trying to do it there and then, and just watched the bright young student sitting next to me. I needed to learn what CAR could do, so I could include this in my new course.

To teach it I brought in Heather Brooke, the ground-breaking freedom of information campaigner who had branched into data journalism. And now one of my students from the very first group on the MA course, James Ball, is teaching it to my current students. He is a perfect example of the success of a course in investigative journalism. He started out on the *Grocer* and broke loads of stories about the grubbier side of the retail food industry. Then he got a job as a researcher at the Bureau of Investigative Journalism. He was spotted as having a gift for CAR, getting stories from data. When the WikiLeaks data exploded on the scene last year he was seconded to the WikiLeaks team to work on the diplomatic dispatches data. He has now got a newly created job at the *Guardian* as data reporter, attached to the investigations desk.

As I try to explain to my students – when they're stressing out with assignment overload – this course is like a giant jigsaw puzzle. Which must be completed in record time. The teaching takes place essentially in two ten weeks terms, with a seven week break at Christmas, when they do work placements, and a four-week break at Easter, when they do more work experience and also crack on with their MA projects, which must be delivered by the middle of June. When I think about it, they are learning in ten months what took me maybe ten years. Plus they get this whizzy new data reporting tool. Nor everyone will excel at this, but they will all have the basics and this is increasingly valued in newsrooms today.

Learning the basics
Like all the students on the other traditional MA courses at City – newspapers, magazines, radio and television – they learn the basics of media law, public administration, ethics and online journalism. Unlike students on these other courses the "investigatives", as I like to call them, also receive an introduction to production in print, radio and TV – the idea being they are equipped with the basic skills so they are at least competent to work in any medium.

The jigsaw also includes pieces or "modules" in journalism practice – news reporting, and feature research and writing. I am extremely lucky to have Melanie McFadyean teaching and tutoring much of the feature writing, with outstanding results. They go to council meetings, courts and inquests, where all human life is there. And as an added bonus they do research for television investigations with David Lloyd, former head of News and Current Affairs at Channel 4 and creator of the *Dispatches* strand, who is positively evangelical in encouraging and coaching the students to work in teams to produce top class investigative stories for television. And, because I am old-fashioned, they also get shorthand. I suspect they hate me for it, when they have a two hour boot camp of shorthand starting at 9am every day.

But the unique selling points of the Investigative Journalism MA are the two modules on investigative reporting. One module is taught by David Leigh, who was awarded the Anthony Sampson Chair in Reporting at City four years ago, at the start of this course. He is absolutely fundamental to it. I have never ceased to be amazed that in four years he has never missed a class, which he teaches for two hours on a Friday morning and then goes back to the *Guardian* to write his latest scoop!

Over the course of six weeks in term one and six weeks in term two he turns out mini-David Leighs. He teaches the basic essential skills in finding people and finding out about people. He teaches how to use the Freedom of Information Act. And he sets them assignments, using public records and databases (from Companies House to Family Records and the Land Registry), and also social networking sites, which would defeat most working journalists today.

The other investigative reporting module is the other unique piece of the jigsaw. For three hours on a Monday afternoon over ten weeks in term two I bring in some of the finest practitioners in the field. These include Anthony Hilton, of the *Evening Standard*, on business and financial journalism; David Henshaw, of Hardcash Productions – perhaps most famous for *Beneath the Veil* – on undercover investigations; James Ball on Computer Assisted Reporting and a line-up including two forensic accountants, Raj Bairolya and John Hudson, and the veteran digger "Slicker" from *Private Eye*, who do a brilliant gig on corporate financial skulduggery. These are masterclasses. They are the cherries on the icing on the cake.

Proof that investigative journalism is definitely alive
So is investigative journalism dead or alive? Well, there's the Centre for Investigative Journalism, exporting the teaching of these skills around the world, and importing top names and practitioners to its summer school held every July at City – its director Gavin MacFadyen should be cloned, he has done so much to spread the word.

There's the Bureau of Investigative Journalism, for which Gavin MacFadyen helped secure funding from the David and Elaine Potter Foundation – Elaine Potter who worked on the legendary "Insight" team in the 1970s, (including the classic DC10 and Thalidomide investigations) and her very generous husband David, who developed the Psion Organiser. The BIJ is a fantastic venture producing ground-breaking investigations for mainstream publication and broadcast and exploring new models of funding for investigative journalism in future. Again we are lucky the BIJ is based at City, thanks again in no small part to Gavin MacFadyen and Head of Department George Brock, ex-*Times* man, who believes in proper journalism.

There's the Paul Foot Award, run by the *Guardian* and *Private Eye*, which every year attracts dozens of entries from journalists from the nationals, trade magazines, freelancers and the regional and local press – yes they are surviving and some are still thriving – (not least the *Chester Chronicle*, I'm very happy to report).

I see a very strong revival of investigative journalism across the media, old and new. There are still some really great, old fashioned, fact-finding, truth-seeking, diggers around. There are the new eye-witness or "citizen" journalists; there are community and campaign groups using the Freedom of Information Act to extract awkward facts from reluctant public bodies. And there are the transparency-seeking and sheer mischief-making hackers. In my view all this has the *potential* for good. We can collaborate, work together, and as journalists verify, as far as is possible, the facts and the evidence. I think it's a very exciting time to be a journalist.

And then there are my students. The next generation of investigative journalists and ace researchers. They all have fantastic potential. They are living proof Investigative Journalism is very much alive, and raring to go.

Note on the author

Rosie Waterhouse is an experienced investigative reporter who has twice worked on the *Sunday Times* Insight team, the *Independent* and *Independent on Sunday*, where she was Investigations Editor, and for BBC *Newsnight*, where she contributed to a BAFTA for a film revealing how BSE spread through the animal feed chain. She has also worked for the *Chester Chronicle*, Chester News Service, the *Manchester Evening News*, the *Mail on Sunday* and the *Daily Telegraph* and contributed a series of articles for *Private Eye* on the Satanic Panic. She is a senior lecturer and Director of the MA in Investigative Journalism at City University, London.

Digging Deeper: Reflecting on the Development and Teaching of Investigative Journalism in a University Setting in the United Kingdom

Eamonn O'Neill examines the roots of the term "investigative journalism" while reflecting critically on the steps he has taken to introduce its study at Master's level at a UK university

This chapter examines the development and teaching of investigative journalism within the setting of a UK university. The roots of the genre and definition of the term "investigative journalism" are explored with particular reference to an interview with the renowned US reporter, the late Bob Greene. It reflects on the steps taken by the author, who is course director of a Master's degree in Investigative Journalism at a major Scottish university, to establish the degree; attract applicants; adjust course content as feedback emerged; and aim to balance theoretical academic study with imparting practical skills.

The chapter also touches on several examples from the author's own professional background working on investigations for all platforms both nationally and internationally. Responses to a questionnaire set by the author to a selection of the current (2010-2011) class of students who are studying on the Master's course are included to reflect individual critical reflections on their own experiences and career aspirations in light of their studying for this advanced degree.

Introduction

Universities within the United Kingdom have been teaching investigative journalism, at both undergraduate and post-graduate level, for at least a decade and probably longer. The shifting offerings down the decades make it difficult to pin down which courses ran when, what each module might have contained, who was teaching it, who was studying and what the perceived outcomes were. There are now two well-established Master's degrees offered at major institutions in the UK: one in London (City University) and the other in Glasgow (University of Strathclyde).

What is clear is that the path to the current landscape has not been an easy one for either the academy or its students. Equally, the relationship with the professional world of journalism in all its forms and the institutions teaching this genre has been a difficult one frequently featuring well-meaning but untested optimism from those organising the courses one one-side, versus often-truthful but nevertheless cynical comments from those already ensconced in a professional career.

One illustration – but a useful one to begin with – of how thorny a subject this can be, is the fact that there is still debate about the roots and even an acceptable definition of "investigative journalism". This suggests that if agreement cannot be reached about such a simple question, then it is little wonder and certainly no surprise, that an agreed procedure, curriculum and set of established outcomes, has not been fully settled upon either. However, it does seem that students currently undertaking these studies in investigative journalism are realistic and hopeful about their career prospects and the usefulness of the degree and the skills they have been taught.

Historical context

The term "investigative journalism" appears to have first entered the professional media and public lexicon sometime during the 1960s-1970s timeframe. Interviews carried out with leading practitioners of the craft indicate confusion and uncertainty over when it first emerged or indeed to whom – individually or collectively – it was first used as a term of description. Literature on the topic, in the UK, USA and, indeed, elsewhere in the world, suggests the precise origins of the term remain frustratingly vague and repeated attempts by various authors, researchers, historians and journalists themselves to pin down the exact origins of the phrase have proven to be almost fruitless.

One of the UK's foremost exponents of what became known as "investigative journalism" is Phillip Knightley, a former member of the famous *Sunday Times*'s "Insight" team. Since both he and the "Insight" team were in their professional heydays around the early 1970s, one would assume he would be as good a judge as anyone to know where the term came from. When I asked him, he replied:

> I wish I knew! And I wish I knew who coined the term! *The Sunday Times* certainly didn't set out to create a team called "Insight" that would do "investigative Journalism". It just sort of grew and there was a wonderful confluence of events…[1]

However, an interview conducted by the author with 77-year-old American journalist Bob Greene in 2006, may well help in identifying one of the earliest usages of the term "investigative journalist" in the 1950s and 1960s. Greene was long regarded as a legend in American journalism circles, and he began his career working on "racket" investigations committees for the government, specifically under the leadership of Attorney General Robert F. Kennedy.

Greene maintains that whilst the terms "investigative reporting" and "investigative journalism" did come into the consciousness of the mainstream media after *All the President's Men* (about the *Washington Post*'s Watergate scoop) was released in print (in 1974) and then in Alan J. Pakula's film (in 1976), the reality was that many journalists were using the same techniques and approaches in earlier decades. He explained that:

> There were major investigative reporters around doing investigative reporting, we maybe hadn't defined it but you knew it by what you were doing…I was giving seminars at the American Press Institute for reporters and editors, on what I called "investigative reporting" in the 1960s…There were well-known reporters who were called "investigative reporters". For example, George Bliss from the *Chicago Tribune*; Todd Link from the *St Louis Post Dispatch*; Malcolm Johnson from the *New York Sun*, to mention only three.

That was before Watergate…I was using techniques I had used in the Senate Rackets Committee to form a squad, a group of reporters. And that was the genesis of the Newsday Investigative Team. Now that was all going on in the 1960s, and we won our first Pulitzer Prize in 1970 with the team called the "Investigative Team" or the "Greene Team"…All I am trying to say is regarding the use and currency of the words "investigative reporting" is that there were investigative reporters who used those words long before Watergate[2].

Greene's model has withstood decades of scrutiny and refinement

By combining the investigative techniques he learned during this tenure, with the press requirements to regularly break fresh stories, and by adhering to a tough legal framework when doing his investigations, Greene came up with a model for investigative journalism which has withstood decades of scrutiny and refinement.

It is the reporting, through one's own work product and initiative, matters of importance which some persons or organisations wish to keep secret. The three basic elements are that the investigation be the work of the reporter, not a report of an investigation made by someone else; that the subject of the story involves something of reasonable importance to the reader or viewer; and that others are attempting to hide the matters from the public[3].

This three-point definition was conceived by Bob Greene during his tenure as president of the Investigative Reporters and Editors (IRE) organisation which was founded in 1975, based at the University of Missouri where it still flourishes today. Greene had, as mentioned earlier, shifted between journalism and working on various investigative bodies which examined labour rackets and abuse of organised labour movements. This led him to see possibilities in marrying formal criminal investigation techniques with the press's usual need for fresh, ground-breaking stories on a regular basis. He set this merging of techniques and demand against a formal legal model of research, verifiable proof and organisation. This was an entirely new approach to newspaper investigation, a model which would eventually be copied by other journalists and publications.

The impact of Greene's approach and style were far reaching and other colleagues from across the industry came to study his techniques and organisational approach. Because Greene had worked for a government agency during his racket investigations, he was aware that a systematic, organised and clearly focused approach was required for an efficient investigation. He was very keen, for example, on an intricate but accessible filing system, which allowed sources to be cross-checked by waves of reporters on his staff. This allowed complex investigations to flow across timeframes and staff changes.

High standard of sourcing needed

He was also well-aware that his investigations, whilst primarily for press publication, would ultimately encounter the law. This meant he adhered to a high standard of sourcing and fair sense of focus. In terms of the former, it meant that multiple sources – not just two, as was applied during Watergate inquiries by the *Washington Post* – were required by reporters. Regarding the latter, he tolerated no skewed fact-picking in order to frame a target. This meant he could never be accused of what later came to be known as "gotcha" journalism, whereby journalists decide the culpability of their quarry before embarking upon an investigation, and therefore consciously – or even unconsciously – sift out awkward evidence hinting at alternative issues and instead cherry-pick only the material which supports their thesis.

This even-handed, professional approach indeed used "detective" methods, in as much as old-fashioned "shoe-leather" was worn out by going door-to-door, street-to-street, for sources and evidence, but it did not ignore the complex context against which the story was told, nor was it ignorant of the subtle power-related issues which moved like tectonic plates underneath everything Greene investigated.

The success of this unique blend of craft and strategy attracted success for him, his team and his publications. What was utterly unique about Greene's approach was that for the first time, newspapers were deliberately organising their staff into teams, led by senior staff members, focused on investigating issues which were of importance to readers but which required serious investment of time and money and which, in all cases, had no sure fire successful outcome in terms of either resolving the issues under scrutiny or, in any case, ever producing a readable story.

Despite these odds, Greene managed to produce stunning work which soon became the model for ambitious papers and editors across the United States. He explained: "The *Boston Globe* came along and studied the way we worked. Then they went back and formed a team that worked the same way – the 'Spotlight Team'. And the year after we won it, they won the Pulitzer Prize in 1971. They sent us a telegram saying 'Thanks teach' for making it possible...' And then the *Providence Journal* came to us and studied the way we did it, and a year after that they won a Pulitzer Prize."[4]

Greene's memory of the genesis of American investigative journalism is useful in more ways than one. His claim that journalists like him were essentially doing this kind of reporting before a specific name was ascribed to it makes sense. Of particular note is the fact that the term "investigative journalist" has been mentioned by other writers, commentators and historians retrospectively, to identify and categorise work carried out by mid-19th century journalists in both the UK and USA[5]. Whilst the descriptive term "investigative journalism" and the attributed and self-designated title "investigative journalist" have been, and remain, in common usage, many professionals in the media industry refuse to countenance the actual existence of either – whether in history or the modern-age

Paul Foot rejects "investigative" as a separate genre

One of the UK's most respective journalists who specialised in investigative projects was the late Paul Foot, who was best known for his ground-breaking columns in the *Daily Mirror*[6]. Whilst becoming well known for his award-winning work on miscarriage of justice cases and difficult cases such as the Lockerbie inquiry, Foot criticised – in fact took some pleasure in publicly *rejecting* – the whole idea that a separate kind of journalism existed with the term "investigative" fixed to it. He explained his contempt in an essay in 1999:

> [Investigative journalism] is a phrase which dates from that time [1960-70]. The expression is often used by jumped-up bylined journalists who want to distinguish themselves from the common ruck. It is in itself a little ridiculous, since all journalism worthy of the name carried with it a duty to ask questions, check facts, investigate[7].

Another journalist, equally well known for his foreign investigations, John Pilger, also took several opportunities to decry what he saw as the inappropriate use of the term. In recent years, however, he edited a compilation of journalism from around the world containing the subtitle *Investigative Journalism and its Triumphs*. In the book's introduction, Pilger said:

> The reference to investigative journalism in the title needs explaining, even redefining…The term, investigative journalism, did not exist when I began my career; it became fashionable in the 1960s and 1970s and especially when Bob Woodward and Carl Bernstein exposed the Watergate scandal…I have applied a broader definition than detective work and included journalism that bears witness and investigates ideas[8].

Whilst understanding and accepting Pilger's effort to enhance and deepen the debate on the definition of the investigative journalism, it is important to consider some of the points he makes. Firstly, it would be ungenerous, possibly even churlish to suggest that Woodward and Bernstein's work on the Watergate scandal amounted to nothing but "detective work". Having said that, Woodward has said publicly on numerous occasions that both he and Bersntein did – in a sense – carry out basic police-type "door-to-door" investigations in order to elicit the information from witnesses they needed. It is important to recognise that one of the reasons that much of the hidden truth and deeper contextual political and criminal meaning behind Watergate could not be featured in their early stories was simply because their stories were news articles. As such, they were constrained by the *Washington Post*'s own news standards to print only factual, accurate stories which served to move the story forward, as and when they discovered more information.

Bearing witness and investigating ideas

This is a constraint which most news reporters traditionally work under. Only if they had branched out into longer news "features" or in-depth articles of greater length (sometimes running into thousands of words for magazine pieces, for example) would Woodward and Bernstein have been able to explore the hidden motives and meanings behind the news articles they were reporting[9]. Instead, it was only with the publication of their book *All the President's Men* which allowed them to explore their facts and themes in greater depth thus partially fulfilling Pilger's stated mission of bearing "witness and investigating [ideas]..."

Secondly, it should also be recognised that both Woodward and Bernstein were relatively young reporters when they investigated the Watergate break-ins – aged twenty-eight and twenty-nine, respectively. Bernstein had had an erratic career until his coverage of the Watergate story and was known to be on the verge of being sacked when he started working on it. Woodward was regarded as being very inexperienced around the time of the break-in in June 1972, and only his reputation as a hard-worker saved him from being taken off the story. It is to Woodward and Bernstein's credit – as well as their various editors – that it remained as focused and productive in revelatory news terms as it did. Consequently, simply labelling it "detective work" is perhaps a little narrow and sounds too dismissive.

However, most journalists – including the author, someone who would happily under most circumstances call myself an "investigative journalist" – would broadly agree with the central sentiments Foot and Pilger express, i.e. that most journalists *should* do investigative work as part of their normal duties and that most journalists *should* report hidden truths and investigate uncomfortable ideas. Yet to agree with these goals is not the same as dismissing the notion that a separate category of "investigative journalism" with its practitioners does exist: the two issues are not mutually exclusive. In the UK Roy Greenslade, Professor of Journalism at City University and *Guardian* media blogger, noted:

> The phrase "investigative journalism" is, in a sense, tautologous because all journalism should involve some kind of investigation that results in the revelation of a hidden truth. Then again, there is no single form of journalism so the separate description is understandable. But let's be honest: there is a qualitative difference between investigative journalism and all other editorial matter that appears in newspapers. It is the highest form of journalism, pure journalism, real journalism, the reason journalism exists. At their best, investigative journalists serve the public interest by revealing secrets, exposing lies (and liars), uncovering uncomfortable facts, evading censorship and, sometimes, risking their lives to act as eyewitnesses to events. Its greatest exponents are muckrakers with a conscience working to that age-old dictum: "News is something

someone somewhere doesn't want published – all the rest is advertising."[10]

Investigative journalism in a university context

If agreeing on the roots and even a definition of "investigative journalism" seems a difficult challenge, then it's fair to say that planning and establishing a Master's degree in this subject within an established university setting in the UK is no easy task either. It is however, a rewarding journey to have undertaken.

I joined the University of Strathclyde in the summer of 2002 as a Lecturer in Journalism within the institution's highly-regarded Department of English Studies[11]. By then I was 35 years old, having worked in the journalism and specialising in investigations in print and broadcast, for 13 years. My credits included major articles for most UK broadsheets and documentaries for network strands including Channel 4's *Dispatches* and *Cutting Edge*.

In the earliest stages of my career at Scottish Television I encountered individuals who (unwittingly) mentored me based on their own experiences carrying out investigations. Particularly important was David Scott formerly of the *Daily Express* and BBC Scotland, and who had worked on the Paddy Meehan miscarriage of justice case and Gus Macdonald, the Chairman of Scottish Television, who'd also been series producer on *World in Action*. Both were tough Glaswegians in the best sense of the term and they dispensed hard-nosed advice but also freely gave of their time to talk me through their own experiences and difficulties. Nearer my own age, another influence was Blair Jenkins, my day-to-day manager, who backed me, financed me and generally believed in me as the projects I embarked grew in scale and ambition.

In London, of equal importance was David Lloyd, Commissioning Editor of Channel 4's *Dispatches* who encountered me in my early 20s and treated me with seriousness and patience as I pitched and produced programmes for him in later years. When I left Scottish TV (and indeed, Scotland for that matter) to live and work in the USA for a couple of years, it occurred to me that it was lessons learnt both in theory and practice from these mentors that had really shaped and underpinned how I perceived and carried out my work.

Another major influence was my experiences working in the USA. In the course of carrying our investigations there, I often spent the early stages meeting US colleagues who had written, for example, a major article or book connected to the subject or theme I was examining. I would have lunch with them or even stay with them for short visits and in the process learn how they entered the profession and then went on to specialise in investigations. A pattern in replies began to emerge and it was clear that most had completed undergraduate degrees, proceeded to a Master's degree and were usually exposed to either a whole course or a single semester class, in investigative reporting.

Importance of being self-starters

These classes varied in depth, length and quality. But they invariably impacted the students disproportionately in comparison to other areas, and the skills made them see the importance of being self-starters; original thinkers; well-organised; able to carry out aggressive and flexible reporting; and see the wider and/or hidden stories which the normal day-to-day deadline pack often missed. One important fact, above all else, was that by and large, the best teachers I was told, were "doers" themselves: they taught from experience, current and constantly knowledge garnered in the field (technical, practical and theoretical) and were still engaged at some level in the industry themselves.

Initially, when I began in 2002, I only taught one class in investigative journalism. Fortunately, the teaching coincided with me achieving a measure of success in the case of wrongfully-convicted Scotsman Robert Brown who had served almost 26 years for a murder he had not committed. Gus Macdonald had handed the file on the case to me in 1991 and I had worked on several STV and later BBC Scotland documentaries investigating the case. My investigations managed to unearth material germane to the case and helped free Brown in November 2002. I was interviewed in Channel 4 News, BBC, ITV and for foreign networks too. My by-lined personal account of the case was given front-page treatment in two major Scottish broadsheets and within days BBC Scotland did a special one-off documentary which in-part, followed my journey and explained my investigative work as the appeal reached its conclusion.

The fact my work was in the media was important only inasmuch as it exposed students to the notion that investigative journalism could create news and lead the cycle of coverage as a result. My walk-on role in the story also conveyed the fact that they were being taught by someone who actually practised what they preached and, as I always emphasise, I was still learning myself.

Inspiration from the US

In subsequent years I taught more classes in investigative journalism and also "road-tested" ideas and strategies at other Scottish universities as a visiting lecturer. Whilst I was keen to begin planning towards a Master's degree, I was aware that other UK universities had tried and failed to start up such degrees[12]. The idea of creating a full-time Master's degree was given impetus however, by further trips to the USA in subsequent years where I saw the establishment of successful courses in various campuses. Usually staffed by veterans who still carried out their own projects and used their past-successes as case-studies for students, these served as something of an early template for me. Making contact with and later meeting in person, Lowell Bergman, of CBS's *60 Minutes* and the Hollywood movie *The Insider* fame, who was running an investigative course at the University of California, encouraged me further. Later, after encouragement from colleagues at the University of Strathclyde – including Professor Brian McNair and Professor David Miller – the MSc in Investigative Journalism was established in late 2007.

It was launched quietly and we began with only a handful of applicants. In later years this would grow to more than twenty-applicants, meaning that some were turned down for various reasons, whilst others never made it through the interview stage[13]. The applicants have come from: UK (including Scotland), Ireland, India, China, South Africa, Palestine, USA, Mexico, Netherlands, Spain, Italy, Poland and Norway. The course itself is broken down into core and optional classes. Students take core subjects like: Investigative Journalism – History & Theory; Investigative Journalism – Project; a class in Manufacture of Consent; Investigative Research; and a Law class. They can mix options from the university's other successful MLitt in Journalism degree (including Media Ethics etc).

All students must successfully complete a Dissertation in the 12,000 to 15,000 word range if they carry on to full Master's status. Those whose grades are failing, or have other issues, may exit before the dissertation and graduate with a diploma. The degree is also offered across two years on a part-time basis. The programme continues to evolve and there has been a concerted effort in the past year to add practical elements from day-one. This, however, raises the dual-concern often asked about how qualified students are when they arrive (i.e. do they have journalism experience?) and what realistically will they be able to do when they graduate? Students must hold (or expect to achieve soon) a good undergraduate degree (normally a 2:1); they are also often asked to attend an interview.

Mix of skills and talents required

Experience has shown that a mix of skills and talents are needed for this course and type of journalism. Passion, for example, is simply not enough, since believing too much in an inquiry can skew outcomes; equally, a purely analytical mind may struggle to grasp the social-justice role often ascribed to this kind of reporting too, a unique position referred to as being "custodians of conscience"[14]. The course does welcome returning or mid-career professionals from the media, although past experience has shown the more basic classes can feel flat and that transferring from a full-time professional environment to the corridor hurly-burly of a major city-centre campus filled with mostly young undergraduate students does present its own set of unique challenges. Students must display a solid understanding of what will be required of them, namely a commitment to produce basic but decent-quality writing; a solid understanding of the academic study of the genre; and the technical capacity to use digital tools at every stage of the newsgathering and publication process.

They are informed from the beginning that this degree will introduce them to the genre; they will learn about its history and theoretical place in society and the wider media industry; practical skills will be learned; they will meet industry professionals[15]; attend networking events; and have the opportunity to mount their own investigative projects as part of their dissertations. The university also offers them the chance to participate in its Innocence Project, allowing them to use their investigative skills in real-cases involving alleged miscarriages of justice[16]. It has made clear the degree does not guarantee a job in investigative journalism but instead imparts skills which will help them become better reporters in their first jobs displaying the ability to source, research and self-start original work and perhaps, down the line, move towards specialising in investigative work.

Questionnaire results

I recently canvassed students via a short and informal questionnaire about why they applied for the course; how they felt about studying history and theory of investigative journalism; whether being taught by someone who had professional experience was a plus; whether mixing academic and practical classes was useful; how they felt participation in the Innocence Project assisted their overall experience; and finally, whether the degree imparted confidence to them to start moving towards their own investigations at some point in the future.

The responses were varied and interesting. Most replies said they wanted to become journalists who dealt in "original" news which they uncovered themselves and not just dealing in "superficial" output. Individual examples (e.g. Nick Broomfield) of professionals who used aspects of investigative skills were mentioned as being inspirational and one Eastern European student stated a leading filmmaker in his country was an example of someone who "engaged" with the audience by not being afraid to show them "the ugly truth". Studying the history and theory was regarded as being "critical" by one student, another said it was "the most important class taught" and the general consensus echoed these views. Being taught by an experienced professional was of "central" importance remarked one student; whilst another said it was "crucial". One student agreed on the importance of this but thought not all lecturers on the course needed such experience. In answer to the question about mixing "academic" and "practical" classes, the responses overwhelmingly indicated they would have preferred more practical classes.

The impact working on the Innocence Project was summed up by one student who said it was "challenging, exciting and rewarding". Another said: "It has also brought home the immediacy of working on a project that will have a huge bearing on someone's life." Two respondents remarked that they found progress on the legal cases "slow" because of the nature of the criminal justice system. Finally, in response to how professionally confident they felt, the following range of replies indicate the general feeling across the group:

Range of replies to survey

Student A: "I feel confident that I have the requisite knowledge and ability to enter into a career as an investigative reporter tomorrow, whether that is taking my lead from an editor as a staff reporter, researching on behalf of an independent production company, or rigorously pursing subjects as an individual freelance journalist."

Student B: "It has provided me with a practical set of skills, an enthusiasm for the subject and confidence that this is a career I want to actively pursue after my degree. However, the course has also prepared me not to expect that this will be achieved quickly or easily."

Student C: "This course helps people to make a choice if thy really want to do it as this course shows the true colours of investigative journalism: difficult, involving lot of commitment and sometimes dangerous. But on the other hand, challenging and very exciting, making it so tempting for the people."

Student D: "It has cemented my desire to work in this genre, from the inspiring figures considered in the history and theory of investigative journalism, to the techniques and the modern platforms of dissemination in reporting - e.g. the use of social networking and Kindles."

One student, in reply to this question, agreed in general with the positive themes aired in the relies above, but did reiterate that more practical experience and skills would have, in this individual case, helped make the student more confident[17].

Conclusions

Investigative journalism, as we have discussed, is clearly a genre of reporting which attracts heated debate, even about its roots and definition. Perhaps this is only appropriate since it does, by common agreement, fulfil a role of great importance in whichever societies it finds itself. Moreover, the motivated and uniquely-skilled kind of individual who tends to practise such reporting is, by and large, probably also the kind of person who would not be slow in adding their voice to such a passionate debate. I would suggest that the differing responses to the merit of teaching investigative journalism I experienced (i.e. positive in the USA and somewhat negative in the UK) are reflected in the historical developments of such courses on both sides of the Atlantic.

Successful degree courses in the USA (both UG and PG) have existed for a number of years but this has not been the case in the UK. Therefore, it is no wonder that opinions differ about what the best process to launch a career in this category might involve, since they tend to reflect the individual's subjective experience. Undoubtedly, it would be unwise for any university, anywhere, to oversell its courses in this area, since to do so would be to ignore the constant difficulties of mounting investigations and the importance of professional experience in undertaking them. The importance of having a professional track-record in this field on the teaching staff seems to be an obvious ingredient for the course developing positively and is reflected repeatedly in the students' responses included in this study.

Investigative journalism is changing at a rapid pace and the use of new digital technology has meant university courses must be aware of industry trends, whilst also be willing to use the campuses to experiment and lead in trying new techniques and approaches. Engagement with industry is vital but the information available also suggests a heartening sense that students do want to learn, understand and explore the roots of this genre, its successes and failures, its heroes and leading players, and understand why it's a unique, relevant and ultimately-respected character in the messy and often bare-knuckle drama of modern journalism.

Notes
[1] Phillip Knightley interview with author, 30 August 2005
[2] Bob Greene interview with author, July 2006
[3] *The Reporter's Handbook – An Investigator's Guide to Documents and Techniques.*, New York: St Martin's Press, 1983., edited by Houston, Brant, Bruzzese, Len and Weinberg, Steve
[4] Bob Greene interview with Eamonn O'Neill, July 2006
[5] For examples dating from mid-19th century in the USA print-press see *Muckraking* (New York: New Press, 2002), edited by Judith and William Serrin
[6] The first-ever dedicated award in the UK's press industry history for "investigative Journalism" was funded in part and named after Paul Foot. The inaugural Paul Foot award was presented in 2005 and I was a runner-up receiving £1,000 from *Private Eye* editor Ian Hislop
[7] Paul Foot, The Slow Death of Investigative Journalism, *The Penguin Book of Journalism: Secrets of the Press.* (London: Penguin Books, 1999) pp 79-80
[8] John Pilger, *Tell Me No Lies: Investigative Journalism and its Triumphs* (London: Jonathan Cape, 2004) p.xiv

[9] For an example of a more recent hybrid article of this nature, see Seymour Hersh's excellent piece from 1993 at: http://www.newyorker.com/archive/content/?020930fr_archive02. This investigation debunked the popular notion – still gaining currency at the outset of the US-led coalition invasion in 2003 – that President George Bush Snr., had been targeted for assassination by Saddam Hussein in 1993. Hersh's piece could only have been published in a magazine such as *The New Yorker* since it demanded space, sympathetic editing, and text-heavy layout context. Ironically, like a tail wagging a dog, such an article ended up generating coverage in news articles

[10] Roy Greenslade: Writers on the Frontline, *Guardian*, 30 October 2004

[11] It was also connected to the Scottish Centre for Journalism Studies which was run in conjunction with Caledonian University until 2008. All journalism degrees are now under the auspices of the University of Strathclyde

[12] See here for example: http://www.guardian.co.uk/education/2001/mar/13/highereducation.uk, accessed on 1 May 2011

[13] In more recent years the course has usually run with student numbers varying somewhere in region of 8-12. The applicant student number has increased 25 per cent year-on-year

[14] See The Reporter's Craft as Moral Discourse, *Custodians of Conscience: Investigative Journalism and Public Virtue* by James S. Ettema and Theodore L. Glasser (New York: Columbia University Press, 1998) p. 3

[15] Including being taught by award-winning visiting lecturers such as human-rights journalist Billy Briggs and have visits from top professionals such as Sam Poling from BBC's *Panorama*

[16] The University of Strathclyde IP was founded by me in 2008 and was the first and only project of its kind in Scotland. It is part of the UK Innocence Network (INUK) involving 30 plus campuses across the UK. I have chaired several national conferences in London in recent years and have trained more than 150 students on the uses of investigative journalism techniques in their cases. Academic year 2010-11 saw Strathclyde students being allowed to use involvement in an assessed piece of coursework for the first time. Approx. 80 per cent of the MSc class participated

[17] This was an open and informal survey conducted for this chapter. Obviously it might be argued that because it was not carried out anonymously the students might feel uncomfortable expressing criticism or negative views. Whilst not arguing with that, I would add that the relationship with the students has been excellent and very transparent;

they understand fully that university courses are not set in blocks of stone and do evolve and develop. Equally they *did* feel comfortable enough to report some criticisms mostly connected to wanting more practical classes. This has been addressed and some additional workshops were organised. I should also point out that the whole class did also complete and submit completely anonymous official university feedback forms earlier in the course. They were universally positive apart from one criticism which asked for longer word-length limits in assessed work. If any colleagues in academia wish to contact me and see the unedited answers to the questions and themes raised in this informal survey, I would be happy to supply the data for closer scrutiny

Further reading

Aucoin, James, L. (2005) *The Evolution of American Investigative Journalism*, Missouri: University of Missouri

De Burgh, Hugo (ed.) (2008) *Investigative Journalism*, London: Routledge, second edition

Ettema, James S. and Glasser, Theodore L. (1998) The Reporter's Craft as Moral Discourse, *Custodians of Conscience: Investigative Journalism and Public Virtue*, New York: Columbia University Press pp 1-16

Macdonald , Gus (1984) A Short History of Group Gropes, *Edinburgh International Television Festival Magazine*, August

Note on the author

Dr Eamonn O'Neill is a Lecturer in Journalism and Course Director of the MSc in Investigative Journalism at the University of Strathclyde, Glasgow. Over a career spanning 22 years, he has been honoured for his investigative journalism in both broadcast and print in the British Press Awards, BAFTAs and the Paul Foot Award. In 2008, he became the first British recipient of an Investigative Reporters and Editors Award (Special category – Tom Renner Award) in one of the USA's premier peer-judged honours for his work investigating miscarriages of justice. In 2010 and 2011 he received honours in the Strathclyde Excellence in Teaching Awards following nominations by students. He is currently producing/presenting a new BBC Radio Scotland series *O'Neill Investigates*. He is married and has twin sons.

What is a Science Journalist for: Communication or Investigation?

Connie St Louis argues that too few journalists are holding scientists properly to account. PR directors now set the agenda and foist their priorities on time-pressed science reporters

The role of a science journalist is a complicated and contested one in the modern world. To understand why there have been recent major failures in the reporting of science, particularly in the area of investigative journalism, I will argue that science journalism operates within a tightly controlled system of constraining narrative conventions.

"Science" itself occupies a muddy realm in the popular imagination – variously invoking areas of study from certain aspects of the social sciences (such as demography and economics) to the so-called hard sciences (such as astronomy and biology). The role of the journalist encompasses a similarly broad field of endeavour, from print to television to radio to the blogosphere.

At the same time, both the world of science and the world of journalism are undergoing major challenges, given technological changes that are proceeding at nothing less than revolutionary speed. The rates of discovery in scientific fields such as genetics or physics present challenges to the descriptive powers of even those with greatest expertise. And as the speed of internet publication has encroached upon the parameters of traditional print media, the ethics and standards of investigative reporting are being tested as never before.

There is no denying the time pressures and information overload on all journalists. A particular problem, however, faces science journalists. It is one that I believe encourages passivity. The amount of research and scientific information that a science journalist has to wade through is oceanic. A glance at the inbox of any science journalist will show the avalanche of emailed embargo press releases and content pages from the exponential growth in science journals.

No time for science journalists to investigate

With so many outlets to file stories to in their publications there is simply no time for journalists to find and investigate stories. That task has been abandoned by publications and it is organisations with media and PR directors who now set the agenda. They drive science journalism and foist their priorities on time-pressed science reporters who, wearily, manage to find time to rewrite the press release by demystifying the complex scientific language or arranging a broadcast interview with the scientist in question which can then be edited for time and clarity.

As a journalism educator I endeavour to equip my students with the skills to produce ethically sound, accurate information for the public good: an increasingly challenging endeavour in an era of social networking technology where facts are sometimes hard to sort from rumour or half-truth, and where the difference is increasingly treated as irrelevant.

So how can the traditional journalistic role of serving a well-informed public be advanced in time of:

a.) confusing information overload;
b.) arcane or nearly untranslatable scientific concepts, and
c.) the propagandising effect of money that literally talks.

Over-reliance on a few peer-reviewed journals

One of the most important constraints is an over-reliance on a very few peer-reviewed journals, owned by large profit-making multinational corporations. The *Lancet*, for example, is owned by Elsevier, the journal *Nature* by NPG. These journals, which are committed essentially to profit-making, in turn, vie for international prestige by seeking not only to publish the latest discoveries but to further publicise those findings popularly, most often via weekly embargoed press releases. There are, however, significant disparities between the vocabulary of specialised scientific disciplines and the common parlance of popular television outlets, chattering-class magazines, and broadsheets. The ability to translate from one to the other ought to be a priority in the education of science journalists, for the impact of such press releases is quite significant in leading or misleading public understanding.

Another complication in conveying scientific information is the tension between academic standards for publication and the high-pressure "scoop" mentality of popular publication. Within the university settings where much scientific discovery takes place, credentials are enhanced by projects that often take years of research, review and editing. In the world of journalism, by contrast, there is value in rushing things to press before anyone else sniffs out a given story.

Somewhere in between, there is the world of scientific discovery that occurs in the research and development sectors of organisations such as pharmaceutical companies and genetic engineering venture capital start-ups. For these latter, where knowledge is packaged as "product", there may be an image-driven desire to suppress certain insights that could depress sales on the one hand, as well as an interest in publicising the investment promise of certain discoveries well before all the facts are known.

Great deference to traditional sources of authority

Another dimension of scientific review is the great deference given to traditional sources of authority amid changing systems of verification and value. Science journalists often assume that the publishing of a paper in a leading journal such as *Nature*, for example, is a stamp of scientific validity and that there is no need to check the underlying data before reporting the story. With the heightened difficulty involved in understanding and interrogating scientific data, journalists must be trained to overcome such challenges.

Reproducibility, of course, is the central concept of the scientific method, and requires the formulation of a hypothesis, a programme of experimentation which involves the systematic observation of those experimental results, the tabulation of information gained, and the final correlation and/or modification of the organised data with the original hypothesis. As a measure of truth, it is in some ways different from tests of veracity in other fields.

Normativity, for example, might be relatively more authoritative in the social sciences. In legal trials, demeanour or appearance passes as a cipher for credibility. And in much of journalism other than scientific journalism, dealing, as it so often does, with singular or exceptional events, it is the rhetorical or persuasive power of words themselves that dictates not just what is "known" or not, but sufficiently and lucidly enough conveyed so as to be conjured and comprehended by those who were not there.

Wide range of skills required for science journalists

Being a science journalist requires an uncommon combination of skills: dedication both to the fact-finding mores of traditional journalism which relies on precision of language, context and innuendo; plus the mores of the scientific method, which require technical precision of an incalculably more refined order. With both feet in two disciplines, I am keenly aware of crucial methodological differences. If traditional journalism relies upon the kind of investigation that allows a complete representation of a particular event or situation, science writing places more emphasis on the underlying empiricism and reproducibility with which outcomes are supported.

The former requires a facility with language as paramount value; the latter requires facility with data. The incredible advances being made in these fields of biotechnology and neuroscience will have repercussions that lay audiences as well as scientific sophisticates will have to be able to discuss. Their political import will or ought to become part of the public domain; these discoveries will become increasingly important foundations for discussing topics as various as genetic modification, eugenics, invasive surveillance and pharmacological products.

The opportunity to design and direct the Science Journalism Masters programme at City University, London, focused my concern that much of what was being produced in the field was about telling science stories rather than investigating science. It was my observation that too many journalists approach scientists as priests rather than as fallible sources thereby rendering themselves as unquestioning vessels as opposed to professional diggers and reporters.

The majority of the students seeking to gain admission on to the MA science journalism course tell me at interview that their primary motivation for wanting to be science journalists is to communicate science. They want to be torch bearers of science, to correct erroneous facts, oversimplified concepts and misrepresentations of science and medicine in the media. They also want to engage the public by ensuring science is understood.

Much of science journalism is PR

These are honourable aims and perfectly reasonable goals but they are ones that should not be the mindset of a science journalist. They are the ambitions of science writers and communicators. Much of the coverage which passes under the name of science journalism is science PR and communications masquerading as reporting. This is to some extent understandable since science journalism began in the nineteen century as science communication consisting of practical information such as farming techniques, home remedies and a sprinkling of sensational stories.

Recently, I attended a "Climategate" event at the Royal Institution in London which brought together the UK's leading scientists and environmental and science journalists. Many of the journalists present recounted their disappointment with the scientists who had all refused to give any interviews when the leaked emails from the University of East Anglia's Climatic Research Unit first broke. It transpired that most of the science journalists were considered to be too partisan by their news editors and other journalists were given the story to report. One journalist complained that the science journalists needed you to talk to them but the scientists went into their bunkers. "Our editors have always suspected that we were too close to you. By refusing to speak to us when we needed you confirmed this in our editors' minds."

This is a perilous moment for science journalism to be confused about its function. It needs clarity and purpose. Too often the stress in science reporting is on new discoveries, new wonders, new devices, new findings, new gadgets and new promises. Where are the investigations which analyse the distribution of scientific and medical resources? Who is scrutinising and calling scientists to account? Who is examining the unacknowledged interdependence between science, medicine and politics? It's time science journalism came of age.

Note on the author

Connie St Louis is a Senior Lecturer and the Director of the MA in Science Journalism at City University, London. She is chair of the Association of British Science Writers (ABSW) and an award-winning broadcaster, science journalist and writer. She worked for BBC Radio 4 for fifteen years as a broadcast journalist. As a freelance she continues to present and produce a range of science and health programmes for BBC Radio 4 and World Service. She is a recipient of the prestigious Joseph Rowntree Journalist Fellowship. Her most recent programme on BBC Radio 4, which she produced and presented, investigated the use of racially targeted designer drugs by pharmaceutical companies. She also presented the landmark Radio 4 series "Life as" which charted the science of life before birth to death. Her recent book, *Reframing Libel*, is a collection of edited papers examining the government's Defamation Bill.

Section 7. The Bigger Picture

Beyond the Daily Rush of Headlines: the Deeper Issues

Richard Lance Keeble

Journalism and literature are too often seen as two separate spheres – one "low", the other "high". Yet, in fact, historically the two spheres have constantly overlapped. Journalistic genres constantly avoid neat categorisations and theorising, thriving on their dynamism, contradictions, paradoxes and complexities. And journalism's functions are diverse and ambiguous being variously associated with democratic debate, education and entertainment as well as myth, fabrication, disinformation, polemic and propaganda.

Indeed, for so many men and women of letters since the eighteenth century, the continuous flow of writing has incorporated journalism, books, reviews, polemics, sociological research or poetry even. Thus, a growing school is emerging in the academe which sees journalism not as a marginal literary pursuit but as a central cultural field which writers exploit for a variety of reasons and where, crucially, they self-consciously construct their public identities.

It is within the context of this debate – which stresses journalism as a specific *literary* genre – that John Tulloch, Professor of Journalism at the University of Lincoln, places his highly original study of investigative journalism. Literary journalism, he suggests, "is concerned not so much with establishing the 'guilty man' or 'defective part' but, rather, with utilising the tools of the imaginative writer – such as narrative, reportage, characterisation and imagery – for investigative purposes to explore the human dimension of the story".

He continues: "Indeed, I want to argue here that it is the literary journalist who takes on the ultimate challenge of the investigative journalist – grappling with issues of causation and evil. And they do this through invoking the tools of history, philosophy and psychology, no less, to serve the journalistic imagination. Stuff you need to read, to keep the title of human being."

For Tulloch, two brilliant example of investigative journalism which cross this boundary into literature are Gitta Sereny's *Into that Darkness*, which centres on the Holocaust through an intense investigation of the death camp commandant, Franz Stangl, and *Somebody's Husband, Somebody's Son*, by the late Gordon Burn, which exhaustively investigates the background of the "Yorkshire Ripper".

We end with a warning. According to Kevin Marsh, director of Offspin Media and former Executive Editor of BBC College of Journalism, journalists have to concede that many in the industry have not made a very good fist of proving journalism's indispensability in the web age. "We have made an even worse fist of proving the value of journalism as our primary means of disclosing what it is that power does in the dark and holding that power to account."

Even so, Marsh stresses, journalists now have to speak up for investigative journalism (just as the writers are doing in this text). Otherwise it will perish in the face of competition from its hollowed-out imitators.

Confronting Evil: Literature and Investigative Journalism

John Tulloch, focusing on the writings of Gitta Sereny and Gordon Burn, argues that it is the literary journalist who takes on the ultimate challenge of the investigative journalist – grappling with issues of causation and evil

> The knowledge of evil is inadequate knowledge...We know nothing to be certainly good or evil save what is truly conducive to understanding or what prevents us from understanding (Baruch Spinoza, *Ethics*, Part III, 1959: Prop. LXIV and Part IV, Prop. XXVII)

How the gist of some conversations stays with you: a large and patrician former *Sunday Times* "Insight" journalist once disabused me in the late 1970s of my enthusiasm for Duncan Campbell's[1] weekly exposés of the British Cold War state in the *New Statesman*, then edited by Bruce Page (1978-82), by squelching me with pained grandeur: "But they're unreadable...so much detail...very boring. How many people get to the end?"

The defence, of course, is that there's some stuff you need to read, to keep the title of citizen. But it's fair to concede that investigative journalism has an overly moralistic sound – obsessive, detailed and patient digging in the public interest. This is, of course, opposed to British journalism's principal claim to fame: the sleaze, hijinks and malice of its tabloid Big Brothers.

It's good for you and it tells you stuff you ought to know: the perfect investigative journalism was summed up, allegedly, by the late Murray Sayle, with his aphorism "There are only two stories in newspapers: 'we name the guilty man' and 'arrow points to defective part'."[2] Indeed, Phillip Knightley, reflecting on the origins of "Insight", defines the enterprise thus: 'At the beginning ["Insight"] was so different from ordinary journalism that people wanted to read it. The idea was to keep them guessing at what the story was about, even, in the first four or five paragraphs, and then you hit them with what it really was. It's been variously described as 'we named the guilty men' journalism, or 'arrow points to defective part'"[3].

But if investigative journalism by that token sounds stylistically quite mundane, there is a class of investigative work which is not. Such work appears from within the debateable and embattled category of literary journalism – namely, journalism which is concerned not so much with establishing the "guilty man" or "defective part" but, rather, with utilising the tools of the imaginative writer – such as narrative, reportage, characterisation and imagery – for investigative purposes to explore the human dimension of the story. Indeed, I want to argue here that it is the literary journalist who takes on the ultimate challenge of the investigative journalist – grappling with issues of causation and evil. And they do this through invoking the tools of history, philosophy and psychology, no less, to serve the journalistic imagination. Stuff you need to read, to keep the title of human being.

Crossing the boundary into literature

Two brilliant example of investigative journalism which cross this boundary into literature are Gitta Sereny's *Into that Darkness*, which centres on the Holocaust through an intense investigation of the death camp commandant, Franz Stangl, and a book by the late Gordon Burn: *Somebody's Husband, Somebody's Son*, which exhaustively investigates the background of the "Yorkshire Ripper".

At first sight, a comparison of a work deriving from the enormity of the Holocaust with one based on a somehow very English case of a provincial serial killer seems hard to justify. Of course, there can be no comparison in terms of the magnitude of historical crimes or significance. But in technique and approach, the narratives possess striking similarities. Both transcend what might be described as their ostensible genre – "true crime" in the case of Gordon Burn and journalistic popular history in the case of Gitta Sereny. Both journalists root their accounts in the human story of an individual to render comprehensible the larger human event of mass murder – events which are frequently described as incapable of being understood.

Both, therefore, run the risk of having their work dismissed as journalistic in the worst sense, where a simple-minded biographical narrative stands in place of historical analysis. Both, however, are committed deeply to the imaginative understanding of the human beings they place at the centre of their narratives and both share a common project – to reclaim "evil" from the unimaginable "other", and root it firmly within the sphere of our shared humanity. Both utilise exhaustively the techniques of the interview: Sereny spent more than 70 hours interviewing Franz Stangl; Burn established relationships of trust with Peter Sutcliffe's father, siblings and friends by spending the better part of two years in Bingley.

Both writers immerse themselves in the story to an obsessive extent: Sereny reports a feeling of danger and contamination as a result (Sereny 2001:93)[4] while Burn, after his involvement with Sutcliffe, was determined not to write another "true crime" book, a resolution the breaking of which he was to regret when he subsequently wrote about the Wests. After this he finally eschewed the "true crime" genre completely and wrote an extraordinary novel, *Fullalove*, based on the antics of the tabloid journalists he observed at the trial of Rosemary West (Burn 1996) - one of the finest exposés in fiction of the systematic betrayals that lie at the heart of "the journalistic *danse macabre*" (O'Hagan 2005). And perhaps ultimately each of these remarkable writers is subject to the same limiting criticism – that in moulding their material to purposes which are in the service of an incompletely realised aesthetic, as well as in the service of historical truth, they compromise both.

Into that Darkness …

> A very disturbing thing has happened to journalism…In anything to
> do with the Nazis, whose doings continue to preoccupy us…any
> attempt at detachment is considered suspect, any degree of
> objectivity reprehensible (Sereny 1988).

George Steiner described Gitta Sereny a few years ago as "our stellar
investigative journalist" whose work is unified by a "fundamental theme":
exploring evil, and "the sources of pathological hatred and unreason"
(Steiner 2000). With characteristic perceptiveness, Steiner emphasises in
her work a special quality of personal exposure:

> When Sereny has cornered her quarry, be he politician, academic or
> sadistic butcher, she closes in with uncompromising acuity, but with
> a seriousness, an intimation of personal vulnerability which establish
> a revealing trust.

While Sereny's presence in her work owes little to the somewhat
hackneyed techniques of the New Journalists in its self-reflective use of
the first person, it is central to her craft: only by placing herself *within the
frame* of her narrative as a moral, historical being, can she establish the
relationship with her subject, and the concomitant ethical dialogue, on
which her work depends. She has been consistent in this approach. At the
core of her work – whether with Albert Speer (Sereny 1995), Mary Bell
(Sereny 1972; 1998) or Franz Stangl – is a dramatic dialogue with another
human being.

One danger in this technique is that it has opened her to regular attacks
of being captured by her principal sources, and of working too close to
her subjects as "not only a confessor but an apologist" (Lyall 1998). It
also raises a serious issue which might be described as "self-
aggrandisement". In particular, her second book on Mary Bell (1998)
drew ferocious criticism, not only from the tabloid press, the inventors of
"cheque-book journalism", on the hypocritical grounds that a £50,000
payment was made to the subject, but from respected fellow-writers such
as Andrew O'Hagan, who accused her of exploiting her subject:

> She thinks all this [i.e. writing the book] would be good for Bell,
> good for society, and good for Sereny. It may be good for Sereny

and it may help society see how wrong it is to simply punish brutalised children who become brutal. But when it comes to the broken girl herself, *Cries Unheard* is a production which is deficient of hearing. The trouble with Sereny is that she has a sensationalist manner and takes pleasure in feeling personally close to the people she writes about. Here we find her messianic role in bringing Bell into the realm of truth (O'Hagan 1998).

This accusation – an intense pursuit of a "good" story and a sensationalist self-aggrandising "messianic" role – haunts Sereny's work, as it haunts journalism, and has surfaced in a number of different guises. I will return to it.

Sereny's career: the basic facts

The basic biographical facts of Sereny's career are well-established and dramatic. Born in Vienna to a wealthy family of Hungarian background, Gitta Sereny left Austria after the Anschluss in 1938 and spent part of the war years working with refugee children in France. As she relates it, the genesis of *Into that Darkness* came when she was working as a child welfare officer for the UNRRA in post-war occupied Germany during the period of the Nuremberg trials (Sereny 2000; 2004). As she discovered what the children had experienced:

> I felt more and more that we needed to find someone capable of explaining to us how presumably normal human beings had been brought to do what had been done. It was essential to before it would be too late, I felt, to penetrate the personality of at least one of the people who had been intimately associated with this total evil. If it could be achieved, an evaluation of such a person's background, his childhood, and eventually his adult motivation and reactions, as he saw them, rather than as we wished or prejudged them to be, might teach us to understand better to what extent evil in human beings is created by their genes, and to what extent by their society and environment (Sereny 1995: 9-10).

Sereny attended the Nuremberg trials for four days in 1945 and saw a portion of the trial of Albert Speer. Twenty-two years later, as a naturalised British journalist, she was commissioned by the *Daily Telegraph* to write a series on West Germany and Nazi Crime trials. As a result, she attended dozens of trials across Germany in Hamburg, Dusseldorf and other cities (ibid: 11). The German chief prosecutor suggested she interview Franz Stangl, the former Austrian policeman and SS man who rose from being head of security at a euthanasia unit to commandant of Treblinka, one of the four Nazi extermination camps in Poland. She interviewed Stangl over several months in repeated sessions in Dusseldorf remand prison and also interviewed his wife in Brazil and one of his daughters. Although this results in a powerful focus on Stangl as an individual moral being, the purpose according to Sereny is to show how individual character can affect political life (ibid: 14) and a substantial part of the book is also devoted to exploring the hidden role of the Vatican in the Holocaust (ibid: 289-333).

Placed fully in the story as a moral, observing being

The main characteristic of Sereny's approach is to place herself fully in the story as a moral, observing being. In the case of such monstrous acts, it is arguable that classic journalistic objectivity is of course impossible. One cannot achieve a "balance" between the Nazis and their victims and would be irredeemably corrupted by the effort. Instead, Sereny attempts to establish a direct relationship with the reader as a sort of moral guide or commentator who reports on her complex states of feeling as the narrative unwinds. This space allows Sereny to admit to feelings of shock and repugnance as she confronts the material but also to feelings of empathy for her subject.

While distancing herself from her own feelings and endeavouring to report accurately in minute detail she also self-consciously engages in building trust with the subject. Ostensibly she is transparent and honest about the terms of engagement. Central to this process is her interview technique: the book is dominated by extracts from the 70 hours of interviews, undertaken in two tranches in April and June 1971. These interviews frequently involve going over the same material many times, a repeated close observation and interrogation of the subject's body language, down to the smallest changes in facial expression and tone of voice. As she explains:

> I wanted [Stangl] to really talk to me; to tell me about himself as a child, a boy, a youth, a man…I told him…that I would promise him to write down exactly what he said, whatever it would be, and that I would try – my own feelings notwithstanding – to understand without prejudice (ibid: 23).

After the first tranche of interviews in April "I knew that in a curious way – and I say this with reflection – I had become his friend" (ibid: 253). She gets him to tell his "story" – and persuades him to repeat it several times:

> The deeper he went into his story, the clearer emerged the picture of the fatal fusion between his own character, and the sequence of events... (ibid: 34).

This testimony is intertwined with Sereny's acute observation of his body language; for example, when she asks him when he realised what Sobibor (the camp he controlled previous to Treblinka) was really for – here he relates his discovery of a gas chamber:

> *But who had built this? How could you possibly not have noticed it before? Or seen it on the plans?*

"The Poles had built it – they didn't know what it was to be. Neither Michel nor I had any time yet to go for walks in the woods. We were very busy. Yes – it was on the plans, but so were lots of other building..." the sentence trailed off.

> *All right, you hadn't known: but now you knew. What did you do?*

His face had gone red. I didn't know whether because he had been caught out in a lie or because of what he was to say next; it was much more usual for him to blush in advance than in retrospect.

"I can't describe to you what it was like," Stangl said; he spoke slowly now, in his more formal German, his face strained and grim. He passed his hand over his eyes and rubbed his forehead (ibid: 110-111).

Expanding the human interest story

She expands the human interest story into a basic philosophical position – well summarised by Richard Blucher – which argues that "the personality and character of individual men and women, high and low, can affect and influence political life, and the tragic consequences that lack or suppression of courage and moral strength in individuals can have on the history of nations" (Blucher 2007). This position, effectively elevating the interview into a form of secular confessional, runs the interviewer into clear risks. This is not Nixon but a Nazi mass-murderer. Reflecting on the Stangl interviews thirty years later, Sereny observed:

> I deliberately kept myself out as far as possible, hoping and believing that the personalities of the men and women in those pages, and the meaning of their words and acts, would best emerge not from my questions, or explanations, but from what they said and how they said it...I asked questions only to the extent that would keep the conversations flowing with increasing intensity. This requires faith in the capacity of your *vis-à-vis* to think, patience to give him or her the time to do so, and finally the determination to tempt them into responding not just with but *to* their own thoughts, which means bringing them to the point where they both ask and answer their own questions (Sereny 2004).

The same sharp concentration is devoted to the setting of a scene. Here is Sereny contemplating the memorial at the site of three gas chambers at Sobibor:

> The air is clear and clean. There is the sound of birds, the occasional whistle and clatter of a train, the far-away clucking of chickens; familiar sounds which, thirty years ago, must have offered momentary illusions of reassurance. But the earth round the mound is terribly fine while the soil under the rest of Sobibor is a light brown sand which gives underfoot. And one is jolted out of any effort at detachment by the sickening shock at realizing that – even these three decades later – one must be walking on ashes (ibid: 116).

This pared away sketch with its slight, terrible details is a restrained exercise of imaginative sympathy – a passing into a historical moment – which is not overtly exploitative or journalistic. But what is rendered problematic by this *modus operandi* is precisely any "effort at detachment" or objectivity – that bad faith at the core of the journalistic enterprise so memorably analysed by Janet Malcolm (Malcolm 1989) where the source is systematically deceived in the interests of the "story" or the book. In what sense has Sereny "become his friend"? The "friendship" is, of course, necessary for Sereny's purposes and – in her self-appointed confessional role – constructed on the rapport without which no cooperation would be forthcoming.

And although it can be argued that Sereny does not fully succeed in securing a clear confession of guilt from Franz Stangl, she does succeed in undermining the myth of a "Nazi monster" in a more convincing way than Hannah Arendt's classic account of the "banality of evil" in Eichmann in Jerusalem (Arendt 1962; Cesarani 2004). On what turns out to be her final visit to Stangl, when she brings him a favourite Austrian soup that she has cooked herself, she presses him to face up to himself in the interests of "truth":

> "I have never intentionally hurt anyone, myself," he said, with a different, less incisive emphasis, and waited again – for a long time. For the first time, in all these many days, I had given him no help. There was no more time. He gripped the table with both hands as if he was holding on to it. "But I was there," he said then, in a curiously dry and tired tone of resignation. These few sentences had taken almost half an hour to pronounce. "So yes," he said finally, very quietly, "in reality I share the guilt...Because my guilt...my guilt...only now in these talks...now that I have talked about it all for the first time..." He stopped...After more than a minute he started again, a half-hearted attempt in a dull voice. "My guilt," he said, "is that I am still here. That is my guilt." "Still here?" "I should have died. That was my guilt."

A convincing portrait of a human being? Up to a point, but as an admission of guilt, Stangl's simple wish for death is deeply problematic and the dramatic structure of the episode tends to undermine our faith in the verisimilitude of the narrative, especially when Sereny reveals that Stangl dies of heart failure nineteen hours later. Although poetically satisfying, the suggestion that she has been the instrument by which he has "faced himself" might also be interpreted as arrogating excessive influence to herself. Nevertheless, this remains an extraordinary, if flawed, exercise in the journalistic imagination.

Somebody's Husband, Somebody's Son

The English journalist, novelist and non-fiction writer Gordon Burn (1948-2009) is among the most original post-modern English novelists of the latter half of the 20th century, although full recognition of his exceptional skills remains limited. A hard-working journalist all his life, and an extraordinarily good one, his work continuously questions the role of the journalist in contemporary culture. Whether writing on sport, art, or crime, Burn established an exemplary rapport with his subjects, to the extent that a common professional charge by rival journalists was that he had been captured by his sources, whether they were artists, sports stars, or the relatives of serial killers.

Along with his interest in sport, and continual arts criticism, Burn achieved some security by working for *The Sunday Times Magazine* as a special writer (*Telegraph* 2009) between 1974 and 1982 and this provided the platform for his first book, *Somebody's Husband, Somebody's Son* , on the Yorkshire Ripper. According to his own account, Burn was drawn in part to the subject by the activities of the popular press: "Fact and fiction had been hopelessly blurred in the weeks and months following Sutcliffe's arrest, largely as a result of newsmen offering hard cash for 'good copy'" (Burn 1993: 375). Burn devoted two years to his research, working off and on in Bingley, where he rented a flat above a pub and established a close rapport with the family of Peter Sutcliffe, notably his father John Sutcliffe, brothers Mark and Carl and sisters Maureen and Jane.

Although the style of the book owes much to the Mailer of *The Executioner's Song* in its deliberate narrative flatness characterised by "simple declarative sentences[s]" (Burn 2004), its principal feature is a dense mesh of interlocking quotes, presented in an ostensibly non-judgemental framework. Ostensibly because, as the narrative progresses, Burn's skillful use of the unspoken and of significant juxtapositions, releases a wealth of possible explanations for the evolution of a person into a mass murderer. Unlike Sereny, Burn rarely places himself within the narrative frame and his approach eschews theorising about the causation of Peter Sutcliffe's terrible acts. But the accretion of artfully placed detail illuminating the dynamics of the Sutcliffe family and their social context provides space for readers to construct moral theories of their own – for example, about the role of Sutcliffe's father John in the family :

> John Sutcliffe spent almost the whole of the 1960s, the decade when Carl was growing up, working nights. Carl, meanwhile, spent most of that time watching television from his mother's lap and resented being sent to bed early by his father when he was around at the weekends. Like the rest of the family (although Maureen, possibly his

favourite, would only admit to holding him 'in awe'), Carl was afraid of his father...

"We were all frightened to death of my dad. He were like a monster. He were never in house, but when he was he ruled the roost. When he came in drunk we'd all sit there in fear; you didn't move. Whatever was on television, no matter how many were watching, was straight off and switched over to what he wanted to see, which was usually sport. If cricket came on, that were it. He used to sort of edge up to telly and sit right in front of it. Nobody dared say owt...(Burn 1993: 114-5).

Burn always sticks closely to accounts that can be directly sourced and restricts his attempts to enter into Sutcliffe's consciousness. Where he does so, the effect is restrained, as in this depiction of the truancy habits of the young Sutcliffe :

Every morning he'd shout "good-bye" and bang the back door...But instead of disappearing down the hill, he'd wait until the coast was clear and then secrete himself in the underdrawing...Lying alone in the dark he'd listen to the weather or the birds, or to the sounds of the house – his mother moving around cleaning, his father, home from the night-shift, snoring in the bedroom alone. Mostly though, as he'd tell his parents later, he just slept, something for which he had an apparently boundless appetite (ibid: 44).

The restrained use of the imaginative touches here, and the explicit sourcing ("as he'd tell his parents later...") are typical, and lend credibility to the narrative, rooting it in a net of links and correspondences that Burn builds up. More skillfully than his contemporaries, Burn's technique of combining intensely researched detail and familial voices allows a space for the story, in the cliché, to tell itself.

Conclusion – rapport and its perils

almost everyone wants or needs to talk about themselves. The result of this approach...is that people develop or indeed discover an increasing curiosity, an increasing need to know about themselves: and this is certainly what happened to Franz Stangl (Sereny 2004).

A crucial distinction between Sereny and Burn is the presence or absence of the persona of the writer within the narrative frame. This is more than a difference of technique. While the choice of narrating style is fundamental to all forms of artistic expression, it is less often perceived as a major issue in journalism – rather an issue of choice, house stylistics or the sub-genre in which the piece is written – column, diary, blog etc. In both books, the choice is, in fact, fundamental to the way in which the material is structured and handled, to the management of our sympathies as readers and – beyond that – to the moral and philosophical posture of the writer.

In his study of Sutcliffe, Burn is punctilious in keeping himself outside the frame of the story, utilising a variety of links between factual information and actuality from his family sources to keep the narrative going and establish a consistent flow of verifiability. In contrast, Sereny figures strongly as the narrator, in a posture that asks us to invest much in her truthfulness and reliability.

Here we face what might be defined as the pre- and post- modern problematic of journalism, handily definable by a date – 1989 – and the letters BJM and AJM – that is pre- and post-Janet Malcolm. In her classic *New Yorker* essay, Malcolm explores the issues of trust arising from what she calls "the deepest structure of the journalist-subject encounter" (Malcolm 1989: 1, 71) – the bad faith involved in the journalist's handling of the expectations of their interviewee and the need to work up stories by imposing novelistic structures.

Sereny, emphatically a BJM person, has clearly found attacks on her integrity and truthfulness deeply shocking and incomprehensible (Sereny 1988, 2004). But the issue is more than a cultural shift that makes us no longer able to trust the journalist because of their cold-hearted pursuit of a good story and the self-promotion which forms an inevitable part of the process. More damaging than O'Hagan's polemics has been the attack by Jacqueline Rose, which identifies an inherent corruption in her posture as a narrator/interpreter and a "crusading aspect of her writing":

> Her aim…is to force the culture to acknowledge the roots of iniquity in an individual life…Sereny represents a form of spectatorship that believes in its own virtue and corrupts itself, what we might call the perverting of curiosity in motion…she believes….that if she can

bring the subjects of her investigation to acknowledge the truth, then their underlying natures, in all their original innocence, will be released (Jacqueline Rose 2003 211-212).

Rose is fully aware of the damning nature of her judgement, and the precise weight that we should attribute to the term "crusading". Of course, for Rose this is nothing personal – Sereny merely becomes a celebrated emblem of the bread 'n circuses sadism and corruption of post-modern journalism, its emphasis on spectacle and the moment of encounter and "our frenzied desire to know" (Rose ibid: 213). Why, she exclaims in exasperation, do these moments have to be lived in the present tense? (ibid).

Yet arraigning Sereny as an arch representative of the sadism of celebrity culture is deeply unfair to an extraordinarily skilful and dedicated journalist. It may be true that this corruption can be avoided in a Burn-like fashion by excluding oneself from the picture or, like Malcolm, adopting the position that if you don't seek to establish a rapport you won't be guilty of bad faith and anyway interviewees don't need to be coaxed to tell their stories (Malcolm 2010: 52). But if there is reason for doubt as to her techniques, there is no reason to doubt Sereny's passionate and risk-taking commitment to the complexity of issues of good and evil and of being human (cf. Bond 2004).

Notes
[1] Not the correspondent for the *Guardian* but the freelance investigative journalist specialising in intelligence, defence and civil liberties. Campbell was a staff writer at the *New Statesman* 1978-1991 and associate editor (investigations) 1988-91. He was prosecuted in the ABC trial 1978 under the Official Secrets Act
[2] See http://www.guardian.co.uk/media/2010/sep/21/murray-sayle-obituary, accessed 18 May 2011
[3] See http://shanecroucher.co.uk/2010/11/02/phillip-knightley-gives-the-insight-on-insight/, accessed on 18 May 2011
[4] Reflecting on the work, she writes: "In the weeks I worked with Stangl, I barely slept; in the years afterwards, when I prepared and wrote *Into That Darkness*, a nightmare of harm coming to my young daughter…pursued me virtually every night. 'If one exposes oneself to the devil,' a kind bishop at the Vatican warned me a year or so later, 'he can invade one'" (Sereny 2001)

References

Addley, Esther (2008) You couldn't make it up, *Guardian G2*, 27 March. Available online at http://www.guardian.co.uk/books/2008/mar/27/fiction.media, accessed on 6 May 2011

Arendt, Hannah (1963, 1977) *Eichmann in Jerusalem: A Report of the Banality of evil*, London: Faber and Faber; revised and enlarged edition, 1977, New York: Penguin

Blucher, Richard (2007) How Helpful is Hannah Arendt in looking "Into that Darkness"? PACEM Vol. 10, No. 2 pp 49-57. Available online at http://www.pacem.no/2007/2/1menneskesyn/4blucher/ accessed on 17 June 2011

Bond, Sue (2004) Review of Jacqueline Rose, On not being able to sleep. Available online at http://metapsychology.mentalhelp.net/poc/view_doc.php?type=book&id=2325, accessed on 17 June 2011

Browning, Christopher (1992) *Ordinary Men: Reserve Police Battalion 101 and the Final Solution in Poland*, New York: HarperCollins

Burn, Gordon (1984, 1993) *Somebody's Husband, Somebody's Son: The Story of the Yorkshire Ripper*, London: William Heinemann; paperback edition 1993, London: Reed Books

Burn, Gordon (1995) *Fullalove*, London: Martin Secker and Warburg

Burn, Gordon (1996) The trial, *Granta 53: News: Scoops, Lies and Videotape*. Available online at http://www.granta.com/Online-Only/The-Trial, accessed on 23 April 2011

Burn, Gordon (1998) *Happy Like Murderers*, London: Faber and Faber

Burn, Gordon (2004) Dead calm, *Guardian Review*, 5 June p. 34. Available online at http://www.guardian.co.uk/books/2004/jun/05/featuresreviews.guardianreview37, accessed on 21 April 2011

Eagleton, Terry (2010) *On Evil*, New Haven and London: Yale University Press

Cesarani, David (2004) *Becoming Eichmann: Rethinking the Life, Crimes and Trial of a Desk Murderer*, London: William Heinemann

Daily Telegraph (2009) Obituary. Gordon Burn 21 July. Available online at http://www.telegraph.co.uk/news/obituaries/culture-obituaries/books-obituaries/5880715/Gordon-Burn.html, accessed on 21 April 2011

Gerrard , Nicci (1998) Mary Bell: The Case for the Defence, *Observer*, 10 May. Available online at http://www.guardian.co.uk/theobserver/1998/may/10/features.review7, accessed on 23 June 2011

Lyall, Sarah(1998) Close enough to evil to look beyond it, *New York Times*, 15 August. Available online at http://www.nytimes.com/1998/08/15/books/close-enough-to-evil-to-look-beyond-it.html, accessed on 22 June 2011

Malcolm, Janet (1989) The Journalist and the Murderer,1. The Journalist, *The New Yorker*, 13 March pp 38-73; 2. The Murderer, *New Yorker*, 20 March pp 49-82

Malcolm, Janet (2010) Iphigenia in Forest Hills, *New Yorker*, 3 May pp 34-63

O'Hagan, Andrew (1998) Her battle with truth, *Guardian*, 22 May. Available online athttp://mg.co.za/printformat/single/1998-05-22-her-battle-with-truth/, accessed on 22 June 2011

O'Hagan, Andrew (2005) Who's sorry now? *London Review of Books*, Vol. 27, No.11, 2 June

Rose, Jacqueline (2003) The Cult of Celebrity, *On not being able to sleep*, London: Chatto and Windus pp 201-215

Sereny, Gitta (1974, 1995) *Into That Darkness. From Mercy Killing to Mass Murder*, first edition, London: Andre Deutsch; second paperback edition with author's preface, 1995, London: Pimlico

Sereny, Gitta (1972, 1995) *The Case of Mary Bell*, first edition London: Andre Deutsch; second paperback edition, London: Pimlico

Sereny, Gitta (1995, 1996) *Albert Speer: His battle With Truth*, first edition London: Macmillan; second Vintage paperback edition

Sereny, Gitta (1988) Kurt Waldheim's Past, *London Review of Books*, Vol. 10, No. 8, 21 April pp 3-8

Sereny, Gitta (1998) *Cries Unheard*, London: Macmillan

Sereny, Gitta (2000, 2001) *The German Trauma: Experiences and Reflections, 1938-2000,* London: Allen Lane: Penguin Press; revised paperback edition Penguin Books

Sereny, Gitta (2004) Into that Darkness 30 Years On. Transcript of a presentation at a seminar *Into That Darkness 30 Years On: The Psychology of Extermination*, conducted by Gitta Sereny, Michael Tregenza, and Anthony Stadlen, 10 October 2004 in Herringham Hall, Regent's College, London. Available online at at:http://www.szasz.com/sereny.pdf, accessed on 8 June 2011

Spinoza, Baruch (1959 [1677]) *Spinoza's Ethics*, trans. Boyle, Andrew, London, J.M. Dent, Everyman's Library revised translation; first published 1910

Steiner, George (2000) Down Among the Dead, *Observer Review*, 17 September. Available online at http://www.guardian.co.uk/books/2000/sep/17/historybooks, accessed on 2 June 2011

Wainwright, Martin (2009) Gordon Burn: Versatile Chronicler of Britain's Seamy side, from serial killers to celebrities and soccer stars, *Guardian*, 20 July. Available online at http://www.guardian.co.uk/books/2009/jul/20/gordon-burn-obituary, accessed on 21 April 2011

Note on the author

John Tulloch is Professor of Journalism and Head of the School of Journalism, Lincoln University. He is co-director of the Centre for Journalism Research (CRJ). Previously (1995-2003) he was Head of the Department of Journalism and Mass Communication, University of Westminster. Edited books include *Tabloid Tales* (2000) (edited with Colin Sparks) *Peace Journalism, War and Conflict Resolution* (2010) (edited with Richard Lance Keeble and Florian Zollmann), and *Global Literary Journalism* (edited with Richard Lance Keeble), forthcoming 2012. He has also written recently on extraordinary rendition and on the journalism of Charles Dickens.

Investigative Journalism: Saving a Craft in Peril

Kevin Marsh argues that journalists have to speak up for investigative journalism. Otherwise it will perish in the face of competition from its hollowed-out imitators

Investigative journalism is a craft in peril. We have to decide whether we want to save it. Whether we can.

Investigative journalism has certainly brought crooks, hypocrites, perjurers and terrorists to account. It has shown itself to be an effective way of scrutinising power and wealth, of shining disinfecting light into dark, secret corners.

Equally, there are reasons enough to think that traditional investigative journalism, say of *The Sunday Times*'s "Insight" team, *World in Action* and *Panorama* has had its day. And that the future lies in industrial-scale leaking such as the Iraq Files and Diplomatic cables via WikiLeaks or the MPs' expenses files. That's certainly the view of everyone's favourite new-media guru Jeff Jarvis of CUNY and Buzzmachine. He sees the future of investigation and transparency – the ultimate purpose of investigation – as:

> …opening up the information and the actions of government at every level by default in a way that enables any citizen to take, analyse, and use that data, extracting or adding value to it and overseeing the actions of those who act in our name, with our money[1].

But is this really the future? Can we really dispense with the agency of journalism? Is investigative journalism now only an historical curiosity?

Holding power to account

Whatever our instincts and however traditional our view of journalism, we have to concede that many news organisations and many journalists have not made a very good fist of proving journalism's indispensability in the web age. We have made an even worse fist of proving the value of journalism as our primary means of disclosing what it is that power does in the dark and holding that power to account.

There is a whole complex of reasons for this. There are the obvious financial pressures. Investigative journalism is expensive. Tough investigations, especially when those being investigated have a very strong interest in an account being silenced, take a lot of time. Much of it not immediately productive and all of it expensive, especially if it's necessary to put a team on the investigation.

All genuine investigations, even those with apparently strong *prima facie* evidence, have to have the right to fail – which can mean money down the drain. And most investigations carry high legal risk which, even if the investigation is well founded, can be translated into cost – such as of a libel action or of fighting an injunction.

There is a hidden financial cause, too. Investigative journalism often grows out of inquiry. A fact check that yields contradictions or suggests a pattern or the role of a single individual. Newspapers' struggling business models have meant fewer and fewer reporters now individually fact-check every line of their copy and, as importantly, pursue new angles. Especially in local papers.

Abusing the language of disclosure

Public indifference to investigation that holds power to account has risen too. In part, for reasons that are nothing to do with journalism, in part because too many journalists and too many news organisations have developed the habit of using the language of disclosure and investigation to misrepresent inadequate, trivial, PR-based journalism – "exposés" of celebrities' lives entirely managed by those same celebrities' publicity agents.

This misuse of language is just one part of a much broader threat – *ersatz* investigative journalism. There is much in modern British journalism that has the look and feel of investigative journalism but is nothing of the kind, significantly cheaper to carry out and more certain of an outcome. Entrapment, for example, which has an important part to play as the last resort in revealing law-breaking, wrongdoing and hypocrisy, is also a relatively inexpensive first resort if your aim is to catch out the witless or ensure that the very conspiracy you are purporting to reveal actually happens.

For every one of the *News of the World's* laudable stings that have brought crooks to justice or exposed the hypocrisy of power and wealth, there have been many more which have simply embarrassed over-testosteroned footballers, trapped celebrities' dim relatives and hangers-on or made the journalists involved appear very close to becoming co-conspirators in crime.

There is also a narrowing and increasingly porous boundary between investigative and advocacy journalism. Michael Moore's films, for example, are quite rightly respected for their belligerence and provocation. Moore presents them as a form of investigation and some even mistake them for the real thing. Yet only the evidence that supports Moore's thesis is ever included in his accounts, irrespective of the contradictions that creates. Of *Farenheit 9/11,* Moore's 2004 film that "exposes" the "true" story of the Bush administration's response to the 9/11 terror attacks, Christopher Hitches writes that Moore seeks only "easy applause, in front of credulous audiences". The film:

> ...bases itself on a big lie and a big misrepresentation can only sustain itself by a dizzying succession of smaller falsehoods, beefed up by wilder and (if possible) yet more-contradictory claims."[2]

Advocacy masquerading as revelation

Hitchens is a known and vociferous critic of Moore and his criticisms should be read with that in mind. Nevertheless, he reminds us of the difference between investigation which seeks facts that may disprove a thesis as well as proving it (and stands the test of fact-checking even by those opposed to it) and advocacy masquerading as revelation. A difference, too, between genuine investigation and the millions of conspiracy websites, each with a title that contains some variant of the word "TRUTH", each of which promises "the facts they don't want you to know".

The last half decade, of course, has seen a new arrival on the scene. Massive leaks such as those on the Iraq war and the US Embassy cables to WikiLeaks or those on MPs' expenses to the *Daily Telegraph*. The scale of these leaks is truly mind-boggling. The Afghan War Diary comprised more than 76,900 documents about the war in Afghanistan. The Iraq War Logs released some 400,000 documents while the US Embassy cables leak placed 250,000 US State Department diplomatic cables potentially into the public domain.

These, while unarguable boons to investigative journalism, threaten the real thing almost as much as they support it. Their release on to the web and the invitation to anyone and everyone to examine them, even to help analyse them, elides the distinction between transparency and investigation. That new individual freedom to explore information and data on the web using ever more sophisticated, ever more personal web tools has allowed a powerful strand of thought to develop that rejects the role of journalism. "We don't need journalists to investigate facts and data for us – we can do it ourselves." It's an enticing illusion.

Reasons to be cheerful

Yet it's also possible to look at the current media scene and be cheered by what one sees and wonder why anyone can argue that investigative journalism is a craft in peril. That industrial scale leaking as well as the many Freedom of Information inquiries that produce real revelation are evidence of greater transparency. And, of course, many public bodies are volunteering more information and data to the public sphere either out of a commitment to openness or out of self-interest – that may be served by flooding the public sphere. Surely, it can be argued, all were are seeing is not investigative journalism in crisis. It's simply happening in different ways, in new places and in unfamiliar formats.

Consumer programmes, for example, featuring detailed investigation and the inevitable confrontation with the guilty, moves investigation closer to our daily concerns. Fly-on-the-wall documentaries "lift the lid" on institutions formerly closed to scrutiny. While crowdsourcing, using the expertise of audiences to fact-check, observe and report, offers the prospect of a whole new way of holding power to account.

None of these are bad things. None is investigative journalism either, with the exception of that subset of consumer journalism that traps the genuinely criminal. But to save investigative journalism, we need to be crystal clear what it *is*. Not just what it is *not*.

There are few definitions of investigative journalism to help us differentiate between "new" formats which are truly investigative and those which are extensions of *ersatz* forms. Investigative journalism tends to be defined by the doing of it – "you know it when you see it". But that simply enables the extension that a definition or description would seek to limit.

Hugo de Burgh[3], in his influential 1999 study, drew together some of the characteristics of investigative journalism and drew close to a working description we could use to differentiate it from other forms of revelation and other forms of journalism.

Revelation – with impact on public discourse
At its most reduced, investigative journalism is revelation carried out by journalists. That's to say, revelation in combination with the assessment, timeliness and salience that journalism adds to the enterprise, ensuring the revelation has impact on public discourse by insisting on attention through mass publication. Revelation is necessary but it's clearly not sufficient; there is much in journalism that's revelatory but not investigative journalism. Most PR – for all its other failings – is in some sense revelatory as are book serialisations; celebrity gossip; long lens photography.

Even if we extend "revelatory" to include some notion of "truth" it still will not quite do. Again, there are many revealed "truths" which are anything but investigative. The confessional autobiography, for example. De Burgh identifies some characteristics that satisfy these criteria and by doing so differentiates investigative journalism from other forms – advocacy, dissenting, analytical and so on. These include that it:

- satisfies the general characteristics of journalism – i.e. proximity, relevance, drama, significance;
- aims to discover a "truth" that has been obscured;
- aims to clarify the distinction in right and wrong – there is always a victim and always a villain;
- seeks an outcome;
- involves a subject not usually on the main news agenda that the journalist has to insist we *should* know about – the basis of the insistence is a moral one;
- is seen as just, as having a right to exist and is competent;
- draws our attention to something that we are not aware of at all or care about something we do not care about at all;
- selects its own information and prioritises it in a way that contrasts with daily journalism;
- differs from other investigative roles in society (police, lawyers, auditors etc) in that its "targets" are not limited, it is not legally founded and is closely connected to publicity.

It is possible, of course, to add many qualifications to these characteristics. The balance between "proximity, relevance and drama" – the "journalism" of the enterprise – and the comprehensive nature of the "truth", the role of counter-evidence and proportion – the "investigative" side. The relative importance of types of source – authoritative and non-authoritative. And so on.

De Burgh's description is a starting point. But it was devised before the massive explosion in the capacities of the web and before the ubiquity of read/write online software enabled us all to become writers, publishers and – some believed – journalists. It assumes the role of "journalist" and "journalism" are not in question. It predates journalism's existential neurosis.

Journalistic impartiality – the crucial ingredient

In 2011, therefore, it is necessary to add a further layer of meaning. That any definition should determine or describe something that is clearly journalism – which tends to entail a paid-for agent of inquiry, assessment and narrative. And tends to entail a degree of impartiality on the part of the journalist as well as disinterest in any specific outcome, other than the revelation of a wrong and the moral demand for its resolution.

So, for instance, in exposing systematic fraud in a government agency, the role of investigative journalism is to point to the villain, hold up the wrong to be righted and insist on justice, not to determine the specifics of any action necessary to bring justice nor to campaign to have the agency wound up or its functions performed by a different part of bureaucracy.

This is certainly what we see when we consider universally acclaimed acts of investigative journalism. Phillip Knightley is one of Britain's most celebrated investigative journalists. He made his name as one of *The Sunday Times's* "Insight" team – the most consistently effective investigative unit in the history of British journalism. When I interviewed him for the Coventry Conversations/BBC College of Journalism conference in the spring of 2011, he described to me how the "Insight" team saw their role as "we name the guilty men" journalism, or "arrow points to defective part". Their impetus, though highly moral in the sense that the team saw a "wrong" or an injustice that had to be put right, was in the direction of final disclosure which would create pressure for the wrong to be righted, not to campaign as an advocate would for a specific type of outcome or resolution.

It's necessary, too, to extend De Burgh's idea of the moral component of investigative journalism to create an indissoluble link between the moral outcome of investigative journalism – righting wrongs – and the questionable morality of some of the its methods. There is a calculus here. The public understands and will extend *post-hoc* legitimacy to the techniques which investigative journalism must sometimes use – invasion of privacy, surreptitious recording, impersonation and deception, "cod-faxes" and so-on – to an end that it agrees is moral, a morality defined in terms of "the public interest".

In an important, but often overlooked, 2002 study for the BBC, the Broadcasting Standards Commission and others, Professor David E.

Morrison and Michael Svennevig[4] found that broadcasting audiences "permitted" relatively high levels of intrusion where public interest was high. They found, too, that it was necessary for the broadcaster to demonstrate the "higher…degree of public interest" and not simply assert it; that underhand tactics should be used only when other methods had failed; and that they should be restricted to the gathering of information that was strictly germane to the story.

The public recognises "the genuine article"

In other words, the public recognises the difference between hollowed out forms of investigative journalism – the forms that entrap for the sake of entrapment, hack into mobile phone mailboxes, or send wired journalists posing as constituents into MPs' surgeries on fishing trips – and the genuine article. There is clearly still a need for investigative journalism. The mass of information and data on the web gives an illusion of transparency. And the web tools that enable us all to interrogate that information and data give the illusion of scrutiny. Mass journalism's ability to convene huge audiences around what is salient, what is morally urgent and pressing remains a powerful tool of our public sphere.

Whether investigative journalism can survive the financial crisis in our industry and sufficiently distinguish itself from its hollowed-out imitators remain an open question. But what is certain is that if we in journalism do not speak up for it, point out the perils that it faces and make positive efforts to save it, it will perish. And an important element in our scrutiny of power with it.

Notes

[1] Jarvis Jeff *A taxonomy of transparency*, Buzzmachine, 23 October 2010. Available online at http://www.buzzmachine.com/2010/10/23/a-taxonomy-of-transparency/, accessed on 27 June 2011

[2] Hitchens Christopher, *Unfairenheit 9/11:The lies of Michael Moore*, Slate http://www.slate.com/id/2102723/, 21 June 2004, accessed on 27 June 2011

[3] De Burgh Hugo, *Investigative Journalism; context and practice* (1999), London: Routledge

[4] Morrison David E and Svennevig, Michael: *The Public Interest, the Media and Privacy*. Available online at http://www.ofcom.org.uk/static/archive/bsc/pdfs/research/pidoc.pdf, accessed on 29 June 2011

Note on the author

Kevin Marsh is Director of OffspinMedia (www.offspinmedia.co.uk) and a host/facilitator at Coventry Conversations/BBC College of Journalism events. He was formerly Executive Editor of the BBC College of Journalism and Editor of *Today*. He produced investigations into the Brighton Bomb, the Cyprus Spy Trial, the Ponting Trial and is currently an executive producing a new investigation into the Nazi's Treblinka camp. His latest book *Stumbling Upon the Truth*, about Lord Hutton, New Labour and the BBC, will be published by Biteback in September 2012.

Afterword

How Investigative Reporting "May Cut Across the Mood of the Times"

Sir Harold Evans, holder of the British Press Awards' Gold Award for Lifetime Achievement, reflects on the collection of essays and reminds us that 'investigative journalism could have rained on the parade before the invasion of Iraq and taken away the punch bowl before the bankers went begging for bail-outs'

There are as many facets to what we call the jewel of journalism, investigative reporting, as there are facets on a brilliant diamond – 58, as I recall, one more than the Heinz varieties. Every facet reflects light in a different way and so it is with the 30 plus essays in this collection which have given such a positive answer to the question in the title page.

We learn much about techniques for exposés on television and from data banks and about going undercover – and we are not confined to this septic isle. I read the contributions soon after sitting in the select committee hearing at Parliament's Portcullis House where Rupert Murdoch, his son James, and erstwhile head of their London operations, Rebekah Brooks, testified to how little they knew of the "dark arts" of phone hacking and police bribery by which the *News of the World* secured too many of its stories or, indeed, could explain why they were still paying money to a convicted criminal.

It was a consolation to know that these scummy practices were exposed by real investigative reporting by the *Guardian's* Nick Davies, importantly sustained by his resolute editor, Alan Rusbridger. As David Cay Johnston reminds us in his sharp survey of US practices, editors – and more often publishers – are sometimes too scared to run the results of an investigation. I like Johnston's term of "journalist-led digging" to define investigative journalism. We should not dilute its meaning by referring to scoops emanating from leaks as investigative. They may require no more effort than opening an attachment on email.

The WikiLeaks stash of State department cables demanded attention. The editing of them for publication was mostly thoughtful and responsible (who wants to get an Afghan villager beheaded for helping the coalition?). But the WikiLeaks were not investigative journalism. Reporters are often unofficially fed an official document stamped "confidential". Prudent reporters will run a few smell tests – is it authentic; is it so partial a picture as to be misleading; what's the rest of the story?

But conventional scrutiny of this kind requires much less effort than the painstaking accumulation of fragments of information and the imagination to build a credible picture of the whole, a task in which a reporter may need comparable skill and patience to that of an archaeologist putting together the shattered fragments of a Grecian vase.

Phillip Knightley tellingly describes how he needed a year to unravel and understand the money tree – the money jungle! – by which the Vestey business family, the largest private multi-national operating in 27 countries, had paid no taxes anywhere for 60 years.

On the other hand, Barnie Choudhury's investigations among minority communities are fine examples of investigative work built not on documents but on human relationships. He had to win the trust of people in Derby to shed light on the practice of honour killings. In Oldham, he found South Asian youths all too ready to talk. They were intent on making some areas of the city no-go zones for whites, but for reporting them Choudhury risked being accused of racism.

It is not axiomatic that investigators will be popular which is one reason it is so heartening to have Neil Fowler's judgement that despite the anxious times in the regions, investigative reporting is "alive and kicking". Let's always remember that the most important investigative reporting may cut harshly across the mood of the times. Investigative journalism could have rained on the parade before the invasion of Iraq and taken away the punch bowl before the bankers went begging for bail-outs.

Yes, I hear the cry that it costs money to do that kind of work. In terms of the broader public interest, if not for the adventurous publisher, the investment is hardly ever anything less than a bargain. The very good news is that where the market fears to tread, philanthropy can come to the rescue – ProPublica in the US, which has won a Pulitzer, and in the UK, the Bureau of Investigative Journalism (BIJ). Launched as a non-profit in April 2010 with a £2 million donation from the David and Elaine Potter Foundation, the Bureau has secured more than a dozen front-page stories and produced a number of award-winning web, radio and television documentaries.

Nine months of research into EU structural funds yielded a report that ran in the *Financial Times*, the BBC and Al-Jazeera as specials and won the Bureau a Thomson Reuters Award in the process. Major press coverage followed the largest-ever analysis of public pay in the UK, a story that became a *Panorama* and one of the most visited BBC web pages of 2010. None of these stories would have received as much investment without charitable backing. The Bureau is still in its infancy and seems set to become a globally important centre for holding power to account, as all good investigative journalism does.

And in the spirit of our trade, I must anticipate the ever-vigilant reader by declaring that I have two associations – one with the BIJ, as Patron, and one with Thomson Reuters, as Editor at Large.

Note on the author
Harold Evans was editor of *The Sunday Times* and *The Times* (1967-1982), and author of *My Paper Chase* (Little Brown, 2009)